CHALLENGE OF GOD
SECOND EDITION

Niall Boyle

GILL & MACMILLAN

Gill & Macmillan Ltd
Hume Avenue, Park West
Dublin 12
with associated companies throughout the world
www.gillmacmillan.ie

© Niall Boyle 1998
0 7171 2662 5

Print origination in Ireland by
O'K Graphic Design
Colour repro by Keystrokes Ltd, Dublin

Imprimatur: Most Rev. Michael Smith D.C.L., Bishop of Meath

The paper used in this book is made from the wood pulp of managed forests. For every tree felled, at least one tree is planted, thereby renewing natural resources.

Contents

Foreword

For three years the Apostles walked with Jesus, listening to Him, observing His deeds and miracles. When He was arrested they lost courage and left Him alone. Following His resurrection they found courage and came back to Him. This was the unlikely group to which He entrusted the task of proclaiming the good news to all peoples. That same good news of Jesus Christ must be proclaimed in all ages.

I warmly welcome this new edition of Niall Boyle's book on teaching the faith to the young generation. As Pope John Paul reminded us on his visit in 1979, 'every generation, with its own mentality and characteristics, is like a new continent to be won for Christ'. Teaching the faith to each new generation is an ever-present challenge for the Church and those entrusted with the task of teaching. This book seeks to present the central truths about faith, about life and about eternity in a challenging and evocative manner for senior students in post-primary schools. Absorbing the content of this book and assimilating it into life should lead to a deeper understanding and appreciation of faith and its central truths. The welcome accorded the first edition of this book by catechetical teachers underlined in the clearest possible manner how successfully Niall had put on paper the insights and experience gained from many years of teaching catechetics to senior pupils in a large boys' school, St Patrick's Classical School, Navan. This new edition will, I believe, also be welcomed by catechetical teachers.

I congratulate Niall on the clear, readable and concise presentation of faith that is to be found in these pages. It would be my wish that this book will find its way into the classrooms of our post-primary schools and be an instrument in leading young people into a deeper knowledge and appreciation of their faith in Jesus Christ.

✠ Michael Smith
Bishop of Meath

Preface

Some years ago, Garret Barden and Philip McShane wrote the following story about a man who invites a scientist to tea:

> *'As the meal drew to a close, the man remarked that he had always wanted to understand Einstein's Theory of Relativity, and since he now had a real scientist to talk to, perhaps he could explain it to him? "Of course, I don't know any physics and I've always hated mathematics, so you would need to avoid all that terminology and the use of formulae. But I know you are an excellent scientist and you surely will be able to explain it to me, in my own simple words."'*
>
> *Towards Self-Meaning*

The point of the story is clear — the man has no concept of what understanding Einstein's Theory of Relativity involves.

The same can be said of some people's approach to matters relating to religion and morality. These are *complex* areas which demand *real* intellectual *effort* in the search for answers. But what are the questions to which people seek answers?

The Second Vatican Council declared that:

> *'In the face of modern developments there is a growing body of people who are asking the most fundamental of all questions or are glimpsing them with a keener insight: What is a human person? What is the meaning of suffering, evil, death, which have not been eliminated by all this progress? What is the purpose of these achievements, purchased at so high a price? What can a human being contribute to society? What can he/she expect from it? What happens after this earthly life has ended?'*
>
> *The Church in the Modern World*

Such fundamental questions deserve to be addressed, however challenging it may be to do so. As with all introductions to religion, this book neither pretends to be exhaustive nor to have the last word — the subject is simply too vast.

It is hoped, however, that this book will play a part in helping students to examine their attitudes towards important matters, on an informed basis, and help them in their development of a more mature appreciation of their Christian faith.

Acknowledgments

The author wishes to thank the following for their helpful assistance and support during the preparation of this book:

Most Rev. Dr Michael Smith, Bishop of Meath; my parents, both my wife's family and my own; Dr Michael Dunne, Ms Pauline McGuinness, Ó Fiaich College, Dundalk; St Peter's College, Wexford and Milltown Park, Dublin; staff of St Patrick's Classical School, Navan; school catechists who reviewed drafts of the text; management and staff of Gill & Macmillan, publishers; and most especially my wife Anne and son Jamie, to whom this book is dedicated.

For permission to reproduce colour transparencies and photographs in this book, grateful acknowledgment is made to the following:

Sonia Halliday; Impact Photos; Greenhill Photo Library; Frank Spooner Pictures; Mary Evans Picture Library; Popperfoto; Dominic Photography; Scala; National Gallery of Ireland; Science Photo Library; Martyn Turner (cartoon); Associated Press; A.F. Kersting; The Stockmarket; BFI Stills Posters and Designs; Pacemaker; British Council of Churches.

Cartoons are reproduced by kind permission of Universal Press Syndicate.

For permission to reproduce copyright material, grateful acknowledgment is made to the following:

Bantam Books for extracts from *Life After Life* by R. Moody; Grossman Publishing for an extract from *Nobel* by N. Halasz; Time Magazine for extracts from three articles; The Sunday Times for an extract from one article and a cartoon by Kipper Williams; Pan Books for extracts from *The Environmental Handbook* edited by J. Barr; Medical and Technical Publishing for the chart of Alcohol Addiction and Recovery; ALERT News for an article; The Sunday Tribune for an extract from an article and the illustration 'Irish Volunteers Abroad'; North Tipperary VEC for extracts from *Learning for Adult Life*; The Sunday Press for extracts from articles by Rev. Colm Kilcoyne, The Irish Times for extracts from two articles by Conor O'Cleary and an extract from a report; Blackie for an adapted extract from *Problems of Christian Living* by R. Taylor; SCM Press for an extract from *Costing Not Less Than Anything* by John Dalrymple; Charles Letts and Co. for adapted extracts from *World Faiths* by Liva Barker; The Word Magazine for adaptation of an illustration; Ward River Press for extracts from *Maximilian of Auschwitz* and *The Mystery of God* by Desmond Forristal; Harper Collins for extracts from *The Christians* by Bamber Gascoigne; Baker Book House for an extract from *Religions of the World* by Earl Schipper; Catholic Truth Society London for an extract from *Can Catholics Believe in Evolution?* by David Jones; Image Books/Doubleday for an extract from *Essential Catholicism* by T. Bokenkotter; Usborne Publishing for an adapted extract from *Essential Biology* by R. Treays; Kairos Magazine for various extracts.

PART 1 INTRODUCTION

CHAPTER 1

Faith and Reason

INTRODUCTION

> How do you know if someone is a witch?
> Because he/she burns.
> What else burns?
> Wood.
> So, why do witches burn?
> Obviously, they're made of wood!
> But how do you know if someone is made of wood?
> Because he/she will float in water.
> What else floats in water?
> Why, a duck, of course!
> Therefore, if someone weighs the same as a duck, then
>   he/she is made of wood and therefore he/she is a witch!

Dialogue from 'Monty Python and the Holy Grail'.

We can tell immediately that this is a nonsensical argument. It is not always so easy, however, to gauge the worth of what we hear and read.

The figure of Aristotle, carved on Chartres Cathedral. Aristotle formulated the theory of Logic, which studies the rules and methods for distinguishing a good argument from a bad argument.

During the course of this book, you will be asked to make your mind up about many arguments on a variety of different topics. To this end, a clear understanding of what distinguishes a good argument from a bad one is essential.

1

What is an Argument?

The word 'argument' means different things to different people. To some, it just means a small disagreement that develops into a blazing row. However, here we will define an argument as:

> 'a carefully thought-out presentation of a point of view, which aims to convince people why they should accept or reject a particular idea or thing'.

Fact and Opinion

An argument must be based on sound evidence if it is to reach a defensible, logical conclusion.

"Today there's a 65% chance of rain, or if you like a 35% chance it won't, not forgetting there's a 50% chance I could be wrong or right!"

Sometimes it's hard to know who or what to believe.

There are basically two types of evidence:

(1) Evidence that is verifiably certain because it is an undeniable, proven *fact*, e.g. the statement of a ballistics expert at a murder trial, identifying the gun used by making a microscopic comparison of the marks on the bullet used with the marks inside the barrel of the gun.

(2) Evidence that *may be true*, but whose truth cannot be established with complete certainty. We should only accept this if we have good reasons for doing so, because it is someone's *opinion*, not a fact.

e.g. Fact: Ireland is a member of the European Union.
Opinion: Ireland should remain a member of the European Union.

An argument may include both types of evidence. Fact and opinion are often interwoven to form the building blocks of an argument. Therefore, it is important to examine each statement of evidence to see if the argument is as soundly constructed as it seems, and whether or not it proves its case.

ACTIVITY

Read each of the following statements carefully, then distinguish which statement is a *fact* and which is an *opinion*:

1   The Roman Catholic Church teaches that there are seven sacraments.
2   Hare coursing should be made illegal.
3   The violence in Northern Ireland is entirely due to religious differences.
4   Hindus believe in reincarnation.
5   Those who leave school without qualifications are less likely to obtain jobs than those who get qualifications.
6   Full employment can be achieved in Ireland within the next ten years.
7   More National Lottery money should be spent on the provision of sports facilities.
8   The Olympic games are held every four years.

KNOWLEDGE AND BELIEF

When someone forms a firm opinion about something, we say that he/she *believes* it. Our beliefs play an important part in our everyday lives, especially in such areas as the law, health care, morality and religion. But when are we justified in believing something?

The philosopher Aristotle made an important distinction between knowledge and belief. He said that while we can hold beliefs which may be true or false, *we can only know things that are true.* In our everyday speech we say we 'know' something if we are *certain* of it. For example:

If we find out that we have been mistaken about something, then we can say, 'I believed it but I was wrong'. We cannot say, 'I knew it, but I was wrong'.

The word *'know'*, therefore, is used only to refer to what is *undeniably*, or *necessarily, true*; e.g.:

> A triangle is a three-sided plane figure.
> **or**
> A whole orange is greater than any one of its segments.

By 'true' we mean that something is the case independently of whether or not anyone is willing to recognise it. Each of the above examples is undeniably true. However, in matters of belief we do not enjoy the same degree of certainty when deciding whether our beliefs are true or not.

Whether or not our beliefs are justified depends on whether the evidence offered to support them is trustworthy. We should always be willing to examine the evidence upon which we base our beliefs to see whether they are justified, and if so, to what extent.

EXERCISE

Consider each of the following situations carefully. Then rank them in order 1 to 3 according to the strength of the evidence offered for holding a belief. Explain your choices: 1 = . . . 2 = . . . 3 = . . .

- David believed that he had won the weekend Lotto draw because his horoscope had said he would.
- David believed that he had won the weekend Lotto draw because the numbers he had selected matched the winning numbers printed in the Sunday papers.
- David believed that he had won the weekend Lotto draw because his next door neighbour told him that his numbers had been picked.

REFLECTION

Just because the evidence upon which we base a belief is weak, this does *not* necessarily mean that we are wrong to believe it. In this case David *had* won the Lotto draw. It just means that we can hold a true belief for strong reasons, for weak reasons or even for the wrong reasons. We should be prepared to look more closely at the evidence upon which we base our beliefs, and try to believe the right thing for the right reasons.

KNOWING A GOOD ARGUMENT FROM A BAD ONE

We express our opinions in arguments.

An argument may look fine at first glance but, in reality, its reasoning may be far from sound.

When reasoning we infer (draw out) a conclusion from a chain of connected

Rodin's statue, 'The Thinker'

statements e.g. *The Giant Panda is an endangered species. All endangered species should be protected. Therefore the Giant Panda should be protected.*

To be sure that an argument proves what it claims, we must know the answers to certain questions:

(1) What exactly is the matter being discussed? *N.B.* Always listen to or read the entire argument before passing judgment on whether it is sound or unsound, right or wrong. Hear the other person out before making up your mind.

(2) Is each of its statements of evidence true? Is there any evidence to support its claims? Does it assume something is true when it is not?

(3) Does the evidence support the conclusion drawn? Example: This argument proves its conclusion because the conclusion can be reasonably said to follow from the evidence:

Mr X drove his car at 80 m.p.h. The maximum speed limit is 60 m.p.h. Therefore Mr X drove his car beyond the speed limit.

An example of the opposite would be:

Some Belgians are married people. Some babies are Belgians. Therefore, some babies are married people!

This is a glaringly false conclusion. There is no sound link between the first two statements and the conclusion drawn from them.

(4) Can you answer the following questions about the language of the argument presented?

   (a)   Do you understand the meaning of the words used?

   (b)   Are emotive words (e.g. 'kind', 'arrogant') used to gain your sympathy or arouse your hostility?

   (c)   Are intimidating phrases (e.g. 'terrorist', 'racist') used to pressurise you into agreeing?

   (d)   Are prestige words (e.g. 'experts say') used to impress you and make you better disposed towards accepting what is said?

QUESTIONS

1   Explain each of the following:

- Argument
- Logic
- Fact
- Opinion
- Knowledge
- Belief
- Truth
- Reasoning

2   When can an argument be said to have proven its conclusion? Give an example.

3   Read the following extracts. In each case, identify those *emotive words*, *prestige words* and *intimidating phrases* used to influence people's response to what is stated.

A. The defence lawyer addresses the jury:

'My client is innocent of the charge of embezzlement. He could not have stolen so much money from his employer's firm. Why? Because he is a decent, well-respected member of his local community. He is a loving husband and father of three adorable children. He is kind to stray dogs. This man has never before been in trouble with the law. He's never even received a parking ticket. He has made generous

donations to local charities. This fine citizen has enjoyed a one hundred per cent attendance record in the firm's accounts department, ever since he was appointed its manager some eight years ago, right up until he was unexpectedly forced to go into hospital for a minor operation six months ago. No one had ever complained about his work until then.

If you choose to send such an excellent, devoted husband and father to prison, you will be depriving his wife and children of his love and support. How could any decent person do such a heartless thing to my client and his family? Only someone with a heart of stone could think him guilty of the crime for which he is on trial here today. I ask you to do for him what you'd want someone else to do for you. I ask you to find him not guilty.'

A scene from the film 'Witness for the Prosecution'

B. An advertisement by the makers of a fictional cigarette lighter:

'It's a great little lighter. Sol – the grand old lighter that's made right here in the good old USA. We truly make an all-American product. The raw materials used in making a Sol lighter are all taken from this great land of ours. We don't use foreign rubbish. No way! Sol lighters are bought by those who are proud to be Americans. If you don't buy one what does it say about you?'

EXERCISE

Read each of the following carefully. Examine each statement in turn. Check whether or not the conclusion can be reasonably said to follow from the evidence offered in each case. Choose which is a good argument and which is not. Then give reasons for your choice.

(1) The local parish church is built of granite. The *nearest* source of granite is eighty miles away. So the building-stone must have been transported *at least* eighty miles.

(2) *If and only if* X drinks large quantities of alcohol, *then* his speech becomes slurred. His speech is slurred. Therefore he has drunk large quantities of alcohol.

(3) *All* important people smoke cigars. Dave smokes cigars. Therefore, Dave must be an important person.

FAITH AND REASON

Where people's decisions are confused or not thought through, reason can help. There are, however, limits to the purely rational approach.

Suppose a woman takes the same bus to work each morning. As she rushes to board the bus, does she ever stop and wonder for a moment if the bus will fail to take her to her usual destination? Probably not. Because the bus is generally reliable she has reason to think that it will most likely do the same today. At the same time, she has to have *faith* that this particular bus will take her to the proper destination.

Faith is *accepting that something is true where one cannot be absolutely certain that it is true*. All religions involve a degree of faith since religious beliefs cannot be 'proved' in the same way that either a mathematical equation or a scientific experiment can be proved. However, faith

St Thomas Aquinas believed in the harmony of faith and reason

is usually based on some evidence which is convincing to the believer, which he/she finds *trustworthy*.

Some people prefer to rely solely on reason and reject any role for faith in their lives. For them, reason seems clear and certain, while faith appears vague and uncertain. Each of us, however, has to put our trust in someone or something. We all make acts of faith each day of our lives. For example:

- When you fly as a passenger in an aircraft, it is an act of faith.

- When you share a secret with a friend, you have faith that he/she will not betray your trust.

- When two people marry, it should be a mutual act of faith, of loving trust in each other.

You may have reasons to support your beliefs about another person or thing, but you still have to have faith.

In our everyday lives, faith and reason complement each other.

QUESTION

1 What is 'faith'?
2 'In everyday life, faith and reason complement each other'. Do you agree/disagree? Explain your answer.
3 Why do 'all religions require a degree of faith'?

SUMMARY

- An argument aims to convince a person to accept a particular idea or thing.
- A good argument is based on sound evidence and will only draw a conclusion which the evidence will support.
- In this context there are two kinds of evidence:
  (1) statements of fact and (2) statements of belief.
- An argument may include both types of statement. It is important to distinguish between them.

- A good argument is one which uses clear and unemotive language to present sound reasons for accepting its conclusion.

- There are limits to the purely rational approach. Reason must be complemented by faith.

- Faith may be defined as the act of putting one's trust in some person or thing.

- A religious person puts his/her faith in God.

- Though faith may be grounded in sound reasons, it can never be proven beyond all doubt.

- While there is more to life and religion than thinking clearly, people do owe it to themselves to think hard about what they believe and why. If they genuinely and passionately believe something, then they must live by it. This is quite a challenge.

PART 2 GOD AND US

CHAPTER 2

Religion in Today's World

A RELIGIOUS CREATURE?

The Mosque: the Muslim house of prayer

It is noon on Friday. In Washington DC, four lanes of traffic stream along Massachusetts Avenue, one of the city's main arteries. A blinking yellow traffic light suddenly turns red.

Impatient to get on their way, irritated by city traffic, the drivers idle their motors, their eyes watching the light. They give the square white building on the corner only passing glances. They drive by it hundreds of times a year, no longer really seeing it. Nor do they hear the strange chant echoing from its tall, slender minaret:

'Allahu Akbar — Allahu Akbar.'

This building is a mosque, a Muslim house of prayer. The chant is the call of the muezzin that first sounded many hundreds of years ago across the sand-swept wastes of Arabia. Friday is the Muslim holy day. From this bustling national capital to the steaming jungles of Bali, from the deserts of Nigeria to the docks of Istanbul, more than one billion people unfold their prayer rugs, face Mecca, the holiest city of Islam, and repeat the words:

'Allahu Akbar — Allahu Akbar' (God is greatest — God is greatest).

Celebrating the Jewish Sabbath

While the followers of the prophet Mohammed pray, a woman only a few streets away lays out her best table linen and the Sabbath candlesticks to prepare for the evening meal. She is a Jew, and she prepares this meal with extra care. For at sundown tonight, the Jewish Sabbath begins. It is the high point of the week for a Jewish family, a time when the cares and burdens of daily living are put away, replaced by the peace and rest of God's holy day.

At the dinner table, surrounded by her family, this woman will light the traditional candles with the blessing:

> *'Blessed are Thou, O Lord our God, King of the Universe, who has sanctified us by Thy laws and commanded us to kindle the Sabbath light.'*

For twenty-four hours, until the first stars twinkle in the Saturday evening sky, this family will be one with a Jewish rancher in Brazil, a lawyer in Germany, an engineer in Russia, a shopkeeper in Hong Kong. There are some 18 million Jews world-wide.

At the same moment, a group of Catholic Christians give their lunch hour to meet with God and with one another for prayer, praise and thanksgiving in the celebration of the Eucharist. The priest and his congregation are only the tiniest part of Christianity, the world's most widespread and, with over 1.8 billion members, its largest religion.

Half a world away, in the holy Indian city of Benares, the banks of the hot, steaming Ganges river are crowded as Hindus wade into the sacred waters to bathe away their sins. It is a holy place of pilgrimage for 750 million Hindus.

In Rangoon, Burma, yellow-robed Buddhist monks, shaded from the tropical sun by umbrellas, walk barefoot along hot pavements, humbly holding out their begging bowls for a few handfuls of rice. They share their belief with 330 million others.

Across the China Sea, in Kyoto, Japan, forty brightly-costumed Shinto paraders tug an enormous float through the streets to celebrate a good harvest. Theirs is the religion of over 100 million Japanese.

And far to the south, in the barrens of the Australian desert, a dark-skinned, curly-haired man, survivor of a long-ago age, sucks a pearl shell and spits into the sky. He believes the sweet-smelling rain will fall now. He is one of 100 million tribal religionists scattered across the globe.

Human beings are religious creatures. It is one of the traits that set them apart from the horse, the pig and the ape. Religion is found among the simplest people on earth and among the most sophisticated.

Adapted from Liva Baker, World Faiths.

In his classic study, *The Variety of Religious Experience*, William James showed definitively that most people in most civilisations, whatever their race or tribe, have all believed in a God or gods of some kind. This sociological fact has led a number of religious thinkers to conclude that it is highly unlikely that something so widespread as the belief in a divine being or beings is without some foundation in reality.

QUESTIONS

1 What do the different people in the extract have in common?
2 What activities would you list as being specifically religious?
3 How many religions are mentioned in the extract? Is one more appealing than another? Why?
4 Do you agree/disagree with Liva Baker's statement that 'human beings are religious creatures'? Give reasons for your opinion.

RELIGION IN TODAY'S IRELAND

Human beings are, by nature, social creatures. We like the company of other people. We are also aware that without the assistance and co-operation of other people, without community, many things would simply not be possible.

Our early ancestors were well aware of this fact. They organised themselves into tribes, otherwise survival in a hostile environment would have been impossible. But not only did they hunt and travel as a community, they also worshipped as a community. Then as now, worship gave comfort to people, gave them a sense of the link between themselves and God. It seemed to confirm the fact that God could be influenced to help them as they confronted the many challenges of life in a hostile world. They may also have realised that faith in God needs to be nurtured and supported if it is to grow. Worshipping together as a community helps to keep faith alive by opening out a person's relationship with God to include other people.

As the extract taken from Liva Baker's book makes clear, most members of the world's great religions feel quite free to carry out acts of worship openly. Religion is generally acknowledged to be an important part of community life and suitable for public display. This was the case in Ireland too, until quite recently.

'When I was a student in University College, Dublin, around 1960, an amazing scene took place every day in the library at noon: everyone there stood and in silence said the Angelus. Even a Buddhist girl from Thailand whom I knew quite well stood in silence. I would love to know when exactly the custom died, but I know that it now would be unthinkable for anyone to make such a public gesture; I wouldn't do it myself. Then only a brave crack-pot would sit down; now only a brave crack-pot would stand up. A different ethos is dominant, which entails the retreat of religion to a largely personal domain.'

M.P. Gallagher, *Help My Unbelief.*

QUESTIONS

1   Does our contemporary Irish society make it easy/difficult for people to show their faith openly or to pray in public?
2   Read *Luke* 12: 1–12 and *Acts* 4: 1–22. What message do you think they contain for Christians in today's Ireland?

CHAPTER 3

The Nature of Religion

THE MEANING OF MYSTERY

To understand the true nature of religion, a person must first be clear about the meaning attached to certain words, especially one such as 'mystery'. The sense of mystery is at the heart of all religions.

But the word 'mystery' is often confused with the word 'problem'. There are, however, important differences between the two of them:

(1) A *problem* is a puzzle for which you hope to find a solution by means of scientific analysis; a question that *must have some rational answer*, even if no one knows what it is yet.

(2) A *mystery* is a fact of existence which you cannot hope to fully understand or fathom, where the methods and tools of scientific enquiry are of limited use; a fact of existence into which you may gain insight but whose *meaning you can never exhaust*; a fact of existence with which you will have to live.

Christian icon depicting the Trinity

Most religions try to help people to grow in their understanding of the mystery of God, of love, of evil and of suffering.

EXERCISE

In each of the following, state which is a problem and which is a mystery:

1. Why do stars eventually collapse into black holes?
2. Why do bad things happen to good people?

3. How can there be three persons in one God?
4. Does intelligent life exist on other worlds?
5. Why have holes appeared in the ozone layer?
6. Is there life after death?
7. Why did the dinosaurs suddenly die out 65 million years ago?
8. Did a person named King Arthur really exist?

QUESTION

What is the most interesting 'mystery' you have yet encountered? Give reasons for your answer.

THE ORIGIN OF RELIGION

Religion is a *human response to the mysteries of existence; an attempt to understand the meaning and purpose of life.* Its precise origin is unknown, shrouded in the mists of time. However, recent archaeological discoveries show that it began very early in human history.

The excavations at the Shanidar caves in the Zagros mountains of Iraq reveal that, over sixty thousand years ago, our distant Neanderthal ancestors practised religion. Why?

'The forces of nature (tornadoes, floods, earthquakes and scorching sun) were frightening to these early humans either in their own right or as forces animated by some mysterious being. Since they had no satisfactory explanation for such recurring natural calamities, they always felt threatened by unseen powers lurking behind visible reality.

There was no way they could control the forces themselves, so they called upon their powers of persuasion to induce these superior beings, as they thought of them, to treat them kindly.'

John Catoir, *World Religions.*

These early humans were aware of the presence of some unseen, higher power in their lives.

Later, when humans like ourselves appeared, about forty thousand years ago, more evidence of religious awareness emerged. At places like

Altamira in Spain and Lascaux in France, people left behind beautiful and intriguing drawings depicting activities such as hunting, and possible religious rituals. This cave art testifies that they too worshipped some kind of higher power.

Did these stone age people worship only one god (monotheism) or many gods (polytheism)? Scholars are divided on this point. They do agree, however, that our ancestors developed religion to show their respect for, and their dependence on, the power of their god or gods. Indeed, the word 'religion' itself is derived from the Latin *religare* meaning 'to tie', because it acknowledges the link between human beings and a divine being(s).

QUESTIONS

1 Many ancient peoples, such as those who built the Newgrange passage tomb, worshipped a sun god. Why do you think they did this?

2 Our ancient ancestors lived in a time before the advent of science. *They made no distinction between a problem and a mystery.* They believed that religion could provide answers to problems in matters such as food and health. Yet they too were faced with many of the great mysteries of life. Can you identify any of these mysteries with which human beings today still have to contend?

RELIGION V SUPERSTITION

Religion should be carefully distinguished from superstition, though the latter can sometimes creep into people's religious belief and practice.

Superstition may be defined as: *'any practice or opinion based on an unjustified or irrational fear of the unknown'.*

Religion, in contrast, is rooted in a sense of respect for the mysteries of life.

Examples of common superstitions include the belief that good fortune will shine upon someone who finds a four-leaf clover, or that some tragedy will strike a person who walks under a ladder.

QUESTIONS

1 What is the essential difference between religion and superstition?

2 Even in our advanced, technological society, superstitious practices still persist. Can you identify any of them?

3 Why do you think superstitious practices still persist? Give reasons for your answer.

4 Read the following extract. Please note that the aim here is not to belittle the religious beliefs of the Aboriginal people, but rather to show the powerful effects of some superstitions.

'Physically the Australian Aboriginal is tough. He can stand any amount of heat, exposure or cold and his incidence to pain is remarkably low. But he has his Achilles' heel. Mental euthanasia. A propensity for dying purely of autosuggestion.

Experiments have proved this: experiments carried out by Australia's leading doctors. On the one hand a group of Aboriginals — voluntarily of course — have spent a day in the desert at a temperature of roughly 95°-100° Fahrenheit, and have spent the night in a sealed-off chamber, thermostatically controlled to a temperature of minus 15°. They slept well without any sort of protection; and though they were naked, felt no cold. On the other hand Aboriginals who are a hundred per cent physically fit have been known to die purely because a tribal medicine man has put the death curse on them. One such man was admitted to a state-capital hospital. Thorough tests proved that there was nothing the matter with him; psychoanalysts tried to instil in him the will to live, the will to fight. But in vain. The medicine man had said he was going to die. And die he did: of self-induced apathy.'

J.V. Marshall, *Walkabout*.

(a) What is meant by the expression 'Achilles' heel'?

(b) What does the author claim is the 'Achilles' heel' of the Aboriginal people of Australia?

(c) What point do you think Marshall makes about the power of superstition among people generally? Do you agree/disagree? Why?

THE ROLE OF RELIGION

An English writer, Charles Colton, once wrote:

> *'People will wrangle for religion; write for it; fight for·it; die for it; anything but live for it.'*

QUESTION

Do you agree with Colton?

If you do, can you give examples?

COMMENT

Colton is not the only person to think this, and he does have a point. But there is more to religion than this.

Read the following extracts:

I. *'Until recent times all people that on earth do dwell have believed in gods of some sort, and always for remarkably similar reasons. Whether the believer is primitive or sophisticated, whether he sits beside a fire in the jungle or the fire in his study, religion has answered his needs in two main areas. It has explained the mystery of what he can observe but not understand — the beauties of nature, the furies of the elements, the unpredictability and injustice of pain, disease, death, the dark obsessions within himself and others, the very existence of all that is. And it has provided the group in which he lives with its identity, its framework, its ethics, backed up by priestly ritual or sacred texts deriving from distant and heroic times. However much different religions may vary, they all fulfil these two basic purposes — answering questions about the universe, and providing a structure for society.'*

B. Gascoigne, *The Christians.*

II. 'Religion is of vital importance to society. Without the civilising influence of religion, the task of the State in maintaining civil order and promoting conditions favourable to true progress becomes immeasurably more difficult. Society depends on religion to foster due regard for lawful authority. It needs religion to inspire respect for the rights of others, to moderate human passions and to restrain selfishness in its many forms. It looks to religion to promote harmony, peace and justice and to foster concern for the needy and the weak.'

Kevin McNamara, *Pluralism.*

Religion fulfils many *positive* functions in society and can be a force for good, promoting understanding and respect between people.

QUESTIONS

1   According to Gascoigne, what are the two basic functions which religion fulfils?

2   In what ways does religion influence society, according to McNamara? Do you agree/disagree that religion has this influence? Why?

3   The journalist and historian, Paul Johnson, once remarked: *'I don't think my Christian faith makes me a better person, but I do think it stops me from being a worse one than I otherwise could be.'* What do you think he means? Do you agree/disagree? Why?

CHAPTER 4

Ways of Thinking About God

THE SPECTRUM OF BELIEFS

Religion has been defined as:

> *'a code of belief which usually involves the worship of God or gods'.*
> Webster's New World Encyclopaedia

With the exception of Buddhism, belief in a supernatural power is an essential element of the major religions. But what do we mean by 'God'?

The writer Frank Sheed once offered this answer:

> *'God is a mystery, an infinite being of whom we can know something, in the knowledge of whom we can grow, yet the truth of whose being we can never exhaust. We shall never have to throw God away like a solved crossword puzzle.'*

While helpful, this is only a vague outline. In their attempts to fill in the details, human beings have produced a rich variety of answers to questions about the nature of God.

People who believe in God (i.e. theists) generally hold one or other of the following views:

(1) *Monotheism* means belief in one God, usually described as the Supreme Being, and Creator of all that exists.

(2) *Polytheism* refers to belief in several gods.

(3) *Henotheism* is where a person believes in one god but does not deny the existence of other gods.

(4) *Pantheism* [also known as 'Monism'] is the belief that all things (people, plants and animals) are part of the one reality, or that they are just 'aspects' of God without an individual identity or value.

Judaism, Christianity and Islam are all monotheistic religions. However, Christians believe that there are three divine persons — Father, Son and Spirit — in one God. This is called the doctrine of the *Trinity*.

The Star of David, symbol of Judaism

Some scholars believe that Hinduism may originally have been monotheistic but became pantheistic, emphasising the oneness of the Universe. Hindus believe that all things, living and non-living, are expressions of the Brahman. Though they worship many different gods and goddesses, Hindus believe that these all emanate from one divine world soul which is all things and which is in all things, underlying everything in our world.

Buddhism began as *atheism* (i.e. *rejection of belief in God*) because its founder Gautama, who had been a Hindu, rejected the very idea of an unseen divine power. Ironically after his death some of his followers, who called him the Buddha, declared him to be a divine being, something it is believed he would have deplored when alive.

Buddha

THE GOLDEN RULE

All the great religions are an attempt to make sense out of human experience of life and death, of good and evil. Each one, with the exception of Buddhism, claims that its teachings are divine in origin. But all claim that faithfulness to their teachings will direct a person's life along the path of goodness.

Indeed, though the major religions differ in their approaches to God, they all share a common belief in what is called the 'Golden Rule', perhaps the most fundamental of moral principles. Though this Golden Rule is worded differently by the major religions, it has essentially the same meaning:

Christianity

> 'In everything do to others as you would have them do to you' [Matthew 7:12]

Judaism

> 'What is harmful to you, do not to your fellow men' [Talmud, Shabbat, 3id.]

Islam

> 'No one of you is a believer until he desires for his brother that which he desires for himself' [Sunnah]

The cross, symbol of Christianity

Hinduism

> 'This is the sum of duty: do naught to others which would cause you pain if done to you' [Mahabharata 5, 1517]

Buddhism

> 'Hurt not others in ways that you yourself would find hurtful' [Udana-Varga 5, 18]

QUESTIONS:

1 Explain the following terms:
   - Monotheism
   - Polytheism
   - Henotheism
   - Pantheism
2 In what way is Christianity different from the other monotheistic religions?
3 Why is Hinduism described as 'pantheistic'?
4 What things do the major world religions share in common?

THE NON-CHRISTIAN RELIGIONS

		Hinduism	Buddhism
BELIEFS	Origin and Location	The roots of Hinduism lie in the highly animistic, polytheistic religion of tribes who migrated to the Indus Valley, bringing their scriptures, the Vedas, and their social system, the caste system. There are presently about 750 million Hindus. Three-fourths live in India, and most of the others live in countries near India. Hinduism is diverse, often called a fellowship of faiths.	Siddhartha Gautama (b. 565 BC), a Hindu prince, left his lavish life to search for truth. On his thirty-fifth birthday, he solved the mysteries of the universe and became Buddha. Buddhism is based in eastern and central Asia. Although Gautama rejected many Hindu teachings, the influence of Hinduism is clear.
	The Supreme Being	Hinduism has assimilated 330 million gods. The most prominent gods are Brahma, Vishnu, and Shiva. Krishna was a loving compassionate incarnation of the Supreme Being. Each Hindu is free to believe in a favourite god or gods.	Gautama ignored the question of a divine being. He taught that speculation about matters of faith was wasteful, and that the time would be better spent helping people with the realities of present life. Ironically, Buddhists have developed complicated forms of worship and deified Buddha himself.
	The Human Predicament	Each human being is like a drop of World Soul, separated from this Cosmic Force and trapped in the dreaded cycle of birth and rebirth. The only way to escape this cycle is to work toward union once again with World Soul (nirvana).	Human beings are slaves to their cravings and their attachment to things. Actually, everything in life is impermanent, and ownership is an illusion. The inability to accept these facts causes craving, and craving causes suffering.
	The Way of Salvation	To achieve nirvana, one may choose from a number of disciplines or paths. These involve various degrees of difficulty. The goal of each is to accumulate karma through one's obedience. The result of an obedient life is rebirth into a higher existence and, ultimately, nirvana.	By accepting the impermanence of all things, people can eliminate desire and achieve 'passionless peace'. This is the state of nirvana, which releases one from the cycle of 'samsara' (birth and rebirth). To reach this state one must follow the Eightfold path.
	Scriptures Distinctive practices	The scripture common to almost all Hindus is the *Bhagavad Gita*, the story of Krishna's incarnation. Worship is broad and ill-defined. Many Hindus visit the Ganges River, believing it has spiritual power. Hindus are widely known for their caste system and their belief that all forms of life are sacred.	At age four, every Buddhist boy goes through a highly symbolic ritual and becomes a monk. He may choose to remain a monk as an adult. Women have an inferior role, and only males can achieve nirvana. There are two sects of Buddhism: Hinayana and Mahayana. Another group, Zen Buddhists, ignore the doctrines of Buddhism and emphasize meditation.

24

Judaism	Islam
The Jews, God's 'chosen people', have a history of persecution, homelessness and mass execution. A religious Jew is one who accepts the teachings of Judaism. Although Judaism began, of course, in Israel, its adherents are dispersed throughout the world today.	There are over one billion Muslims in the world today. Since its foundation in the seventh century AD, Islam has spread rapidly, influencing every race and continent. Its roots lie both in the animistic, polytheistic religion of the nomadic Arabs and in Judeo-Christian teachings. Both affected its founder, Mohammed.
The cornerstone of Judaism is the Shemah: 'Hear O Israel: The Lord our God is One Lord.' Everything centres on God. He is a moral God Who demands reverence and obedience, but He is also a God of love. He shares His glory with no other. Adherents of traditional Judaism believe they are still exclusively God's chosen people.	Among the early Arabs, Allah was the supreme God. For Muslims, Allah is the one and only, the God of absolute unity, who sees all, knows all, is all-powerful and unchanging. He shares his glory with no other.
The Jews have endured tremendous suffering for centuries. Their view of the human predicament is that of the *Old Testament*. All human beings are sinners in need of a saviour. Suffering is the result of sin. The world is in a state of chaos, rushing headlong toward destruction.	Human beings must accept the teachings of the last true prophet, who taught that one must submit to Allah or be lost. The greatest sin is refusal to acknowledge and praise Allah, unwillingness to submit to his perfect will. Allah is supreme and deserving of constant praise. He rewards the submissive with a heaven of sensual delights and punishes the disobedient and irreverent with a hell of gruesome agonies.
Adherents of Judaism anticipate the coming of the Messiah, who will restore the Jewish people and, through them, the world. Until his coming, obedience to the law is the only way of salvation. This obedience will bring righteousness in this life and will give eternal life in heaven to the faithful.	In order to gain eternal life in heaven, one must practise complete submission to the will of Allah. This includes obedience to the Five Pillars and the Shari'a, an extremely strict code of ethics, morality, and civil and criminal law.
Although Jews believe all of the *Old Testament*, the Torah (the law) is by far the most important part. The Talmud contains sixty-three books which explain the Torah. Jewish boys are highly educated while girls are taught to be homemakers. Judaism emphasises family and community.	Islam accepts four scriptures: the *Torah*, the *Psalms*, the *Gospel* of Jesus, and the *Koran*. Only the *Koran* is considered Allah's complete revelation. Muslims are known for their prayers, said five times daily. They also go to the mosque every Friday at noon. They give alms to all who ask, fast for the month of Ramadan, and attempt to travel to Mecca at least once in their lives.

Earl Schipper, *Religions of the World.*

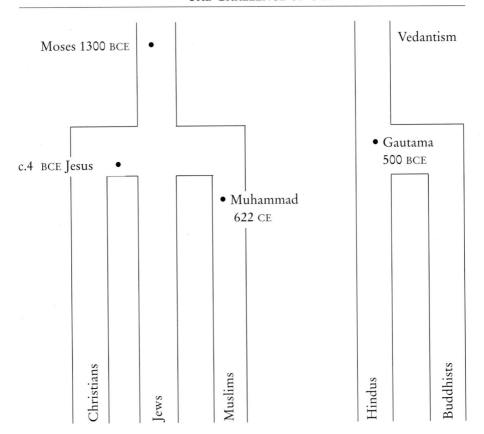

Moses 1300 BCE

Vedantism

• Gautama
500 BCE

c.4 BCE Jesus

• Muhammad
622 CE

Christians

Jews

Muslims

Hindus

Buddhists

Major Religions of the World

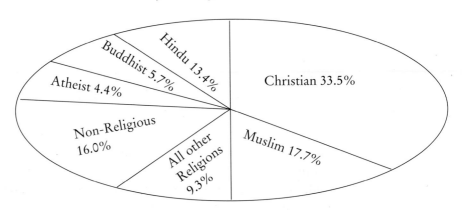

Hindu 13.4%

Buddhist 5.7%

Atheist 4.4%

Christian 33.5%

Non-Religious
16.0%

All other
Religions
9.3%

Muslim 17.7%

**Estimated Religious Population of
the World**

Source: *Encyclopedia Britannica Book of the Year*

EXERCISE

Read the following statements of belief carefully. In each case identify the particular religion to which it belongs.

- One must be obedient to the Five Pillars and the Shari'a to gain eternal life in heaven.

- The result of an obedient life is rebirth into a higher existence and ultimately nirvana.

- The goal of life is to achieve 'passionless peace'.

- God will send a messiah to restore his chosen people and through them the world.

- Allah is the one and only God and only the Koran is Allah's complete revelation.

- All human beings are sinners in need of a saviour. All suffering is the result of sin.

- Human beings are slaves to their cravings and attachment to things. Craving causes suffering.

- The Lord is a God who demands reverence and obedience, but He is also a God of love.

IS THERE ONLY ONE GOD?

Three of the major world religions, Judaism, Christianity and Islam, believe that there is only one God.

The most famous argument in favour of monotheism was put forward by Thomas Aquinas. He said that God *must* be one because by 'God' we mean a being who is infinite and perfect in every way — *unique*. If another god existed, that god would have to be perfect in a way that God is not. This would mean that God would be lacking in some way as God would not be completely perfect and so would not really be 'God' at all. God, Aquinas said, must by definition be completely perfect, unique and therefore *one*. Consequently, there can only be one God.

Christians believe that this truth was first revealed to the Jews, from whom all the great monotheistic religions have sprung.

Questions

1 Why does Thomas Aquinas argue that there can only be one God?

2 In his book *Human Destiny*, John Hammes claims that monotheism is a more believable form of religion than polytheism. Do you agree/disagree? Why?

Relations between Christians and Non-Christians

The Second Vatican council (1962-65) called on Christians to build '*bonds of friendship*' with non-Christians of good character, and stated that Christians should '*reject nothing of what is true and holy in other religions*'.

But a question now arises: why choose to be a Christian and not, say, a Jew or a Muslim?

In his book *An Approach to Christianity*, B.C. Butler tackles this question.

He points out that a person's actions and words can tell us a great deal about his/her character. The most complete act of revealing one's true nature to another person is when we say or do something which reveals how much we really love that person. Our words and deeds reveal our love.

Christians believe that Jesus revealed the love of God in a way and in a depth never before experienced *by what he said and did*. God became a human being and lived among us. He died for our sins and rose from the dead. Butler claims that we will not find anything like this in any other religion.

It is Christian belief that God has most fully revealed the truth about his nature through the life, death and resurrection of his Son, Jesus Christ.

Questions

1 Why should Christians build 'bonds of friendship with non-Christians of good character'? Explain your answer.

2   Why do Christians believe that Jesus is unique?

3   Why does Christopher Butler choose to be a Christian? Do you agree/disagree with him? Explain your answer.

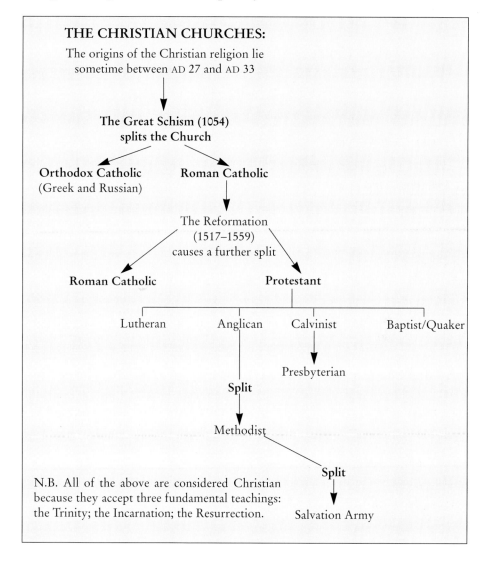

THE CHRISTIAN CHURCHES:

The origins of the Christian religion lie sometime between AD 27 and AD 33

The Great Schism (1054) splits the Church

Orthodox Catholic (Greek and Russian)   **Roman Catholic**

The Reformation (1517–1559) causes a further split

Roman Catholic   **Protestant**

Lutheran   Anglican   Calvinist   Baptist/Quaker

Presbyterian

Split

Methodist

Split

N.B. All of the above are considered Christian because they accept three fundamental teachings: the Trinity; the Incarnation; the Resurrection.   Salvation Army

THE AUTHENTIC OUTLOOK

A truly committed, religious person exhibits certain signs which testify to a genuine faith in a loving God. These include:

- A stronger desire to build an ever-closer personal relationship with God through prayer, and to demonstrate one's love of God through helping one's fellow human beings.

- A greater willingness to take responsibility for one's own actions, and a greater care about the moral example one sets for others.

- A sharper awareness of the capacity for doing good or evil, both in oneself and in other people.

- A greater ability to admit to failure and weakness without threatening one's sense of self-worth.

- An increased respect for the sincerely-held religious beliefs of other people and a willingness to demand that they treat yours with equal respect.

- A greater ability to recognise what is good and true in the beliefs of others while remaining firmly committed to the teaching of one's own religion.

HOW TO DISTINGUISH THE CHRISTIAN CHURCHES FROM SECTS CLAIMING TO BE CHRISTIAN

A *Church* is characterised by:
- A balanced, comprehensive range of doctrines informed by centuries of deep, prayerful reflection on the teachings of Jesus Christ.

- Membership which is open to and includes people of all nations and social classes, requiring only their willingness to honestly follow their consciences informed by the teachings of their faith to qualify for membership.

- A critical attitude to the values of contemporary society but a willingness to work with and through its institutions to build a better world for all, members and non-members.

A *Sect* denotes a group with such characteristics as:
- An extreme, narrow emphasis on a few aspects or teachings of the Christian tradition at the expense of others.

- Personal conversion must be accompanied by a willingness to follow all the dictates of its teaching unquestioningly, without any reservations.

- Severe restrictions are placed on the personal freedom of members in all aspects of their lives.
- Condemnation of the values of contemporary society, usually accompanied by a withdrawal from active involvement in its institutions and a restriction of interest to its own members' welfare.

Further Reading

M. Evans, *Are Jehovah's Witnesses Right?*

F. J. Ripley, *Jehovah's Witnesses*

Both are published by the Catholic Truth Society, London

CHAPTER 5

Religion and Science

INTRODUCTION

Until the Enlightenment, religion provided most of the answers to the questions which concerned people.

Since then, however, science has made remarkable strides in understanding our universe, with the result that it has shaken many people's confidence in religion as a source of answers.

By science we mean:

> *any systematic field of study or body of knowledge that aims, through experiment, observation and argument, to produce a reliable explanation of phenomena (i.e. objects and events) in our world.*

Our purpose here is not to question the adequacy of the procedures and theories of any particular science, but rather to challenge the belief that the sciences and technology provide the *only* sure and worthwhile knowledge for understanding ourselves and our world, and that they alone will eventually provide the solutions to all human problems.

While religion and science have tended to go their separate ways since the 1600s, the twentieth century has witnessed a gradual realisation that they have much to offer each other. A belief persists, however, that science alone can provide the solution to all human problems.

In his book, *Understanding the Present*, Bryan Appleyard challenges those scientists who think that, given enough time and money, science will be able to explain not only the nature of the universe but also the reason for its existence. He maintains that some scientists try to devalue the important questions science cannot answer, such as the meaning of life, the existence of God, or the nature of the human soul.

Sadly, narrow-mindedness and prejudice on *both* sides of the religion-science debate have done much harm, confusing and misleading people about the true nature of the relationship between them.

QUESTIONS

1 What is the purpose of science?

2 What are the main concerns of religion?

THE SCOPES 'MONKEY TRIAL'

In 1925, John Scopes, a high school science teacher in the American state of Tennessee, was arrested and charged because he had violated state law. Ignoring warnings from local officials, he had persisted in teaching Charles Darwin's *theory of evolution*, i.e. that human beings had gradually developed in both physical appearance and intellectual capacity from primitive ape-like ancestors over a period of millions of years.

The law of the state of Tennessee would only permit him to teach a fundamentalist (i.e. literal) reading of the story of Adam and Eve in *Genesis* (Chapters 2 and 3).

Scopes was vilified and branded an atheist for refusing to teach the Bible literally. Fundamentalist Christians misrepresented his position. Scopes, like many other Christians, had come to understand that the Bible had been inspired by God but not dictated by God. He realised that it was never meant to be an eyewitness description of what had happened at the creation of the world. The stories of how God created the world in six days and made the first human beings are not historical or scientific accounts but a beautiful poetic statement of religious belief, that *all life comes from God and depends on God for its continued existence*. While science tells us *how* our world was created, the Bible tells us *who* created it and *why*.

Scopes was put on trial, and was prosecuted by the leading fundamentalist lawyer and politician, William Jennings Bryant. However, Scopes was fortunate to have the services of the greatest defence lawyer of the period, Clarence Darrow.

After an extraordinary court case, in which the defence actually cross-examined the prosecuting counsel in the witness box, Scopes was found guilty as charged by the jury. However, the court did not imprison him, only imposing a fine of $100 which was then set aside on a legal technicality.

Fundamentalist Christian groups were outraged. Scopes had evaded prison and had succeeded in showing that the law restricting teachers from teaching about evolution was both unjust and unworkable.

QUESTIONS

1 What is Darwin's theory of evolution?

2 What did Scopes believe was the real intention of the author(s) of *Genesis*?

3 In your opinion, does the theory of evolution pose any real difficulty for people's confidence in the Bible or religion in general? Explain your answer.

4 Read the following story:

One bright summer's morning the philosopher Ludwig Wittgenstein was out walking with one of his young students. The latter remarked that all those people in times past who understood the Bible literally, and so believed that the sun rotated around the earth, must have been complete morons. Wittgenstein stopped, looked up at the sun above them and replied: '*Really? And just what do you think it would look like if the sun did rotate around the earth, as they believed?*'

(a) What point do you think Wittgenstein was making?

(b) How can it help us to understand the frame of mind of people in earlier times who read the Bible literally?

5 In his book *The Early Earth* (published in 1972), Professor John Whitcomb stated that the story of Noah's Ark (read *Genesis* 6:5-8 and 19) happened exactly as the Bible author said. He calculated the capacity of Noah's Ark as 1,400,000 cubic feet, commenting that this is about equal to the capacity of 522 modern railroad boxcars. On this basis, he argued, two of every species of air-breathing creatures on our planet could have been transported within the ark with room to spare for food supplies.

To anyone who doubted this straightforward, literal or 'fundamentalist' reading of *Genesis*, Whitcomb said that to do so would seem '*to imply that God is not a trustworthy witness of what happened at the time of creation*'.

(a) Would it be fair to say that Whitcomb believes the account in *Genesis* to have been dictated by God (note the use of the word 'witness') to some ancient Jewish scholar? Give reasons for your answer.

(b) What makes it difficult to believe that *Genesis* is *literally true*, word for word?

RELIGION AND SCIENCE IN PERSPECTIVE

The film *Inherit the Wind*, directed by Stanley Kramer, is a dramatised version of that famous court case, known since as the *Scopes Monkey Trial*. Kramer shows remarkable insight into the whole affair. After the Clarence Darrow character (played by Spencer Tracy) has outwitted the prosecuting counsel, he is about to leave the courtroom. Just before he leaves he gathers his books and papers. He picks up Darwin's *Origin of the Species* with his right hand, pauses a moment, then picks up the Bible with his left hand. He considers both books, puts them together in one hand, places them under his right arm and walks out of the courtroom. In that brief scene the director makes a striking statement about the relationship between science and religion.

Spencer Tracy in Inherit the Wind

The conflict between the two is gradually being seen for what it is - no contest at all. Both have important roles to play in human life.

Much of the clash between religion and science can be traced back to the distinction we made earlier between a *problem* and a *mystery*. Too few people grasped the importance of this distinction, so that when, for example, scientists challenged a literal reading of the *Old Testament*, e.g. the story of Adam and Eve, it was assumed, often wrongly, that they were attacking the very idea of religion itself.

'The Italian astronomer Galileo Galilei (1564-1642) was condemned by the Holy Office in Rome when he said that the earth moved round the sun, not the sun round the earth. Because the Bible always speaks of the sun moving around the earth, Galileo was forced to withdraw his theory and was put under house arrest. The Church officials had failed to realise that the Bible was not *speaking scientifically but using everyday language; just as we ourselves still speak of the sun rising or setting although we know it does nothing of the sort.'*

Des Forristal, *The Mystery of God.*

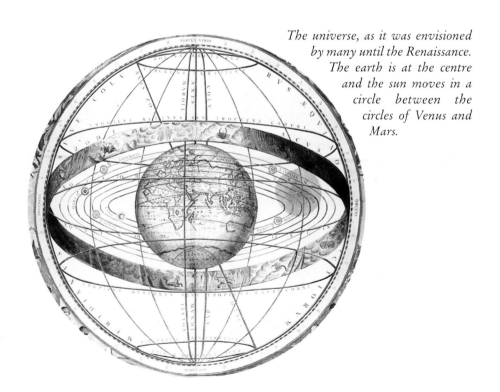

The universe, as it was envisioned by many until the Renaissance. The earth is at the centre and the sun moves in a circle between the circles of Venus and Mars.

Such events soured relations between many scientists and religious believers. It also led some people to think that we have to choose to base our lives on either science or religion. In fact, we need *both*.

'Science and religion are friends, not enemies. They share a common concern for truth, and both are seeking to understand the world. Science is concerned with the impersonal, repeatable side of experience and with finding out how things happen.

Religion is concerned with the unique, personal side of experience and with finding out the value and purpose of what is happening.

We need both if we are truly to understand what is going on'.

John Polkinghorne, *The Sunday Times* 15.8.94

QUESTIONS

1 Why were relations soured between much of the scientific community and the Catholic Church after the condemnation of Galileo?

2 Do you agree/disagree that we need both science and religion if we are to 'truly understand what is going on'? Explain your answer.

FAITH AND SCIENCE

Religion and science have more in common than is often realised. There is a growing awareness of the role of faith in science too.

In his book *Science and Belief*, Michael Poole points out that science itself involves a number of basic beliefs about the world which are *not proved* by science, but are *assumed* by it. They are:

1. *Rationality*
Rationality implies that our thought processes make sense and are basically reliable. This presupposition is central to all branches of study. You cannot even discuss whether rationality is a correct assumption without committing yourself to the assumption that it is!

2. Intelligibility
Whereas rationality assumes we can understand, intelligibility assumes the world can be understood. If we did not believe that, then there would be no point in trying to do science.

3. Orderliness
The belief that nature is orderly, that it is cosmos not chaos, makes it worthwhile searching for patterns which can be summarised in scientific laws.

4. Uniformity
Belief in the uniformity of nature is the assumption that, even though the world changes, the underlying laws of nature remain the same in time and space. For example, although gravity has resulted in both the birth and the death of stars at different times, the law of gravity itself has remained the same.

5. Worthwhileness
Without the presupposition that science is a worthwhile and legitimate activity, people would not carry out experiments.

The foundations of science, therefore, are not beyond questioning. A scientist may have *good reasons* for believing that these assumptions are correct. Indeed, without them scientific research would be impossible. But he/she cannot be completely certain. The scientist has to make an act of *faith* in them.

CONCLUSION

Science is concerned with describing and understanding the workings of our world, whereas religion is concerned with matters that science cannot answer — what is the meaning, purpose and value of life?

Science and religion are not in conflict, they are *complementary*. As Dr Martin Luther King put it:

> *'Science investigates; religion interprets. Science gives us a knowledge which is power; religion gives us wisdom which is control.'*

QUESTIONS

1 What are the five basic beliefs about the world which science assumes?

2 What have you learned about the foundations upon which science is based? Is it true to say that science involves a degree of faith? Explain your answer.

3 The great scientist Albert Einstein once wrote: 'Science without religion is lame, religion without science is blind.'

(a) What do you think he meant by this?

(b) Do you agree/disagree? Why?

Professor Stephen Hawking, author of A Brief History of Time, *who acknowledges that scientists have asked the question:* How? *but have neglected the fundamental question:* Why? *He is open to the probability that God exists.*

CHAPTER 6

The Mystery of God

THE PRESENCE AND ABSENCE OF GOD

'One of the baffling things about the life of a believer is the way in which belief in God comes and goes. As a believer I hold that God is Creator of the World and so is present in every particle of his creation. But it is one thing to believe in God's presence and another to have a sense of that presence.

Many people could draw up a list of experiences which have led them to believe vividly in the presence of God. My own list would consist in grand experiences like the sight of the Alps one winter's morning from an aeroplane, twenty thousand feet up — silent and vast, majestically independent of human beings; but also in the sight of tiny delicate things like a new-born baby's finger nails.

God is even more powerfully present in human relationships, and, like most people, my list of positive experiences of God would chiefly consist in my experiences of human trust and friendship. Inevitably we take love's existence for granted, but it is, in fact, an almost miraculous experience.

And yet our sense of God's presence among human beings can evaporate as quickly as it came when we are confronted with all the ugly facts of life in this world, both the ugly facts we read about in the newspapers and see on television, and the ugly facts in our own lives — private events like the breakdown of trusted friendships, public events like the awful massacres, torture, gross inhumanities which happen all around us.

One way of describing this world which both reveals and hides God is to call it the sacrament of God. Sacraments are signs which speak of God's active presence and so can be said to show him. But they are only signs pointing to him and they do not always point plainly — they have to be read. This is how the created world appears to believers: as a sign of God's creative activity which has to be read. If we read the signs correctly, then we recognise God's active hand in everything around us.'

John Dalrymple, *Costing Not Less Than Everything.*

QUESTIONS

1 What are the experiences which encourage John Dalrymple to believe in God's presence in our world?

2 What are the *'ugly facts of life'* that make people doubt God's existence or goodness?

3 What does the author mean when he describes our world as *'the sacrament of God'*?

4 What does he say we will recognise if we *'read the signs correctly'*?

IS GOD JUST AN ILLUSION?

Sigmund Freud

The French writer Voltaire once jokingly remarked:

'If God did not exist, it would be necessary to invent him.'

Later, Sigmund Freud and Karl Marx decided to pursue seriously a remark made in jest.

Karl Marx

Freud said that our ancestors invented God to provide them with an imaginary father figure to help them cope with the pain and disappointments of life, and provide reassurance that people will be rewarded for making sacrifices in this life by enjoying a better life in the next world.

His contemporary Karl Marx reached the same conclusion, and developed it further. He said that belief in God and the practice of religion acted as a 'brake' on human progress, as a sort of drug to keep the impoverished masses quiet and subservient. Lenin stated this view forcefully:

Lenin

> *'Religion is the opium of the people. It is a kind of spiritual gin in which the slaves of capital drown their human shape.'*

Once Lenin and his communist followers seized power in Russia in 1917, they sought to undermine popular religion. Here is an example of the methods they used:

> *'Some hungry children in Georgia were told to ask God to give them their daily bread. Three times they asked and nothing came. Then they were told to make the same request to Lenin, and lo and behold, a truckful of food came round the corner.'*
>
> B. Gascoigne, *The Christians*.

When this kind of tactic failed to achieve the desired effect, the Communist regime began to imprison and execute Jews, Christians and Muslims by the hundreds of thousands. Yet it failed to eradicate religious belief. Indeed, even more ruthless attempts to do so have also failed. Read the following story:

THE JAPANESE MARTYRS

'The history of the Christian missions to Japan has been an amazing saga of heroism since the first Christian gospel preached there by Francis Xavier in 1549. For nearly a century the Catholic Church made great progress in spite of sporadic persecutions. But in 1638 the Shogun Hideyoshi decided to exterminate Christianity. When the Christians rebelled, 35,000 of them were massacred. Some of the victims were subjected to the intolerable torture of the pit: hung upside down, suspended in a hole in the ground and kept in agony for days by torturers who bled them slowly from their temples. There were many martyrs until

42

finally all signs of Christianity were obliterated. Japan was sealed off from all foreign contacts for two centuries.

The signing of a commerce treaty with the United States in 1854 finally re-opened the country to foreign missionaries. A group of French clergy opened a small chapel in Nagasaki.

One day a remarkable thing happened: A small group of Japanese visited the little mission chapel. One of the priests welcomed them and began talking with them. What he learned stunned him. These Japanese were devout Christians who had secretly managed to hold on to the essentials of the Christian faith for two centuries, although without priests and totally isolated from the outside world. There were other groups of these Christians scattered across Japan, finally numbering some 10,000 in all.

When news of this reached the Japanese authorities they reacted with fury, for membership of the Christian religion was still an illegal act. Some of these heroic believers were cruelly persecuted and killed while others were forced into exile. World opinion stirred up by press reports, however, finally brought an end to the persecution, and in 1889 complete freedom of worship was granted.'

Adapted from: T. Bokenkotter, *A Concise History of the Catholic Church.*

It is remarkable how totalitarian states have used all their resources to destroy belief in something they say does not exist.

QUESTIONS

1 Did Marx have a point when he talked about religion being abused by some powerful groups to control the poor? Explain your thinking.

2 Does Marx's criticism necessarily mean that God does not exist and that religion is a mistake? Give reasons for your answer.

3 Why do you think people are prepared to suffer great persecution and even death for their religious beliefs? Explain your answer.

THE COLDNESS OF A UNIVERSE WITHOUT GOD

I. The mathematician and philosopher Bertrand Russell once wrote the following description of a universe without God:

'No heroism, no intensity of thought and feeling can preserve an individual life beyond the grave ... all the labourers of the ages, all the noonday brightness of human genius are destined to extinction in the vast death of the solar system, and ... the whole temple of man's achievement must inevitably be buried in the debris of a universe in ruins.'

Sceptical Essays

Bertrand Russell

II. In his famous play, *Waiting for Godot*, Samuel Beckett tells of two tramps who are waiting for a mysterious person called Godot whom they believe will come and save them. While they are waiting, they meet a blind man who is guided by another man who cannot speak. When they ask the blind man how his companion became mute, the former bursts into an angry speech about what he believes is the meaninglessness of human life.

Waiting for Godot: The two tramps, Vladimir and Estragon, with Lucky, the blind man.

'When! When! One day, is that not enough for you, one day like any other day, one day he went dumb, one day I went blind, one day we'll go deaf, one day we were born, one day we shall die, the same day, the same second, is that not enough for you? They give birth astride of a grave, the light gleams for an instant, then it's night once more.'

Beckett claims that human life is no more than a brief flash of light which is all too quickly swallowed up by the darkness of the grave.

QUESTIONS

1 Express Russell's and Beckett's ideas in your own words.

2 (a) If people genuinely believed in their viewpoint, how would it influence their attitude to life? Give reasons for your answer.

   (b) Do you agree/disagree with them? Why?

SEARCHING FOR SIGNS OF GOD'S PRESENCE

Over the centuries people have tried, with varying degrees of success, to advance sound reasons for believing in God's existence. However, before considering them, we must distinguish our approach to the mystery of God's existence from the approach adopted by scientists when they pursue the answer to some particular problem in astronomy, engineering or medicine.

'Science enjoys the use of the great weapon of experiment, but in the realm of the personal, testing has to give way to trusting, as we know in our encounters with each other. Setting little traps to see if you are my friend will destroy the possibility of friendship between us. It is the same with God.'
   John Polkinghorne, *Serious Talk: Science and Religion in Dialogue*

There is no possibility of a clear-cut, undeniable proof of God's existence. God is a mystery, not a problem to be solved. Rather, Christians and non-Christians believe that we can find what John

Dalrymple calls 'signs of God's active presence in the world', and that these point towards God's existence. But where should we look for these signs of God's presence?

If we reflect on our experience of the world, a number of questions arise:

(1) Why should there be order in our world?

(2) Why should our world exist at all?

(3) Why should we have a moral awareness?

But before we begin our search, we should remember that:

'Any kind of questioning about the existence of God needs a special spirit of reverence. Since we are tackling a question that touches everything about us and our lives, unless our approach is filled with a kind of wonder, it will stay superficial. A famous philosopher used to insist that any argument about the existence of God had to start from a sense of amazement that I am here at all. In his opinion, waking up to the surprise of my own existence is the beginning and basis for all the more worked-out reasonings about God. Therefore I can be on the wrong wavelength in my search unless I sense something the strangeness of my being alive at all'.

M. P. Gallagher, SJ, *Questions of Faith.*

QUESTIONS

1 Why is the idea of 'trust' important in our search for signs of God's presence? Explain your answer.

2 Why is there no possibility of a 'clear-cut, undeniable proof of God's existence'? Explain your answer.

3 What kind of approach to our search for God does Gallagher advise us to adopt? Do you agree/disagree? Why?

Sign One: The Evidence of Order in Our World

Some recent writers have attempted to show that our earth and human life itself are simply freaks of nature, accidents that happened by blind chance when our solar system was formed billions of years ago. But the scientist A. C. Morrison gives the following example of how enormously figures multiply against chance:

'Suppose you take ten pennies and mark them from 1 to 10. Put them in your pocket and give them a good shake. Now try to draw them out in a sequence from 1 to 10, putting each coin back in your pocket after each draw.

Your chance of drawing no. 1 is 1 in 10. Your chance of drawing no. 1 and 2 in succession would be 1 in a 100. Your chance of drawing 1, 2 and 3 in succession would be 1 in a 1,000. Your chance of drawing 1, 2, 3 and 4 in succession would be 1 in 10,000 and so on, until your chance of drawing numbers 1 to 10 in succession would reach the unbelievable figure of one chance in ten billion.'

Mark Link, Man in the Modern World

Morrison believes that so many factors are necessary to allow life to arise and develop on our planet that it is simply mathematically unthinkable for the order of our universe to have happened by chance. The theory of evolution gives us an explanation of how life developed on earth but it does not tell us why this happened, why there is order and purpose in our world. As another scientist has written:

'Science tells us that evolution is not enough to explain the coming to be of life. Such a thing could not happen in any old world, for it requires a very specific, finely tuned balance in the fundamental laws of nature. This remarkable insight is called the "Anthropic Principle". Religion makes this intelligible by recognising that the universe is indeed "not any old world", but a creation endowed by its creator with just the special physical fabric that has enabled life to thrive on earth'.

John Polkinghorne, Sunday Times 15.8.1994

Science is built on laws which we can observe at work in nature: physical, chemical and biological laws such as the laws of evolution. A law demands a lawmaker. Scientists do not make the laws which give order to nature, they only discover those laws which are already in existence.

47

Because of this, Christian philosophers argue that all life, especially human life, was *deliberately created* and that its evolution has been *guided* for a purpose by God.

Sign Two: The Fact that our World exists at all

The following extract is taken from a piece written by Maximilian Kolbe. (There is some overlap here with Sign One, above.) The extract describes a conversation he had in a railway carriage with a fellow passenger who claimed that we cannot find any worthwhile evidence for belief in God's existence. Kolbe draws his attention to the wonders of our world which we so often take for granted.

KOLBE: *What would you think of a man who argued this way about this watch of yours: 'This metal case has come from the gold mine of its own accord, it has melted itself down and purified itself and formed itself into its present shape by chance. The inscription was engraved on it by chance. The glass was moulded and polished by chance. Likewise the delicate wheels and springs all made themselves by chance. Finally, all the different parts were assembled together by chance and without the assistance of human mind or hand. In short, it is entirely by chance that the watch tells us the time of day.' If a man were to say this in all seriousness, what would you think about him?*

PASSENGER: *I'd think he had taken leave of his senses.*

KOLBE: *Well now, in nature we have organisms that are far more complex and intricate. In studying anatomy, you must have been struck by the design of the human eye, how many different parts it has, how delicate they are, how marvellously they work together to enable us to see. In the whole of nature there are millions and billions of organisms which live and grow and multiply. How could it be claimed that these wonders of nature are mere accidents? Someone might say: 'Such a thing does not happen without a cause, but its cause has another cause and that has another and so on.' But even if this series of causes could reach back into infinity, don't we have to look for some sort of First Cause? These other causes do not give any perfections from themselves but only hand down what they have already received. What we have to look for is the source of all perfections. There must be some sort of First Cause and that is God.*

D. Forristal, *Maximilian of Auschwitz*

However, Christians believe that God is not simply the *creator* but also the *sustainer* of all that exists.

Consider the following:

Suppose you walk into a room on a winter's evening and there is an electric light shining. You know that someone has had to have switched on that light. But the light continues to burn only because there is a continuing flow of electrical current to sustain it. Similarly, God did not simply create our world, God also *sustains* it. Without God's constant support, everything would cease to exist. God's creation is evolving i.e. dynamic, not static. God continues to be actively involved in our world but invites us to co-operate in the work of its completion.

Sign Three: The Fact that Human Beings Have an Awareness of Good and Evil

The sense of right and wrong is found in all people, whether they are the Aborigines of the Australian outback or the Inuits of the Canadian Arctic. It speaks to astronauts orbiting the Earth, as well as to doctors treating their patients. This inner voice of *conscience* is not limited to any particular time, place or race of people. It is a *universal* thing. Even the most hardened individuals have been known to be so tortured by the realisation of the evil they have inflicted on others that they have confessed their crimes rather than continue to experience their anguish and guilt. For example, the group of Japanese war veterans who publicly confessed to atrocities they had committed in China in the 1940s (*Irish Independent*, 14.8.1997).

Cardinal Newman argued that the fact of conscience points to our awareness of some fundamental, universal order of right and wrong. This order cannot be explained adequately except by concluding that there exists some higher being who *established that order*, and who gave us a sense of obligation to its *Orderer*. This being, he concluded, is God.

QUESTIONS

1 What are your reflections on Morrison's and Polkinghorne's claims that the existence of *order* and *life* in our universe is a reason for belief in God's existence?

2 Do you find the arguments for belief in God as the *creator* and

sustainer of all that exists convincing or unconvincing? Give reasons for your answer.

3 What argument does Cardinal Newman raise in favour of God's existence? Do you find it convincing or unconvincing? Explain your answer.

SUMMARY

There are no clear-cut undeniable proofs for the existence of God. But we can find signs of God's presence in our world and these point towards God's existence.

1. The existence of *order*, and the awesome *complexity* of conditions necessary to support life in what can appear to be a chaotic world, support the case for belief in God.

2. The very *existence* of our universe can only be accounted for if we accept the existence of a First Cause — God, the creator and sustainer of all that exists.

3. The reality of *conscience* and our awareness of a universal moral order point towards the existence of the One who created them.

   These arguments are said to have a *cumulative force* which amounts to a strong probability that God exists, especially if we consider the evidence of the *universal nature of religious experience* (see chapter 2). In the end, however, belief in God is, like most of our important beliefs, an act of faith, of trust in God, though grounded in reason.

TALKING ABOUT GOD

How can we say anything worthwhile about God if God is so unique, so unlike anyone or anything else?

Thomas Aquinas offered an answer based on an analysis of the way we use language. He divided words up into three different types:

Univocal: where two words are used in exactly the same sense, e.g. David is *tall*. Mary is *tall*.

Equivocal: where two words are used in altogether different senses, e.g.: Peter *types* a letter. A cat is a *type* of animal.

Analogical: where two words 'share' a sense of meaning, e.g.: God is *good*. Susan is *good*.

Here Susan is not understood to be 'good' in exactly the same way as God is 'good'. All the great monotheistic religions believe that God's goodness far surpasses human goodness. Yet Susan's goodness does point towards and helps us to appreciate something of God's goodness. This type of analogy is called a *metaphor* (unlike a simile, it does not use the words 'like', 'as' or 'than').

The scriptures make extensive use of metaphor. Jesus told us that '*God is our Father*'.

Christians believe in a God who is infinite, perfect, loving and good, the creator and sustainer of all that exists. But this raises a serious question: *Why does such a God allow evil things to happen?*

QUESTIONS

1 Explain each of the following ways of using words:

- Univocal

- Equivocal

- Analogical

2 Why is the use of metaphor important when talking about God?

3 What are the *positive* and *negative* aspects of using the metaphor 'God is our Father'?

4 What idea of parenthood do you think underlies Jesus' description of God as 'Our Father'? Explain your answer.

CHAPTER 7

The Mystery of Evil

INTRODUCTION

'The real argument against Christianity is the experience of darkness. I have always found that behind the technical arguments levelled against Christianity ... there are always various experiences of life causing the spirit and the heart to be dark, tired and despairing.' Karl Rahner, SJ

The mystery of evil in our world has caused many people to doubt either the goodness of God or the very existence of God.

ACTIVITY

Here are four statements on God and the mystery of evil. In each case state why, in your opinion, some people feel this way.

God does not exist, so there is no one there to notice or help.

'Nothing happens, nobody comes, nobody goes, it's awful.'
Samuel Beckett, *Waiting for Godot*

God does exist, but is unaware of our suffering and so does not intervene.

'God is a sadist. The tragedy is that he doesn't even know it.'
Sven Hassel, *Cross of Iron*

God exists, knows about our suffering but is simply not interested.

'God has no face, but instead a pair of enormous spectacles, which pass over a non-existent nose.'
F. Scott Fitzgerald, *The Great Gatsby*

God exists, knows about our suffering, cares for us but is unable to do anything about it.

'With stupidity the gods themselves struggle in vain.'
Johann Schiller, *The Maid of Orleans*

COMMENT

Though perfectly understandable reactions to the mystery of evil in our world, it can be argued that these all suffer from a fundamental flaw — they are not based on a clearly defined idea of what constitutes evil.

The word 'evil' is defined as whatever is: *'morally bad; wicked; harmful or tending to harm, especially intentionally or characteristically'.*

(Concise Oxford Dictionary).

Christians make an important distinction between two kinds of evil:

(a) **moral evil**, i.e. any *harmful action* which is *intentionally* committed by human beings; and

(b) **non-moral evil**, i.e. any *harmful event* which occurs because it is a *characteristic* of our world (part of its make-up), e.g. a natural phenomenon which is beyond our power to prevent.

QUESTIONS

1 Match the following examples to the two categories of evil set out above:

- murder
- disease
- war
- volcanic eruptions
- storms
- theft
- earthquakes

2 Read *Genesis*, Chapters 3 and 4, which tell the stories of Adam and Eve, and of Cain and Abel, respectively.

Who is responsible for the existence of *moral* evil in the world according to the author(s) of *Genesis*? Explain your answer.

Wasting Wealth:

1 tank = equipment for 520 classrooms

1 jet fighter = 40,000 village pharmacies

1 destroyer = electricity for 9 million people

WORLD HUNGER AND A LOVING GOD

Many people find it hard to believe in a loving God because so many people are starving to death.

An estimated 35,000 people die of hunger every day, and half of humanity goes to bed hungry every night. How, people ask, could a loving God allow this to happen? Christians believe that it is *human beings* who are responsible for famine and misery in our world. There is plenty of food, enough to enable everyone to live well. However, human beings have abused the freedom God has given them and refuse to share their wealth with each other as God wants.

The causes of world hunger have been identified by economic analysts for some time. At the heart of it is the deep division that exists between the rich North (USA, Canada, Europe, Japan, Australia and New Zealand) and the poor South (most of Asia, Africa and Latin America). The countries of the South are sometimes called the 'Third World' or 'Developing Nations' because of their high levels of poverty.

North and South: A Comparison		
	North	South
Percentage of world population	25%	75%
Percentage of world income	80%	20%
Average life expectancy	70 years	50 years
Percentage of world manufacturing	90%	10%
Level of formal education	At least 2nd level	Basic to none
Position in international economics system	Dominant	Dominated

Even many people who admit that the world economic order is unfair often shrug their shoulders and say that the people of the Third World are their own worst enemies. People who adopt this attitude are accepting some of the misguided beliefs about world hunger.

The first misguided belief

There are too many people; that's why some are starving!
Where? In Somalia or the USA? The latter has 6 per cent of the planet's population yet consumes 25 per cent of its resources.

'Why do people in poor countries go on having more children than they can afford? The answer is: they don't, usually. Where you are living without any aids to living which we have, where each day is a long grind of many hard jobs, just to survive, children are needed as helpers. Where

there is only a 50-50 chance of your children living past five years, you've got to plan to have many children. And when there is no social security, old age pension or health insurance, who else is going to look after you if not your children?'

Susan George, *How the Other Half Dies*

Some people think that the only solutions to what they think is over-population are:

- the promotion of artificial methods of family planning

- abortion

- compulsory sterilisation.

In sharp contrast, Christians argue that present levels of poverty can only be reduced by a massive redistribution of our planet's wealth. However, few people or their political leaders are prepared to make the *sacrifices* that are required to achieve a morally just distribution of the world's resources.

The second misguided belief

There is not enough food in the world to feed everyone
On the contrary. Our world enjoys a surplus of food, though only 44 per cent of all arable land is cultivated. Indeed, a United Nations report concluded that our planet is capable of feeding six times its present population. There could be plenty of food for *all*.

The third misguided belief

Famine is caused by climate
Droughts and floods are natural occurrences that people in developing nations have coped with since ancient times. The problem now is that the people of Africa and Asia have less capacity to cope with each new crisis,

as the world trading system is making them poorer and poorer. Further, global warming and depletion of the ozone layer could cause severe climatic changes in the developing world, which they would have great difficulty coping with.

The fourth misguided belief

Famine is caused by incompetence

It is fair to say that inexperienced governments in many developing nations have made errors of judgment in economic planning and management, but so too have governments in the rich North. In 1997, for example, over 18 million people in the European Union were unemployed.

Once African and Asian states gained their independence from colonial rule after World War II, they were eager to develop their agriculture and expand their industries. From the 1960s onwards, Western banks loaned massive sums of money to Third World countries, but afterwards charged exorbitant interest rates on these loans.

Third World governments were forced to adopt drastic measures, such as massive cuts in health and social welfare expenditure. These affected the poor, especially children. To pay their debts, African nations have had to grow cash crops such as coffee, tea and pineapples purely for export, *not for domestic consumption*. Since all available arable land is used to grow these 'cash crops', the poor are forced to move either into arid bush country or into the hill forests to farm. Without either fertilisers or proper techniques (e.g. terracing hill slopes to prevent soil erosion in the rainy season), the land is soon incapable of feeding them, so they face starvation.

Further, too many poor nations are competing with each other to sell the same cash crops. It's a buyer's market, where the prices are set in advance by Western nations and the prices are forced down. The poor suffer.

To make matters worse, many Third World nations are still reeling from the old Cold War rivalry between the USA and the former USSR. Each superpower destabilised democratic governments in the developing world and backed ruthless despots, reopened old political wounds and helped to wreak havoc on the poor of these countries.

THE CYCLE OF POVERTY

More than 60 countries in the Third World are governed by military dictatorships. Most of these countries have followed the same tragic path to poverty.

→ Widespread poverty and starvation.

→ Political upheaval and military coup

→ Military leader sets up dictatorship

→ Arms then bought from rich nations with loans provided by Western banks. These arms are used to strengthen the dictator's grip on power.

→ Creates large debts to these banks and rich nations.

→ As debt mounts, government spending on health, social services and education is cut drastically to pay interest on loans.

→ Country spirals downward into even greater poverty, and famine results.

ARMS SALES

Arms in a Third World Country

World-wide annual military spending amounts to around £512 billion.

Since World War II 40 million people have died in civil wars in developing countries using mainly imported weapons. Nine of the ten largest arms manufacturers are in the USA.

Over the past 35 years, 79 of the 82 wars fought were civil wars. During that same period developing countries have increased their military spending at three times the rate of developed countries.

The Economist 1995

QUESTIONS

1 Who do you think is responsible for the famine and misery of the Third World: God or human beings? *Give reasons for your opinion.*

2 Earthquakes and volcanic eruptions are beyond human capacity to prevent at this time. Are there any steps which can and should be taken to reduce the pain and suffering they cause?

3 Read *Luke* 16: 19-31. What is the point Jesus makes and how does it apply to the way the world economy is run today?

4 Find out about the work of organisations such as Action Aid, Concern, Goal or Trocaire.

THE CHALLENGE OF EVIL

Christians believe that:
• Moral evil is caused by the immoral actions of human beings. While God is all-powerful, God is also all loving and because of this God chooses to give human beings the freedom to make moral decisions, i.e. the power to choose between good and evil.

   'Free will makes evil possible, but it also makes love possible. If we were not free we could not love.' Rod Kissinger SJ.

• God calls on human beings to use their talents to build a better world and so complete the work of God's creation. Christians must work for progress in health care, education and social justice.

However, a difficulty remains:
We are left with the suffering caused by both moral and non-moral evil
Why would a loving God put us in a world where pain and death occur?
There is no easy answer.

A RESPONSE

Christians believe that we have no choice but to accept pain and death as an integral part of the balance of life and death in our world.

   'God does not hold in being a world which is just a puppet theatre, in which God pulls every string. Physical or non-moral evil is the tragic but necessary cost of an evolving world. The same processes which enable

some cells to mutate into new forms of life, will allow others to mutate into malignancy' (John Polkinghorne).

Christians do not believe that God causes suffering. They believe that things such as cancer and droughts are sadly part of the ordinary functioning of nature. But God has given us the ability to understand, anticipate and respond to them. We must learn all we can about our world and make the necessary effort to combat these phenomena if our world is to be a better place for all.

Yet, people long for a world without pain — no more people being born with a severe disability or dying slowly from cancer.

Christians admit that there are many terrible injustices in our world, but argue that whether or not this denies God's existence depends on our understanding of the meaning and purpose of life itself. If we believe that life is confined to the period between conception and death, then there really is no justice to be had. But if our concept of life reaches out to include life after death, where our eternal destinies are decided by the way we have lived in this world, *then there is justice*. This does not make the experience of evil in our world any easier to undergo. But Christians take comfort from their belief that throughout life's struggles, God is there with them. Even when people think that they are alone, God is there to offer comfort and support (Read *Psalm* 22 or 23).

QUESTIONS

1 If our world was without pain and death it would be a wonderful place. But would it also be an impossible, cartoon-like world? Explain your answer.

2 Without death: (a) Would our planet be over-populated and so incapable of supporting life?

   Statisticians have calculated that the dead outnumber the living by 30 to 1.

   (b) Would human life itself lose any of its value? For example, would we appreciate good health if we never experienced sickness? Give reasons for your answers.

SUMMARY

Christians believe that:

- the mystery of evil in our world does not mean that a loving God cannot exist. However, they do recognise that it poses a great challenge to faith in a loving God;

- belief in God and religious worship cannot explain away evil, but it can give people some understanding of it and a means of helping them cope with it;

- God calls all people to use their talents to reduce the impact of evil (moral and non-moral) in the world.

CHAPTER 8

Jesus of Nazareth

THE CHRISTIAN IDEA OF GOD

I '*In 1947, some Bedouin Arabs were smuggling goats into what was then Palestine, and they were passing through the Qumran area on their way towards Bethlehem when one of the goats strayed. A boy clambered along the cliffs to retrieve the animal. Idly he threw a stone into one of the caves. There was a sound of something breaking. Inside the cave he found tall clay jars containing bundles of manuscripts, sewn together in long scrolls and wrapped in linen. They are what we now know as the Dead Sea Scrolls.*

When the precious scrolls were unrolled, they revealed much about religion in the time of Christ. Four dots on the manuscript replace the name of God, which for the Jews was too holy even to be written. These four dots say a great deal about the difference between the Jewish and Christian religions — at any rate in their beginnings. The original God of the Old Testament was a distant awe-inspiring figure. If he appeared on earth, it was only to speak to prophets — and then, likely as not, from inside a burning bush. The God of the Muslims, Allah, would be equally remote.

But the Christians went to another extreme. It was a most startling change. A human being, they said, had given birth to God: not a princess, not long ago, not far away in some distant land; but a simple girl, quite recently, near by. It was, they insisted, a historical event — the sort of thing that in other times you would read about in your local paper.'

B. Gascoigne, *The Christians*

QUESTION

In what way is the Christian God different from the God of the Jews and the Muslims, according to Gascoigne?

WHY DO CHRISTIANS CALL GOD 'OUR FATHER'?

II *Christianity is the only major religion to have as its central event the suffering and degradation of its God. Crucifixion was a barbarous death, chiefly used for agitators, for pirates and for slaves. Part of the victim's punishment was to be whipped, and then made to carry the heavy cross-beam to the place of his own death. When the cross was raised, a notice was pinned to it giving the culprit's name and crime — INRI in this case — Iesus Nazarenus Rex Iudaeorum (Jesus of Nazareth, King of the Jews).*

However familiar the Crucifixion may be, it remains a profoundly moving subject — an inspiration over centuries of many of Europe's greatest artists. But its familiarity does prevent our noticing quite how remarkable this scene is as an image of God. When a Jesuit missionary told the story of the Crucifixion to an Indian emperor, the emperor was shocked that the God of the Christians should have allowed this to happen to him. By the standards of most religions his surprise is understandable. But the power of this scene is part of that same humanity of the gospel story — that sense of sympathy, even intimacy, which is made possible by a God who is also a man. Devout Christians of all centuries have wept tears of pity for their God, and that in itself is unusual.'

B. Gascoigne, *ibid*

QUESTIONS

1 Why is it considered strange that Christians worship a crucified god?

2 Write a brief account of the Christian understanding of God and include the points mentioned in both the extracts above.

An eleventh-century mosaic inside Hagia Sophia, Istanbul. The central image, as here, is always of Jesus Christ (represented by the Greek letters IC XC). He is always shown as Pantocrator – meaning 'Ruler of All'.

QUESTIONS RAISED ABOUT JESUS

Since the publication of David Strauss's *Life of Jesus* in 1835 there has been no shortage of books attempting to undermine the belief of Christians that Jesus is the Son of God. It has been said that:

(1) Jesus never existed;

(2) the Gospels are unreliable;

(3) Jesus did not perform miracles;

(4) the resurrection did not happen.

We will examine the first charge now and each of the others in the following chapters.

Did Jesus Really Exist?

Since the heart of Christian faith is trust in the person of Jesus Christ, it is only natural that people will want to know as much as possible about him.

A person named Jesus really existed. It is a historical *fact*. He was born in what is now the state of Israel, sometime between the years 6 B.C. and A.D. 6, and he died sometime between A.D. 27 and A.D. 33.

It is difficult to be more precise about dates. The Gospel writers did not share our modern fascination with precise dates for events such as birthdays and so on. They may have felt that such details were of little importance, preferring to concentrate on the *meaning* of Jesus' life and message.

Most of our historical information about the life of Jesus is derived from the *New Testament*, sources written by Christians. However, there are other *non-Christian sources* which independently confirm his existence and give some historical details. This is what they say about Jesus:

- *'He was a doer of wonderful deeds (miracles) ... He drew to himself many Jews and many of the Greek race ... Pilate at the instance of the foremost men among us sentenced him to be crucified ... and even now the tribe of Christians named after him is not extinct'.*

  Josephus, Jewish historian of the 1st century, AD

- *'He was executed at the hands of the procurator (governor) Pontius Pilate in the reign of Tiberius.'*

Tacitus, Roman historian of the early 2nd century, AD

Neither Josephus nor Tacitus could ever be described as friends of Christianity. They wrote about a *real person*.

QUESTIONS

1 What evidence do we have that Jesus really existed?
2 What, in your opinion, are the things that have made Jesus such an attractive figure for people over the centuries? *Give reasons for your answer.*

CHAPTER 9

The Gospels

ARE THE GOSPELS RELIABLE?

While it is true that non-Christian writers of ancient times state that Jesus really existed, they provide little information about his life. Most of what is known has been extracted from the four *Gospels*. But some writers have challenged the authority of the *Gospels* on a number of grounds:

1. **The *Gospels* were not written down for at least forty years after the death of Jesus. How can they be accepted as reliable sources of information about him?**

It must be remembered that since books were scarce in ancient times, Jews were taught from an early age to memorise and accurately recall the important stories of the *Old Testament*. Jesus' Jewish disciples would have naturally taken great care to set down his message and record the key events of his life accurately. The people who actually knew Jesus and were still alive when the *Gospels* were written would certainly have reacted badly if the written *Gospels* were inaccurate or misleading, as this would have been a terrible insult to the Son of God.

2. **We only have *copies* of the original *Gospel* manuscripts. How do we know if the *Gospels* we have are the same as the originals?**

Sadly the original manuscripts (handwritten documents) are unavailable to modern scholars. They either decayed with use as all books do, or were destroyed in one of the many periods of religious persecution suffered by the early Christians. Our earliest *complete* manuscripts date from the fourth century AD.

The fact that these are only copies of the original gospels should not lead us to fear that they are not genuine, faithful copies of the original. Fortunately, archaeologists have discovered a few precious fragments of very early copies of the original *Gospels*. The oldest is a section of St John's gospel, known as the Rylands papyrus No. 457, which dates from AD 134. This page therefore dates only thirty-five years or so after the original was written, a relatively short period that allows little time for copyists' errors or distortions to occur. This and other odd pages surviving from later copies have been used to act as a 'spot check' to confirm the accuracy and reliability of those fourth-century manuscripts on which we depend. These very old manuscripts show that the *Gospels* we have today are genuine and reliable.

3. If the *Gospels* are supposed to be an accurate account of the life of Jesus, why do they not tell us more about Jesus as a person?

The *Gospels* are not biographies in the modern sense of the word. They do not offer a physical description of Jesus, because the authors were not themselves interested in such personal details, preferring instead to concentrate on the words he spoke and the miracles he performed. Little wonder that ever since then, artists such as Giotto, Michelangelo and Dali have presented so many different versions in plaster or on canvas of the same person. It is unlikely that any show Jesus as he really was, but rather how people since have imagined him to look.

Christ Crucified

4. If the *Gospels* do not offer a biography or history in the modern sense, then what value do they have?

It has already been said that the *Gospel* authors had a very different approach when compared to modern authors. Their main aim was to explain the meaning and importance of Jesus to the people of their *own time*.

They probably had quite a lot of information to draw upon, such as eyewitness accounts, sometimes their own memories and one or more collections of Jesus' teachings which have long since disappeared. But they did not use all of it. Rather, they selected those things that they believed were most important and then wove these into the *Gospel* accounts we have today.

While they were keen to know what Jesus said and did, they were not particularly interested in setting each saying or event down in the exact order in which it was said or happened. For example, some scholars believe that the story of Jesus being tempted by the devil in the desert, which *Matthew* and *Luke* put at the start of Jesus' ministry, really concerned important decisions which Jesus faced at a later date.

St Matthew divided his Gospel into three sections:

(a) Jesus' moral teachings

(b) his miracles

(c) his parables.

This was done to suit the tastes of people in his time and not ours. Matthew's audience liked to have things set out in just such a formal way.

It is important to remember, also, that the four evangelists wrote with the benefit of hindsight. They firmly believed that Jesus was the Son of God, and this affected the way they wrote about his life. Those who had experienced the risen Jesus saw all he had said and done before his death in a different light. This is *not* to say that they invented incidents to support their case, but rather that they now saw the real meaning and significance of the things that Jesus had said and done, which they probably had not seen before. They wrote the *Gospels* with the intention of making clear to the reader that Jesus was the Son of God (Read *John* 20:31.)

5. How can we be confident that the *Gospel* writers recorded the actual words and sayings of Jesus?

If the four evangelists did not record the actual sayings of Jesus, then they recorded the closest possible approximations. Non-Christian writers of ancient times, as we have noted earlier, spoke of Jesus' reputation as a miracle-worker and holy man. There is no evidence that the *Gospel* writers did *not* faithfully record the words and deeds of Jesus to the best of their ability. They may, however, have expanded upon some of the things Jesus said to make it clearer what he meant. As Henry Wansborough explains:

'For instance Jesus, speaking to Jews, forbade men to divorce their wives. By Jewish law a wife could not initiate divorce proceedings, so there was no need for Jesus to add that it is equally wrong for women to divorce their husbands. But Mark, writing for non-Jewish communities, where either partner could divorce the other, extends the prohibition to women too, so that readers will not misunderstand what Jesus was saying. So though Mark alters the actual words of Jesus, he is faithful to his message, which is that divorce is always wrong, whether it is demanded by the husband or the wife.'

Jesus: The Real Evidence.

People at the time the *Gospels* were written would have been aware of this. They could distinguish between Jesus' actual words and the statements of the evangelists, written down after years of prayerful reflection.

QUESTIONS

1   Do you believe that the *Gospels* are reliable sources of information about Jesus of Nazareth? Explain your thinking.

2   Choose any extract where Jesus is teaching.

For example, *Matthew* 6: 1-4, 9: 10-13;

Mark 9: 33-37;

Luke 6: 1-5, 6: 36-42, 8: 8-15.

What is your response to what he says?

3   Would a young person's response at the time of Christ be different from or the same as your response today?

4   List *three* words which describe the character of Jesus as it is conveyed in the extract you have chosen.

5   Could you apply any/all of these words to your own character/life? *Explain.*

CHAPTER 10

The Miracles of Jesus

1. How can people be expected to believe in miracles in this day and age?

While the people of Jesus' time were not at all surprised that miracles could happen, our modern western society is very sceptical. Jesus' miracles were faith-enhancing signs of hope to people two thousand years ago, but they raise serious and disturbing questions for people today. We live in an age when many people doubt the very existence of God, and this poses a problem when we start to talk about a subject such as miracles. By definition, a miracle is:

> *an unusual and unexpected event, where the normal laws of nature are suspended and which can only be explained by saying it happened because God intervened directly in human affairs.*

However, modern science is not necessarily hostile to the idea of miracles. Read the following extract by a lecturer in science education at University College, London.

'SCIENCE SAYS MIRACLES CAN'T HAPPEN.'
It is a common belief that science says miracles can't happen because miracles are said to 'break' scientific laws. But can scientific laws be 'broken'? And what are scientific laws anyway?

The word 'law' is used in more than one way, and this leads to confusion. The most familiar use is in the 'laws' of the land. Here the laws state what should happen. People should not murder or steal from others. These laws are prescriptive *because they prescribe what should happen — much as medical prescriptions state what drugs should be used. These laws can be broken, as in the case of homicide or robbery.*

The laws of the land can be compared to a plan. An architect's plans are prescriptive, showing what the building should be like when it's finished.

Scientific laws are completely different. They are descriptive, as they describe what normally does happen. Scientific laws can be compared to a map, which describes how the land lies. Like a scientific law, if a map does not agree with what the world is like, then the map needs to be altered. Map-making is a useful comparison with the work of the scientist. For, as the lie of the land determines the shape of the map, so the scientific data determine the form of the law — not the other way round.

Boyle's law says that 'the volume of a fixed mass of gas at constant temperature varies inversely with the pressure'. It is a well-known scientific law. But there is nothing fixed and unalterable about scientific laws. If later experiments do not fit in with a law, then it is the law that needs to be corrected. At high pressures it turns out that Boyle's law does not hold and a more complicated formula is needed.

Scientific laws no more make events take place the way they do than a map makes a coastline have its shape. Boyle's law does not make the volume of a gas get smaller. The increased pressure does that.

The descriptive/prescriptive distinction should not be pressed too far. There is one sense in which scientific laws do prescribe something — our expectations. On the basis of what has happened before, scientific laws enable us to prescribe (that is, write down beforehand) what is rational to expect.

Scientific laws may indicate what to expect, but they offer no guarantees that things could never be any different. Consequently they say nothing more about the possibility of one-off events like miracles than was known a long time before there was any great interest in science, namely that miracles are not what we would normally expect.

Michael Poole, *Science and Belief*

Christians believe that miracles do not occur in the ordinary course of events in our world. But we cannot conclude from this that miracles are impossible. We cannot rule out the possibility that they occur. Science cannot say that miracles can't happen.

Miracles can happen in our time. People have made incredible recoveries to full health after tottering on the very brink of death due to some terminal illness such as cancer. Less obvious but just as important are the many cases where people have found the strength, through coming to know Jesus in prayer and study, to turn their entire lives around, out of the darkness of sin and into his light of peace.

QUESTIONS

1 What do you understand by the word '*miracle*'?

2 What are scientific laws?

3 Is modern science necessarily hostile to the possibility of miracles? Explain your answer.

2. How can we take all these miracles at face value?
There could have been exaggerations or errors and they could have happened quite easily.

Take, for example, the case of Jairus' daughter (*Luke* 8: 41-56). According to the story, the girl's family sent for Jesus as she was near death. But, while Jesus was still on his way, news reached him that she had died.

There seemed to be no point in continuing on his journey, but Jesus went on to the family's home anyway. On his arrival, he told the assembled mourners:

Christ healing two blind men
(Matthew 20: 29–34)

'She is not dead, merely asleep.' Then he amazed them all by raising her to full life and health.

Perhaps, a modern sceptic might remark, she was not really dead at all, but in a coma (i.e. a prolonged deep sleep, from which she could not be awakened). The evangelists and the witnesses who told them the story of Jairus' daughter might have made an understandable mistake. All they might have witnessed was a purely coincidental recovery from a coma, which happened quite by chance after Jesus had arrived. It only appeared to be a miracle. That is one explanation, but there is another — she *was* really dead and Jesus brought her back to life.

If the story of Jairus' daughter was just a once-off incident, we might well lean towards the 'coma recovery' explanation. But the *Gospels* tell us that such 'coincidental recoveries' happened to people who asked Jesus for help virtually every day of his public ministry.

Before deciding if a cure is miraculous, the modern Catholic Church asks a number of questions:
  (a) Was the disease serious?
  (b) Was the cure sudden and unexpected?
  (c) Is it a complete cure?
  (d) Has it lasted at least 3 years?
  (e) Has it been proven by medical investigation?
  (f) Did any medical treatment assist the recovery?

3. Why should people believe in these stories of Jesus as a miracle-worker?

Christians believe that there are good reasons to accept these accounts:

(a) These stories are supported by historical records, as non-Christian writers referred to Jesus as a 'wonder worker' who greatly impressed people by his actions.

(b) Even Jesus' greatest opponents — the Pharisees — did not deny his power to work miracles, although they did claim that he had been given this power by the devil and not by God. These accusations are recorded in the Jewish *Talmud*.

(c) Many eyewitnesses to Jesus' miracles came to firmly believe in him as a result of their experience of his goodness and power. Indeed, they were so convinced that later they were prepared to travel to the furthest parts of the known world to spread his message and even lay down their lives for him. There was a factual basis for the miracle accounts, and a general consensus existed, among Christians and non-Christians alike, that Jesus was a *'miracle worker'*.

4. Might there not be a psychological explanation for these events that has nothing to do with miracles?

It is true that there are *different kinds* of 'miracles'. Thanks to modern psychiatric medicine, we know that many illnesses such as paralysis can be caused in a person suffering from an unhappy mental state. Some terrible tragedy or bitter experience can so affect a person's mind that it has a physical effect, causing the body, in a sense, to 'go on strike'. In such a case it is not possible to cure the person's physical ailment without solving the mental problem first. It is quite likely that many people with just such a problem came to see Jesus. He did not give them a lengthy course of counselling and prescribe drug treatment; rather, it is likely he simply sat and talked to them, radiating a unique goodness and peace, pinpointing the cause of their mental distress, so that they came to see themselves differently. Then the cause of their unhappiness faded away and so also did their paralysis. This may not sound spectacular, but it is none the less a miracle. In a very real sense, Jesus gave them back their lives.

But not all illnesses are psychosomatic, i.e. caused by a person's mental state affecting their body's health. Yet, Jesus could cure any person of *any illness* and even raise Lazarus, a man who had been dead and buried for several days, back to life (*John* 11: 1-44).

5. What was the purpose of Jesus' miracles?

Jesus did not use his miraculous powers of healing to provide some 'magic short-cut' to faith for those who sought his help. Rather Jesus responded to and sought to strengthen the faith people *already* had in him.

St John refers to Jesus' miracles as signs that God is present and at work in our world, that God loves us and that God has come to free us from sin and death (read *John* 5: 36). Christians believe that the miracles of Jesus are an essential part of his message. Through them we can see that what Jesus described as the 'Kingdom of God' has begun.

QUESTIONS

1 Why do you think Jesus worked miracles?

2 '*A miracle that takes place in a person's heart is just as important as a spectacular physical cure*'. Do you agree/disagree? Why?

3 Evaluate the evidence for and against Jesus as a miracle-worker. Which side do you find the more convincing? Give reasons for your answer.

CHAPTER 11

The Resurrection

1. Isn't it quite possible that Jesus survived the crucifixion and was rescued from the tomb by his followers who then concocted the story of his resurrection?

If one accepts the *Gospels* as trustworthy sources, they support the assertion that Jesus died on the cross.

(a) The story of the crucifixion is so familiar to people that it is easy to forget how truly awful it was. The prisoner was forced to carry the wooden crossbeam to the place of execution, where he would be nailed through the wrists and feet to the cross and then secured with ropes to prevent the body tearing free later. A small 'seat' would be fastened to the upright post on which the victim could rest his body weight. But this was not an act of mercy; on the contrary, it had the effect of *prolonging* the person's life and so his agony, as the victim was constantly struggling to breathe.

(b) Even before this ordeal Jesus was in a gravely weakened state, having been scourged on Pilate's orders. A Roman scourging was a horrific experience: the victim was repeatedly struck upon the back by a multi-stranded whip, which had jagged pieces of metal inserted into each leather strand, so that the lashes not only cut the skin, but tore off strips of flesh each time they made contact. A scourging alone was sometimes enough to kill a person.

(c) While it is true that a person could linger for days on a cross before dying, Jesus' ordeal lasted about six hours. His death was due to a combination of massive blood loss, exhaustion (he had to be helped to carry the cross) and suffocation.

To make sure he was dead, the Jewish authorities requested that the usual practice for ensuring death by crucifixion should be followed. This meant that the legs of the victim would be broken so that he could not hold himself up to breathe and would swiftly suffocate.

When the Roman guards had done this to the two thieves, they came to Jesus but found it unnecessary, as he was already dead. Ever cautious, however, they pierced his side with a spear to make certain (*John* 19: 34).

(d) Neither the Jewish nor the Roman authorities were going to allow Jesus to escape to cause trouble some other day. Pilate had given in to the Sanhedrin's demand for Jesus' execution because they had threatened to report him for disloyalty to the emperor (*John* 19: 12). Pilate knew that since Jesus posed a serious threat to their authority they were in deadly earnest. To protect his career, he had to make sure of Jesus' death. Tacitus records Pilate's decision, Roman executioners were nothing if not thorough.

2. Even if Jesus did die on the cross, couldn't the apostles have stolen the body and then invented the story of the resurrection?

This accusation was recorded in *Matthew* 28: 13. Scholars believe it to be untrue for the following reasons:

(a) The Sanhedrin persuaded Pilate to place a guard on the tomb of Jesus to prevent just such a thing happening. It is unlikely that these Roman soldiers would have fallen asleep on duty, as it was an offence punishable by death. Further, they certainly would have resisted any attempt to steal the corpse (see *Matthew* 27: 63–66).

Poussin's painting 'The Entombment'

(b) But supposing there was no guard present, would the disciples have done it? Again, it is highly unlikely.

The execution of Jesus had had a shattering effect on their morale. Their Messiah had died a shameful death and, worse still, they had abandoned him when he most needed them. Peter publicly denied that he had ever known Jesus, not once but three times (*John* 18: 15–27). They were not expecting to see Jesus ever again and were too afraid to even stir out of doors until they were given the news that Jesus' corpse was missing. Such shocked and frightened people would not have gone anywhere near the tomb until some considerable period of time had lapsed, for fear they too might be arrested and suffer the same fate. They would not have gone to the tomb to steal the body, any more than they would have wanted to help take his body down from the cross and bury it there in the first place. The *Gospels* portray them as wanting to put the whole business behind them until Mary Magdalen's news galvanised them into action.

(c) If the gospel writers wanted to concoct some elaborate phony story about the resurrection, they would not have identified Mary Magdalen, or any other woman, as their primary witness to the empty tomb. In contemporary Jewish law, the testimony of women was not acceptable in a court. Any writer who wished to convince people that a hoax was actually genuine would *never* have chosen a woman as his principal witness, as they did not carry any credibility in this male-dominated society.

(d) Even if the disciples had wished to conduct an elaborate hoax to win mass support, they chose a very strange way to go about it. For there was considerable disagreement among the Jewish people and within the Sanhedrin itself about the whole idea of life after death.

Essentially, there were two schools of thought:

• the *Sadducees*, who controlled the Sanhedrin, did not believe in life beyond the grave, stating that this life is all there is and when we die, that is the end of our existence.

• the *Pharisees*, and the greater majority of ordinary Jews, did believe in life after death, but they thought two specific things about the resurrection:

   (i) it would only take place when the end of the world had come;

   (ii) it would be a shared experience, i.e. everybody who had lived a good life would be raised up to new life together.

So the claim of Jesus' followers that a single, individual person had risen from the dead before the end of the world was an unheard-of idea, which would have greatly challenged the beliefs of their fellow Jews. If they had deliberately set out to win friends and influence people by fraudulent means, they would never have chosen such a completely novel idea as Jesus' resurrection.

3. How can people trust the gospel accounts when they don't seem to agree on the details of the story?

No one actually saw Jesus rise from the dead. The Gospels only tell us what happened *afterwards*. They all agree that shortly after dawn on what we now call 'Easter Sunday', Mary Magdalen and some of Jesus' woman disciples went to the tomb to embalm his body properly. To their great surprise they discovered that the tomb was open (*Mark* 16: 4), the corpse missing and the linen cloths in which it had been wrapped lying on the floor of the tomb (*John* 20: 6). Here the gospel accounts diverge.

Diagram of the tomb of Christ

ACTIVITY

Read and then compare the following scripture passages:

Matthew 28: 1–20

Mark 16: 1–20

Luke 24: 1–48

John 20: 1–29

1 In what ways do they differ from each other?

2 In what ways do they agree with each other?

RESOLVING THE DIFFICULTIES

That the *Gospel* accounts of the resurrection differ in certain respects should not really surprise us. Then, as now, no two people ever see or remember an event in exactly the same way. This said, however, we can see that these different accounts agree on a number of crucial points and so they render any small differences in detail between them unimportant.

(a) *The Fact of the Empty Tomb:*

- When different groups of people went to the tomb, they all discovered the same thing — that Jesus' corpse was gone.

- Those who discovered the empty tomb were either told by an angel (*Matthew*, *Mark* and *Luke*), or came to realise by themselves (*John*), that Jesus was risen from the dead and that they would soon see him again.

Women disciples at the empty tomb of Christ

(b) *The Post-Resurrection Experiences:*

- The people to whom Jesus appeared were all deeply upset and depressed by what had happened, quite convinced that Jesus was dead and that all their hopes for a better future had died with him.

- Jesus then decided to reveal himself to them, usually greeting his astonished hosts with some reassuring words, such as 'Peace be with you' (*John* 20: 21).

- At first, all the witnesses were shocked and frightened when they saw the risen Jesus — a natural reaction in the circumstances. But this quickly faded to be replaced by a remarkable inner peace. It really was Jesus, not dead, but alive. Yet, and this they found hard to explain, he was not alive now in exactly the same way as before.

- Jesus clearly wanted his followers to spread the news of his resurrection and ordered his disciples to 'Go, therefore, make disciples of all nations' (*Matthew* 28: 19).

N.B. It is important to realise that both the empty tomb and the post-resurrection appearances are needed to support the value of each other as evidence for belief in the resurrection event.

- If the tomb was not empty, then the appearances of Jesus could be considered to be mere hallucinations, or the fanciful imaginings of people who refused to accept the death of their leader.

- Without the appearances, the empty tomb could have been explained away as a simple act of grave-robbing by Jesus' followers, who wanted to perpetrate a hoax and hoped that people would be gullible enough to swallow it.

(c) *The Transformation of the Apostles:*
Perhaps the most significant fact of all is that something quite extraordinary happened to the disciples in the days after the crucifixion. They had been hiding away from public view, frightened and demoralised by the death of their leader. Then, in the weeks that followed Easter Sunday, a gradual change came over them, until they gained the strength to go out into the marketplace and begin preaching that Jesus had risen, even though they knew that to do so would be to put their own lives at risk. Frightened people had been transformed into courageous missionaries. Only their experience of the risen Christ could have caused such a change of heart. By his resurrection, Jesus had shown them that all he had said was true. Now they too wanted to live his kind of life.

4. Could the 'post-resurrection experiences' have been ghostly apparitions?

Like most people at that time, the disciples believed in ghosts. At a glance, the stories of Jesus' various visitations might seem to lend credence to claims that they were merely 'ghostly apparitions'. For example:

The *Gospels* show that Jesus could appear in two places at the same time (*Mark* 16: 9-12), or walk through a closed door (*John* 20: 19-20), or vanish at will (*Luke* 24: 31).

But a careful reading shows that the *Gospel* writers went to great pains to impress upon their readers that the risen Jesus was *not* some disembodied apparition who simply popped back to our world to say a proper goodbye to his followers. First of all, the evangelists tell us that Jesus was really physically present, he was a tangible person. (Read *Luke* 24: 36-43; *John* 20: 24-29 and 21: 9-14.)

Secondly, the fact that the risen Jesus could do things that are impossible for a human being to do makes perfect sense. Remember, the disciples often remarked throughout the accounts of his appearances that, though it was really Jesus they met, in some way he was different from the person they had known. Indeed, on occasion they did not immediately recognise him (see *John* 21: 4 and 12).

Yes, Jesus was alive. Just like Lazarus or Jairus' daughter? No. The disciples had seen Jesus bring these people back to life and they made it quite clear that Jesus had *not* been restored to his old mortal life as had Lazarus or Jairus' daughter. Unlike them, Jesus was no longer restricted by the laws of space and time that limit our human freedom of action, so he could pass through objects or become tangible at will. He was alive, but we can say that, through his resurrection, his human body was transformed and glorified. Jesus was living a completely new kind of life.

QUESTIONS

1   What is the evidence to support the Christian belief that Jesus died on the cross on Good Friday?

2   Why do Christians believe that the apostles would not have stolen the body of Jesus to perpetrate a hoax?

3   (a) What were the two schools of thought about life after death within the Jewish community in the first century AD?

   (b) How did these two groups react to the claim that Jesus had risen from the dead?

4   On what points do the four *Gospel* accounts of the resurrection agree?

5   Why do Christians believe that both the empty tomb and the post-

resurrection appearances of Jesus are needed to support the value of each other?

6 What is meant by the 'transformation of the apostles'?

7 Why do Christians deny claims that Jesus' post-resurrection appearances were merely ghostly apparitions?

THE IMPORTANCE OF THE RESURRECTION

The belief that the resurrection really happened is central to the whole Christian religion. As St Paul wrote in the mid-first century AD:

> *'If Christ has not been raised, then our preaching is useless and your believing it is useless.'* (1 *Corinthians* 15: 14)

But the Christian story does not end with the resurrection. It is not simply an historical event. Christians believe that the resurrection is an *ongoing story* of hope and salvation which includes all of us today.

The resurrection of Jesus should not be considered simply as a demonstration that Jesus was God made human. It is that but also much more.

'The resurrection is the completion of the sacrifice Jesus made on the cross. Because Jesus remained true to his Father's word, his Father raised him from the dead to a new life of glory. Jesus is re-united with his Father for ever. And because Jesus is our representative, he has re-united the fallen human race with God. Our redemption is achieved.

But if humankind has been redeemed why are there still wars? Why do people still hurt each other and fail to love? Why is there still suffering and death?

These are complex questions. Here we can only give a brief indication of the answer to them.

We said that Jesus made it possible for us to overcome the power of sin. He made salvation possible. *He didn't make it easy!*

Salvation comes to us when we accept Jesus. And when we accept him we are changed. We begin to share in the relationship he now has with his Father.

We enter into that life by being reborn in Baptism. Jesus has made salvation possible for all. His life and his love are freely available to anyone who will accept him. And sin persists in us, and in the world, in so far as we refuse to accept him.

Of course, our full and complete union with Christ will not be achieved until, we like him, have passed from this world to the next. But salvation has begun already. The seed of the new life of Jesus has already been sown in us. Our task here and now is to foster its growth so that even on this earth we become more and more like Jesus.'

Adapted from: *Your Faith*, Redemptorists of London Province.

QUESTIONS

1 Imagine that you are either Mary Magdalen or Thomas the Doubter. Write a letter to a friend to convince him/her that Jesus is risen from the dead. Use the evidence examined in this chapter.

2 Why is belief in the resurrection of Jesus of central importance to the Christian religion?

SUMMARY

Christians believe that:

- Jesus is unique, the Son of God, the second person of the Trinity.

- Jesus possesses two natures, one fully human and one fully divine, yet is one person.

- Through Jesus' teachings, miracles, suffering, death and resurrection, God offers humanity the only real solution to the mystery of sin and death.

- God offers us healing and redemption through the gift of faith in Jesus as our Lord and Saviour.

THE GIFT OF FAITH

Christian faith in the risen Jesus involves more than a mere rational examination of the *Gospels* and an acceptance of the testimony they present about a unique event in human history. Faith is a gift, an illuminating insight which God freely gives to all those who genuinely and sincerely seek it.

However, though faith is described as a gift, it does not mean that a person's decision to have faith in Jesus is in some way forced upon him/her. On the contrary, no one is compelled to have faith in Jesus. We are all *invited* and are *free to choose* how to respond.

Faith is not an irrational act. But precisely because faith is understood as a 'gift of God', we are unable to achieve it purely by our own intellectual efforts. If we are to believe in the risen Jesus and experience the difference this can make in how we live our lives, we need God's help and strength (i.e. God's grace). This is why Christians believe that it is important to *pray* for the gift of faith.

QUESTIONS

1 Why do Christians describe faith as a 'gift? Explain your answer.

2 Why do Christians believe that we need God's help to have faith in Jesus? (Read *Mark* 9: 17–27 and *Hebrews* 11: 1).

CHAPTER 12

Prayer

WHAT IS PRAYER?

It is said that prayer is a mystery. Why? Because it is so simple that any child can do it, yet so difficult that no adult can fully understand it.

Prayer has been described as: *'a communication with God and an awareness of God's loving presence in our lives'.*

Prayer is closely connected with worship. By worship we mean: *the prayerful honour and the recognition that God has created all that is. Through worship human beings seek to respond to and be in union with God.*

R. Ekstrom, *Concise Catholic Dictionary*

Generally speaking, when people pray on their own or in small groups we call it 'prayer'. However, if people come together in larger numbers it is called 'public worship', e.g. Sunday Mass where Catholic Christians celebrate the sacrament of the Eucharist.

At prayer, Iona Abbey, Scotland

WHY DO PEOPLE PRAY?

Often people turn to God in prayer because they experience

- evil and suffering in their own lives;

- sorrow for having let someone down in an important situation;

- gratitude when something important goes well;

- helplessness when they are powerless to help someone they love;

Muslim worship

- a sense of mystery and wonder through a loving relationship or an encounter with nature;
- how short and easily ended a human life can be.

QUESTIONS

1 What is your personal definition of prayer?

2 Read *Matthew* 6: 5-6 and *Mark* 11: 22-24. What does Jesus have to say about prayer?

Reflection: Each of these different circumstances gives rise to different kinds of prayer. If we rearrange their order we can identify six types of prayer:

(1) *adoration*—a sense of mystery and wonder;

(2) *intercession*—love for other people and a wish to help them;

(3) *petition*—an awareness of our own physical and spiritual needs;

(4) *contrition*—a realisation of where we have gone wrong in our lives;

(5) *protection*—a sense of the power of evil and a realisation of the suffering it causes;

(6) *thanksgiving*—a deep-seated gratitude for all those people and things that are important to us.

The Holy Trinity. Here the three triangles are joined into one circle to symbolise the idea of the Three Persons in the unity of God.

APPROACHING PRAYER

Even those who believe in God can sometimes feel that prayer is

Prisoners at Dachau concentration camp praying following their release.

irrelevant, a waste of time. But this is to misunderstand the nature of prayer. Christians believe that God is always there for each of us and that God's love is constant and never-tiring. As the poet Patrick Kavanagh wrote in *The Great Hunger*: '*God is in the bits and pieces of Everyday.*' Through prayer people can develop a strong awareness of God's presence in their daily lives and from this gain the strength to face up to the challenges with which life confronts them.

Prayer should not be approached in a spirit of self-centredness, but this is not to say that we should not ask God for things. On the contrary,

> '*The person who prays with hope ...*
> *might ask for everything ...*
> *like nice weather or a promotion.*
> *This concreteness is even a sign*
> *of authenticity.*
> *For if you ask only for faith, hope*
> *and love ... without making them concrete in the nitty-gritty*
> *of life,*
> *you probably haven't involved God in your real life.*
> *But if you pray with hope,*
> *all those concrete requests are merely ...*
> *ways of saying that we trust in*
> *the fullness of God's goodness ...*'
>
> Henri Nouwen, *Prayer and Hope.*

QUESTIONS

1 Why is it important for Christians to approach prayer in a spirit of hope?

2 Why does Henri Nouwen say that we should pray for 'concrete requests'? Give examples in your answer.

3. Read the following extract: *The Kingdom and Prayer*

The idea that Christians need have little concern for this world is an absurd caricature. It would be like an individual who would pray for a miraculous cure of his pneumonia rather than sending for a doctor. To pray for something implies that we are prepared to play our part in bringing it about.

Prayer cannot be an evasion of our own responsibilities. On the contrary, unless it includes a recognition of our own obligations, it is a lie. Thus when Christians pray, as they were taught, 'Thy kingdom come', they are undertaking a commitment. They are recognising an obligation to work for the growth of the kingdom of God and to create among people the sort of relationships which are acceptable to God.

Adapted from Donal Murray, *Jesus is Lord*

(a) What point does the author make in his first paragraph?

(b) When Christians pray 'thy kingdom come', what do they mean? What obligation does it place on them?

ON BEING HOPEFUL

Sometimes, however, it can be very difficult to see any reason for hope, but St Paul reminds us that: *'What seems to be God's foolishness is wiser than human wisdom, and what seems to be God's weakness is stronger than human strength'* (*1 Corinthians 1:25*).

The story of the great American president, Abraham Lincoln, seems to bear out St Paul's words. Mark Link SJ writes: 'Abraham Lincoln knew failure. For 30 years it dogged his every footstep. It walked the streets with him during the day. It went to bed with him at night.

A partial list of his failures reads like this:

1832 defeated in election for the legislature

1833 failed in business

1836 nervous breakdown

1843 defeated in nomination for Congress

1854 defeated for Senate

1856 defeated in nomination for vice-president

1860 elected President of the United States.

Lincoln was well prepared for the defeats and setbacks that battered and bruised America during the Civil War years. Another man might have collapsed under the ordeal.

Of himself, Lincoln said: *'God selects his own instruments, and sometimes they are strange ones; for instance, he chose me to steer the ship through a great crisis.'*

QUESTIONS

1 Read *Matthew* 21: 22. How would you apply its message to the story of Abraham Lincoln?

2 What, if anything, do you think people today can learn from Lincoln's life story? Explain your answer.

WHEN IT IS DIFFICULT TO PRAY

Even when people want to pray, they can often find it difficult to do so. If they are upset about something or if they have had a row with someone, they can find it difficult to concentrate. These thoughts seem to crowd in on them. Since it is not possible to put them out of their minds, the best thing is to *include* these thoughts in their prayers.

'Lord, I had a row with X today. I am very upset. My mind keeps going back to the quarrel and she was wrong. But was she? Isn't that my pride speaking? And even if she was wrong, am I not ready to forgive? Lord, how often have I wronged others, how often have I wronged you? You did not hold back your forgiveness so why should I now? Help me, Lord, to make the first step, to hold out a hand of friendship. She probably feels as bad about it as I do. Lord, give me the courage to forgive.'
T. McGivern, *Day-dreaming or Praying?*

A distraction need not be a distraction. It can help us to grow closer to God and to find the courage to show forgiveness and kindness. This is real prayer.

DOES GOD LISTEN?

Sometimes we think that our prayers are not answered, that God does not listen to us.

Our prayers may seem unanswered because our own behaviour may be getting in the way of an answer. We may not be willing to pay the price, i.e. to get what we want our character would have to change and we may not want to make the effort required.

God has given human beings the gift of free will. God will not take this gift away from us. Rather, God asks us to exercise our free will in a loving fashion, co-operating with God to build a better world. God does listen to us, but so too should we listen to God.

QUESTION

Some people find the whole idea of prayer difficult to accept. Some people think: *'Prayer is just talking to yourself.'*

Some people believe: *'Prayer is a waste of time because even when you ask for what you want, nothing changes.'*

(a) Why do some people hold these views?

(b) Do you think they understand what prayer is actually about or not? Give reasons for your answer.

CHAPTER 13

Cults

WHAT IS A CULT?

On 18 November 1978, more than nine hundred members of an American religious group known as the *'People's Temple'* committed mass suicide in the jungles of Guyana, South America.

They all followed the orders of their self-styled messiah Jim Jones, committing an appalling act of blind, irrational fanaticism. People who thought that this was just a once-off event were sadly proved wrong by the events at the *Branch Davidian's* headquarters at Waco, Texas, in April 1993, and at the *Order of the Solar Temple's* retreat at the Swiss town of Cheiry, in October 1994. Yet again, people followed some self-proclaimed messiah to their deaths. Such incidents have heightened public awareness of the potentially destructive nature of these new groups called *'cults'*.

But what is a 'cult'? Jean Merritt, a psychiatric social worker with considerable experience in this area, offers the following definition:

More than 900 people, followers of Jim Jones, committed suicide at the People's Temple, Guyana, in November 1978.

'I define Rev. Moon's Unification Church, the Way International, Children of God and other such groups as being cults. I do not consider them a religion because the loyalty of the members is not to a formalised doctrine, but solely to the demands of the leader, one person. Because of this, rules, regulations and beliefs vary with the whim of the leader. Power and control are in his hands and no one else's. The closest analogy is that of a dictatorship or of a totalitarian state.'

Quoted in: Steve Kemperman, 'My 3½ years in the Moonies', *Sign*, Vol. 59, No. 4, December 1979.

This chapter will focus on those groups which, their critics claim, abuse the idealism and enthusiasm of young people.

QUESTIONS

1 What is a 'cult'?
2 Before reading further, draw up what you consider to be four likely characteristics of the kind of person you think would be likely to join a cult.

METHODS OF RECRUITMENT

While cults seem to hold a special attraction for people who are psychologically disturbed, these kinds of people form only a small minority of their membership. The bulk of their membership consists of young people between the ages of 18 and 25, who are of average or above average intelligence, have no history of mental illness or serious emotional problems, and have enjoyed relatively good and stable family lives.

Cults tend to seek out idealistic young people who are receptive to new ideas and who sense that there must be something more to life than the pursuit of wealth, power and pleasure. Cults are particularly interested in young people who have just left home, are new to a college or work setting, are unsure of themselves, and have not yet developed new friendships. They target likely recruits, then appear sympathetic and comforting. They shower him/her with interest and concern, invite him/her to social events and so engage his/her interest in the group. This is a highly practised technique called 'love bombing'.

The new recruit is persuaded to attend a free, residential weekend 'workshop' at one of the cult's centres. Once there, the person is isolated from the company of any acquaintance to prevent him/her sharing any doubts or suspicions. The cult workshop leaders ensure that the intended recruit never has a free, unaccompanied moment to stop and reflect. This is to stop him/her standing back from the situation and prevent him/her figuring how he/she is being manipulated, how he/she is being moulded to suit the cult's own hidden agenda.

No one is forced to join a cult. A person is slowly *persuaded to convince him/herself* that it is the best course of action for him/her to take. The cult seeks to convince a prospective recruit that their community is the ideal environment in which to develop his/her full potential, the place where you will get support when things get you down. Above all, the cult offers ready-made, often *simplistic* answers to life's mysteries.

The workshop leaders are usually quite skilled in techniques of manipulation, exploiting the fact that most young people have little background in their own religion, so that they find it difficult to detect the flaws in the arguments with which they are bombarded. In time, they can begin to take on the thought pattern of the group and begin to think and act the way the group requires them to do. At any time a new recruit can break away but only if he/she wants to do so.

David Koresh, who died with many of his followers in April 1993 in the fire at the compound of his Branch Davidians in Waco, Texas.

Once a person chooses to join, the cult becomes his/her 'true family', and he/she must cease all contact with his/her family and friends. Former cult members have reported that they were told that they would be walking out on God or would be lost forever if they left the group.

> '*At first, new members are welcomed by permanently smiling cult members, then gradually made to feel unworthy and persuaded to give up all their worldly goods. Members are encouraged to report on each other, and attend sessions where they admit to their unworthiness. This encourages an intimacy based on revealed weaknesses. Then the leader can use everything to manipulate them. Abuse comes to be accepted by the followers as tests of their loyalty. David Koresh, for example, tested the loyalty of his Branch Davidians in many ways. Once he found a cult member eating a hamburger in Waco, in violation of the spartan food regime he had ordered. Koresh humiliated him with a lengthy lecture in front of the assembled group. Sometimes he ordered male members to allow him to have sexual intercourse with their wives and daughters.*'
>
> Conor O'Clery, *The Irish Times*, 24.4.1993.

QUESTIONS

1   What kind of person is targeted by a cult?

2   How do cults go about recruiting new members?

3   At Waco and Cheiry, as at Jonestown earlier, people unhesitatingly obeyed orders that were absurd and suicidal. This has led American cult-critics Flow Conway and Jim Siegelman to claim that such groups exercise a form of *'mind control'* over their members. How, in your opinion, could the methods described above be used to achieve this degree of control over cult members?

THE CULT LEADER

Each cult is dominated by a strong 'father-figure', who usually claims divine powers. For the Unification Church, the cult better known as the 'Moonies', this is Sun Myung Moon, a South Korean whom his followers believe is the *'perfect man'* sent by God to establish *'The Family'* of *'saved'* human beings who *alone* will survive the coming holocaust.

Those who have left the Moonies describe it as a harsh, militaristic, right-wing, fascist and only vaguely religious movement, which uses deception techniques to recruit new members. Like most cults, the Moonies teach that the end justifies whatever means they deem necessary to complete the orders of their leader.

The cult's primary function appears to be to use its young members to raise funds for the 'divine purposes' of its leader.

Moon is not modest. He claims to be the *messiah*, and tells his followers that since the creation of the world, virtually all the great religious figures, including Jesus, have failed God. Moon, however, describes himself as being morally perfect, and claims that only by following him can people be saved from hell. Moon

Wedding of 6,516 couples by Sun Myung Moon. Usually the bride and groom only meet each other shortly before the ceremony. Marital breakdown rates are, not surprisingly, quite high.

was imprisoned for tax evasion by the US authorities in 1984. By 1997, some 2 million people in more than 100 countries were convinced enough to declare him their saviour.

(Figure source: CNN, 29.11.97)

QUESTIONS

1 Describe the role played by the cult leader.

2 Commenting on these cults, theologian Alan Davies remarked: *'Nothing is as bad as bad religion'*. What do you think he means? Do you agree or disagree? Why?

3 Often those who leave cults are deeply disillusioned and cynical about religion and life in general. Some have suffered considerably. One American study of 400 former cult members found that about a fifth had feelings of self-destruction. They required considerable counselling and support to help them rebuild their lives. Why, in your view, was this the result of their membership of a cult?

4 Read the following:

'Quite often, the unpaid debts of the Christian Churches end up on the doorsteps of the cults. No doubt the widespread success of cults is due in part to their frequently manipulative methods of recruitment. But the main reason for their success seems to be the fact that in our society people are more and more being treated like mere numbers; rarely are they treated as people. The result is a coldness and a loneliness that can become unbearable. This is where cults come on the scene, with an approach that is emotional rather than rational. They nourish the logic of the heart rather than the mind.'

Joseph Cardinal Daneels, *Christ or Aquarius?*

(a) What does Cardinal Daneels identify as the main reason for the success of cults in the Western world?

(b) Do you think he is reading the situation right? Explain your answer.

(c) What steps do you think the Christian churches should take to help people feel part of a community in which they are considered important and wanted?

CHARACTERISTICS OF A CULT

- Requires total, unquestioning obedience from its members to the orders of its leader.

- Uses highly manipulative recruitment techniques and training programmes to shape the personality of any new recruit to suit the leader's plans.

- Demands a sudden and complete separation of the new recruit from his/her family and friends to prevent them from encouraging him/her to think again about involvement in the cult.

- Encourages a strong dislike, even hatred, for anyone outside the cult.

  'Commonly, cults teach their members that the outside world is evil, corrupt and even satanic. Only the cult group itself is pure and good. Thus the cult promises to protect its members from all the forces that will lead them to hell. As a consequence, new cult members often try to convert their parents and friends; then, if they are not successful, they shun families and old contacts as lost souls.'

  Sr Loretta Pastva, *Great Religions of the World*

- Preoccupation with fundraising, not to help the poor and the sick, but to fund the lifestyle of the cult leader and his senior advisors.

- Considerable difficulty for members who leave the group. Tremendous pressure is exerted on them to stay.

ACTIVITY

Compare and contrast the actions of Jesus with those of modern day cult leaders:

(1) What was Jesus' attitude to power and wealth? Suggested Readings: *Matthew* 6: 24; *Mark* 8: 27–30, 9: 33–35, 10: 41–45; *Luke* 12: 13–21, 18: 9–14; *John* 2: 13–16, 18: 33–37.

(2) How would you describe Jesus' relationship with his disciples? Suggested Readings: *Luke* 17:4; *John* 6: 1–14, 14: 27–28, 20: 19–21

(3) How did Jesus treat those who were outcasts on the fringes of society or those who were not members of his religion? Suggested

Readings: *Luke* 5: 27–32, 6: 27–35, 7: 1–10, 7: 36–50, 10: 29–37, 19: 1–10; *John* 8: 2–11, 9: 1–7.

(4) What kind of influence did Jesus have on his disciples? Suggested Readings: *Matthew* 14: 22–33, 26: 56; *Mark* 4: 35–41, 16: 8–15; *Luke* 8: 22–25, 24: 9–11.

(5) Jesus said: *'I have come into this world that you may have life and have it to the full.'*

(a) What do you think he meant by this?

(b) How does this compare to the vision of earthly life presented by cults to their members? Give reasons for your answer.

CHAPTER 14

The Occult

WHAT IS THE OCCULT?

In recent years there has been a remarkable upsurge of interest in the occult. The word itself is derived from the Latin word *occultus* meaning 'the hidden', and this provides a clue to its attraction. Occultists claim that there are hidden or invisible forces from a spirit world beyond ours, with which they can make contact and from which they can gain access to secret sources of knowledge and so gain greater power.

Occult practices can be examined under two headings:
1 *Divination*
2 *Witchcraft.*
We will examine divination first.

Divination is any activity that calls upon some non-human being or force to: '*discover information inaccessible to normal inquiry, e.g. about the future, lost objects, hidden character traits*'.

Penguin Dictionary of Religion

The principal forms of divination are:
• Astrology
• Palmistry
• Fortune Telling (Clairvoyancy)
• Cartomancy
• Ouija Board
• Spiritualism (Seances)

QUESTIONS

1 What do occultists believe?

2 Have you ever heard of any 'occult' happenings or events? If so, what do you think about them? Explain your answer

3 Read the following: '*Medieval people saw God in the mysteries of nature: wind, storm and stars. In their scientific innocence they tended*

to see God everywhere. Today, perhaps we have just the opposite problem. Lost in the concrete canyons and captivated by our knowledge of science we tend to see God nowhere.'

Mark Link, Man in the Modern World.

Do you think this sense of 'the absence of God' has led some people to turn towards occult practices, such as ouija boards, to fill a void in their lives? Give reasons for your opinion.

THE DANGERS OF DABBLING IN THE OCCULT

Some people seem to think that along with smoking cigarettes, experimenting with Ouija boards or taking part in seances is just a normal part of growing up, a bit of harmless fun. This is to completely misunderstand the true nature of such activities.

In using the Ouija board or taking part in a seance, a deliberate attempt is made to make contact with forces about which little is known. In a seance the group employs the services of a *'medium'*, i.e. someone claiming to possess psychic abilities that enable him/her to contact the spirts of the dead. Whether genuine contact is made with the spirit world or whether people delve into as yet unexplored aspects of the human mind, we do not know.

Christianity has always discouraged such practices, chiefly for two reasons:

- They place confidence in forces *other* than God and as such encourage behaviour contrary to the first commandment, i.e. 'I am the Lord your God. You shall not put false gods before me.'

- They involve a person becoming completely passive and open to unknown influences in order to communicate with some mysterious and potentially dangerous spiritual force. This exposes a person to manipulation or even, as it is traditionally called, 'possession'.

While avoiding alarmism, Christianity has always acknowledged the possibility, though rare, of demonic possession. The majority of reported incidences are either hoaxes or due to some psychiatric disorder (e.g. schizophrenia), but there have been *some* genuine cases recorded.

Catholic Church authorities go to great lengths to establish whether a genuine case of possession exists or not. The local bishop nominates a priest with training in psychiatric medicine to examine the case. He will look for a combination of certain factors in the person suspected of being possessed:

- the ability to speak in a foreign or ancient language of which he/she has no previous knowledge and has never studied;
- unusual physical strength;
- knowledge of private/secret matters which the person under examination could not possibly know by ordinary means.

Only if these conditions have been met will permission be granted to carry out an *exorcism*, i.e. a ceremony to cast out an evil spirit that has taken possession of the person.

Read this extract:

A PARTICULAR CASE OF POSSESSION AND EXORCISM

'If, on the one hand, we cannot be certain that a case of demonic possession has occurred, on the other hand we cannot rule out the possibility of this happening. Prayers for deliverance from evil, whatever the evil may be, have been an important part of Christian worship from the beginning; they are for our benefit. Such prayers, when seeking deliverance from alleged possession, need not be said because we are sure of an evil spirit's presence; the possibility of such a presence is enough. In any case the evil is a reality, whatever its full explanation.

An Italian exorcist informed me that his peasant origins were an insult to the devils he had exorcised. The proud devils generally insisted that the Pope or at least a Cardinal perform the exorcism!

The same exorcist held that it would be risky for an individual to attempt an exorcism. He explained that it is Christ who conquers Satan, hence the exorcist must have the authorisation of the Church, of the Body of Christ, for the performance of the exorcism. He is also accompanied by other devout Christians who pray with him during the exorcism, for wherever two or three are gathered in Christ's name there is a special strength and effectiveness to their prayers.

The Italian exorcist found performing exorcisms a most difficult and exhausting task. After his last exorcism, he coughed up blood for a month. His throat was raw after prolonged shouting at the demon.

The voice of the demon, he stated, came from all parts of the room, much like stereo sound. The body of one possessed person was as white as a sheet of paper and his eyes were like fire.

The exorcist prayed that there would be no harm done to himself and to the possessed person. As a result of this prayer, a man whose head smashed a church pew was not harmed by a blow that might have killed him; similarly, another man, hurtled by a demonic force from the top of an altar to the pavement far below him, was also unharmed.

The exorcist produced a photo of a goat's head scorched upon the wall of the bedroom of the possessed person whom he had exorcised. He explained that at the end of the exorcism a flame leapt across the room, accompanied by a sound like a thunderclap, and scorched this image which indicated the departure of the demon. The exorcist had taped some of his exorcisms. One involved a young man purportedly possessed by the spirit of a damned soul, of a man named 'Matteo' who had lived centuries before. This spirit did not wish to reveal itself, and did so only after the exorcist's insistence that he do so in the name of Christ. His voice was that of an old man in the body of a young adolescent. When the exorcist asked Matteo what was the main obstacle to the damnation of souls, Matteo replied 'grace', 'the divine mercy'.

Given the context, these responses were quite remarkable. The dialogue between the exorcist and the voice ('Matteo') revealed a violent battle between two spirits: it is by no means a tranquil exchange of views and information. Even those who listened to the tape without understanding Italian were deeply impressed by the violence of the exchanges.'

Adapted from John Navone, 'Possession and Exorcism', in *The Way* Vol.15 (1975)

QUESTIONS

1 What are the dangers of dabbling in the occult?
2 Having read the above extract, now read *Mark* 5: 1–20 and *Luke* 4:31–37. What lessons do you draw from these readings about the power of Jesus Christ over evil? Explain your answer.

WHO IS SATAN?

The Hebrew word *'Satan'* and its Greek equivalent *'Diablos'* or devil means something like 'slanderer' or 'enemy'. The Fourth Lateran Council (1215) affirmed the belief of Catholic Christians that Satan exists and that he is a *spiritual being*, i.e. *he does not have a physical body*. The council further stated that Satan was created good but that he abused the gift of free will and rebelled against God. The poet John Milton later encapsulated Satan's choice in the immortal line: 'Better to reign in hell than serve in heaven' (*Paradise Lost*, Book 1.)

The 'Omen' series of films and such TV programmes as the 'The X Files' have created a totally misleading impression of Christian teaching about Satan. Quoting from non-existent biblical texts and distorting the meaning of genuine texts, they transform Satan into Angra Mainyu or Ahriman, the god-like evil spirit of Zoroastrianism, the religion of ancient Persia. Christianity has *never* taught that Satan has the power to control nature or make people do things against their will. Rather it has stated that Satan can only suggest to or *tempt* a person to do something. While a spirit, Satan is *not divine, not the equal of God*.

Jacob Epstein's sculpture of St Michael and Lucifer

Christian teaching states that *a person cannot be demonically possessed against his or her will*, that he/she must *freely choose* to let it happen. Dabbling in occult practices is believed to expose a person to such danger.

However, surveys in recent years have shown a steady decline of belief in the devil's existence. Reflecting on this change and in an effort to encourage people to take seriously the devil's existence, the English writer C.S. Lewis wrote a book in which an 'old devil' offers the benefit of his experience to a 'younger devil'. At one stage the former offers his apprentice this advice:

'The fact that "devils" are predominantly comic figures in the modern imagination will help you. If any faint suspicion of your existence begins to arise in his mind, suggest to him a picture of something in a red costume, and persuade him that since he cannot believe in that (it is an old method of confusing them), he therefore cannot believe in you.'

C.S. Lewis, *The Screwtape Letters*

QUESTIONS

1 What is Christian belief about Satan?
2 'The devil's best asset is that many people no longer believe in him'. What do you think this means? Do you agree/disagree? Why?

WITCHCRAFT

The modern image of witches and witchcraft is largely derived from the annual practice of dressing-up in black robes and a pointed hat at Hallowe'en. Witchcraft's origins, however, have been traced back to the primitive nature cults of prehistoric times.

The word *'witch'* means *'wise one'*, and it can be applied to both men and women who form themselves into a group known as a *'coven'*. Witches claim to possess what they call the *'craft'*, that is, magical powers over the forces of nature. During the Middle Ages, superstitious people would often pay those whom they believed to have magical powers to find them a place to dig a well, or ask them to cure a sick animal. Then as now witches claimed that they could use their supposed powers to do either good or evil, giving rise to the distinction between *'white'* and *'black'* magic.

Practitioners of white magic claim that they draw on their natural psychic powers to make magic solely for the purpose of doing good. Black witches claim that they can call on the assistance of an evil spirit to inflict harm on others.

Christianity has always opposed witchcraft in any form. In common with the other monotheistic religions it has considered those who engage in such activities to be completely misled, clinging to a mistaken belief in magic that is without any real foundation. Above all else, however,

Christian teaching rejects any form of witchcraft, whether white or black, because it encourages people to place their trust in forces other than God, with the danger of exposing them to psychological and moral harm.

QUESTIONS

1 What is *'witchcraft'*?

2 Why does Christianity reject the practice of witchcraft? Explain your answer.

VICTIMS OF THE OCCULT

Help is available to victims of occultism. Occult practices are dangerous, and experts in the field have identified two main types of victim:

(1) Those who *freely* choose to get involved in occult practices and suffer psychological and moral harm as a result;

(2) Those, especially young children, who are *forced* to take part in barbaric rituals where they are subjected to various forms of physical and/or sexual abuse, sometimes leading to their murder to provide a human sacrifice.

Generally speaking, witches are *not* involved in such activities, which are usually the work of *Satanists* who reject God and worship the devil. These reject any civilised code of behaviour and place little, if any, value on human life.

Research carried out by psychiatrists shows that casualties of the occult suffer from depression, their personalities change, they experience violent mood swings, and they are more likely to become schizophrenic.

QUESTIONS

1 What kind of psychiatric illnesses can afflict victims of the occult?

2 Read the following statement: '*Most people, it seems, whether children or adults, are drawn to the occult's promise of power. Satanists in particular are power-oriented. Wanting some belief system, today's teenager may turn to the occult because it promises power, influence*

and strength. Christians, on the other hand, depend on God for their strength and have a decidedly non-modern habit of putting other people before themselves'.

Rachel Storm, 'Debating the Devil', *The Catholic Herald*, 1989.

What is the attraction of occultism vis-a-vis Christianity in today's world, according to Storm?

Do you agree/disagree? Why?

3 If dabbling in the occult is liable to expose people to both psychological and moral harm, why do some still persist? Explain your answer.

PART 3 THE MORAL LIFE

CHAPTER 15

Introduction to Morality

THE CHALLENGE

A famous atheist, Jean Paul Sartre, once wrote:

'Human beings are condemned to be free.'

But some people since have wondered if we are not just condemned. They believe that another writer, Thomas Hobbes, summed up human life exactly when he described it as:

'Solitary, nasty, brutish and short'.

A quick review of the week's newspaper and television reports make it clear that this is only too true for many people. In an era of high unemployment, economic uncertainty and violent crime, many feel powerless to control and direct their *own* lives, never mind hope to make an impact on the many problems that afflict others, both at home and abroad.

It would be less than honest to try to down-play the challenges people, both young and old, have to face. The different *personal* problems each individual has to cope with put a variety of *limitations* on his/her freedom.

Christians admit the problems of today's world; but they are not fatalistic, they believe that something can be done, even if only gradually, to improve both our own society and those of others elsewhere. This is not due to any false, simplistic optimism, but to their faith in the person and teaching of Jesus Christ. It is this which gives them the hope and strength they need to try, starting with their own lives, to work for a better world.

Christians believe that whatever scope for free choice people have, life still presents them not only with problems to confront, but also with opportunities for growth and development if they use their different talents wisely. They believe that, when confronted with difficult choices, people should *think carefully* and *act responsibly*, confident that God is always with them, guiding and supporting them.

So it is important to begin this section on morality by examining the meaning of *freedom* and what constitutes a *moral action*. Read the following article by Dr Donal Daly.

FREEDOM

Morality is basically concerned with *the rightness or wrongness, goodness or badness of human actions*. One does not need to be a professional moralist to know that some things a person may do are wrong (e.g. to deliberately murder an innocent person) and other things are right (e.g. to raise money for charity). Such actions are moral actions, the first a morally bad action, the other a morally good one.

Not every action that a person may perform is a moral action. Moral actions are a *particular kind* of human action. To see where the difference comes in we might consider, for example, the difference between jumping into a river to help save a person in danger of drowning and accidentally falling down a flight of stairs. The first is a moral action (morally good), the second is neither good nor bad. Falling down a stairs is something one does, but it is not a moral action. If we ask why it is not, we have to see the *difference* between the two kinds of acts.

One difference stands out immediately when we consider the two actions which serve as examples. A person who trips and falls down a flight of stairs does so by accident and not from choice. It is something he/she does (in a sense) but the person who does it is *not in control* of what is happening. He/she does not decide to do it, but rather it is something that *happens to* him/her. In the case of a person who jumps into a river to help another, that person *is in control*. It is something one *chooses* and decides to do. It is not something that just happens accidentally.

Control of the action is the major characteristic of those human actions which are properly called moral actions, and which can be said to be either good or bad, right or wrong. *Moral actions* are those which are *in the control of the person performing them.*

An action is controlled when the person *knows* (at least to some extent) what he/she is doing and *wills* (at least to some extent) to do it. Moral action is the product of human choice. When a person is in control of his/her actions one is *responsible* for them and can be blamed if they are bad, or praised for them if they are good. The implication of the fact that a person can choose a course of action is that one is *free*. Responsiblity and freedom go hand in hand.

Human freedom is quite an awesome responsibility. By one's free moral actions the individual can shape oneself — one's character and moral worth, the kind of person one is. People, collectively, by their free moral actions can shape their society and the kind of world they live in. Human freedom has often been denied, of course, in favour of some form of *determinism*. But even when denied in theory, human freedom must be assumed in practice. It is assumed every time we encourage anyone to do a particular thing or to follow a particular course of action, and also when we blame anyone for doing something we think is wrong or harmful.

Because human actions following from human choice can be either morally good or morally bad, human freedom is ambiguous. As Dr John Macquarrie says, '*We can help our neighbours or injure them; we can use the resources of nature or abuse them; we can beautify the world or we can ravage and pollute it. And because there is a risk in all action, since we cannot see all the results that will flow from our action, we sometimes effect evil when we mean to do good; and ... what we intend for good may turn out to have unexpected destructive side effects.*'

Because of this ambiguity, increasing human freedom will entail the risk that some will abuse it. But nevertheless since the capacity to act freely and responsibly is essential to being a human person, where freedom to act is denied there is a lessening of humanity. There will be no full humanity without freedom to act.

There are, however, obvious limitations to human freedom in concrete situations. When we wish to ask whether a person is to be blamed and perhaps punished for a bad action, or praised and rewarded for a good one certain questions have to be asked:

- The first thing to be decided is whether or not one is responsible for what one has done. Was one in control of what one was doing?
- The second thing is whether one knew what one was doing and did one choose to do it?

There are instances where a person who has done something wrong will say, 'I couldn't help it', or 'I just didn't know what I was doing'. If that really is the case, then one cannot be blamed because one was not in control, and was not responsible.

But *when one knows what one is doing and choses to do it then one is performing a moral action — one which will either be morally good or morally bad —* and *one is responsible for it.* Human freedom controls one's moral action. It can be used for good or evil. The choice and the responsibility are one's own.

Adapted from: *Kairos*, November 1987

QUESTIONS

1 Explain each of the following:
- Morality
- Determinism
- Freedom
- Responsibility
- Moral Action

2 Choose which of the following is a moral action. You are *not* asked to decide here whether they are morally right or morally wrong:

(a) Refusing to wear a seat-belt when driving, (b) collecting money for charity, (c) verbally abusing a classmate, (d) defending oneself against an uninvited attack, (e) becoming a blood donor, (f) taking money from your mother's purse without her permission, (g) choosing not to take an illegal drug when offered it, (h) taking time off when you are supposed to be at work.

3 Why does Dr Daly describe freedom as an 'awesome responsibility'? Do you agree/disagree? Explain your answer.

CHAPTER 16

Thinking About Thinking

INTRODUCTION

Christians are called to have a *positive, hopeful* but *realistic* view of human nature, beginning with their own selves. It is useful, therefore, to examine the way in which human beings think, how this affects their decisions and the actions which flow from them.

The aim of this chapter is to make people more aware of the factors that influence their decision-making and ultimately their behaviour towards themselves and others.

LANGUAGE: ITS USES AND ABUSES

When Dr David Attenborough presented the final episode of his acclaimed television series, 'Life on Earth', telling the story of human evolution, he decided to call the human race the '*Compulsive Communicators*'. Most people seem to enjoy communicating with each other, whether it is in conversation about a favourite topic (*speech*), waving 'hello' to a friend (*gesture*) or typing a message to someone via the Internet (*writing*). We call all these different forms of communication '*language*'.

Most people seem to enjoy talking, whether it is about sport, clothes, fashion, hair-styles, music, politics or whatever.

Since language is our medium of communication, let us examine some of the different ways in which it can be used:

(1) *to state a fact*, e.g. 'Ireland is an island.'
(2) *to ask a question*, e.g. 'Why are there no snakes in Ireland?'
(3) *to express emotions*, e.g. 'I love you.'
(4) *to give an instruction*, e.g. 'Open your textbook.'
(5) *to make a commitment*, e.g.: 'I will be there on time.'

Dramatists and poets have long appreciated the power of language to affect people positively. However, language can be a major source of conflict because of the way in which some people deliberately or unthinkingly confuse the different ways of using language. For example, if I say that my next-door neighbour owns a dog named Rex, I am stating a fact. But if I were to say that my next-door neighbour owns a *mongrel*, I could be saying more than just passing on information about the dog's mixed breeding. I could be implying that I do not think much of the dog, or of my neighbour's judgment either. So many small incidents have erupted into full-scale rows, or worse, because someone used an inappropriate word or phrase, either accidentally or deliberately.

QUESTIONS

Read the following extract:

> *There is a way of using bad language that is a weapon of attack on either the person or the opinions of another. For my money there is far too much of it about and if we are serious about the roots of violence, we must have an honest look at the way we use language.*
>
> *Martin Luther King said that the way white people talked about blacks did more harm than all the repressive laws in the state legal documents. He said you could change all the bad laws in the books and it would be a waste of time if you didn't first change the language of the whites. Not just the language, but the attitudes that triggered the language.*
>
> *When Hitler wanted to create a climate where public opinion would tolerate his rape of the Jews, he started by calling them crude names. Language. The day someone somewhere, laughed at the crudity was the day Hitler got permission to open Auschwitz. Then he went on to daub Jewish shops with threats. Sign language. When few objected, he knew he had permission for the Holocaust. Language had been his main weapon.*
>
> Colm Kilcoyne, *Sunday Tribune*, January 1996

1 What does the way in which a person uses language tell us about him/her?

2 What does this tell us about the power of language to help or to hurt?

REFLECTION BEFORE RESPONSE

The philosopher Aristotle once described human beings as *'rational* creatures', but that is not the full story. We are also *'emotional* creatures'. Those who wish to influence people's thinking and behaviour, for good or ill, try to tap into one or other and sometimes *both* aspects of the human mind. They can either convince people to *think* a particular way by bombarding them with seemingly convincing arguments based on complicated statistical evidence, or else make them *feel* they should do a particular thing or support some action.

Unfortunately, people often seem to think that if someone says something, there are only two ways for them to respond:

(a) they can *accept* what they say; or

(b) they can *reject* it.

But there are *other options* open to them:

(c) they can *qualify* it because it may be true only up to a point and not tell them the whole story; or

(d) they can *question* it, suspending final judgment until they can find out more information.

Whatever their response, people need to stop and consider what is the right way to think and act, *as we are responsible for what we say and do.*

The Importance of the Media

The media have a tremendous potential to influence public perceptions on a whole variety of important social issues.

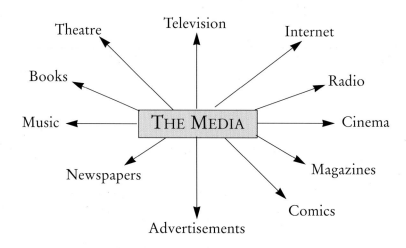

QUESTIONS

1   Can you identify any important issues where news media have performed a valuable social service by highlighting injustice and abuse of power?

2   Look at two newspaper reports of the same story, one in a 'tabloid' and the other in a serious 'broadsheet'. Do you notice any differences in the way they present the same story? What are they?

3   Do you think that a 'free press', where a government cannot enforce its particular point of view on the media, is worth preserving? Explain your answer.

THE INFLUENCE OF THE MEDIA

The mass media (especially TV) can powerfully influence our opinions on a whole range of topics by determining which events are given exposure to the viewing, listening or reading public. We should be aware of the following:

(1) Some essential facts might be left out of a report, so that a fair account might not be given. The 'edited' analysis of the facts might be made to look as if it is complete.

(2) Some minor incident or small error might be blown up out of all proportion and made to appear as a major occurrence.

(3) A radio or TV presenter's opening remarks might put a particular *slant* on the discussion that follows. Instead, a brief, accurate and balanced outline of the facts should be given.

(4) An interviewer might interrupt someone answering a question before that person has been given a fair chance to develop his/her point.

(5) The expression 'well-informed sources' might be used to give credibility and respectability to anonymous, sometimes vicious, rumours.

(6) Loaded words might be used to *label* people, for example, calling someone a 'conservative' or a 'liberal' in an effort to influence how we will react to what he/she has to say.

This has led media analyst David Porter to conclude that:

113

'If by "truth" we mean an accurate, totally unbiased, comprehensive and objectively presented version of events, then we will never find perfection in the media.'

MORALITY AND THE MEDIA

The Christian churches call on people to search for the truth and to live according to its demands.

'The eighth commandment forbids misrepresenting the truth in our relations with others. Christians are called to bear witness to their God who is the truth and wills the truth. Offences against the truth express by word or deed a refusal to commit oneself to moral uprightness: they are fundamental infidelities to God.'

Catechism of the Catholic Church

Human beings can work together for harmony and unity among humankind only if they deal with one another honestly and sincerely. Truth is a basic requirement for all communication. Communicators and their audiences need to develop a critical sense that is fair-minded but determined to get to the truth.

When informing public opinion, the media should provide information that is *full*, *accurate* and *true*. Where the interpretation of this information is controversial there needs to be honest debate where the different viewpoints are represented. In this way people can make decisions that are more soundly based.

QUESTIONS

1 Why is it argued that sincerity and truth are a basic requirement for all communication?

2 What do you understand by the expression 'honest debate'? Explain your answer.

3 Read the following extract written by Conor O'Clery during the US Presidential campaign in 1992:

'SOUNDBITE FROM THE BIBLE BELT'
I had intended arriving an hour early for the Vice-President Dan Quayle's rally at Auburn University in Alabama, but overlooked

114

the fact that I was driving west across a time zone and arrived two hours early instead.

Mr Quayle, for his part, turned up an hour and a half late, which meant I had most of a morning to observe the build-up to what was a fairly typical campaign stop for the Vice-President. It was a revealing experience.

Mr Quayle's task is to show the flag and rally the faithful in the Republican heartlands. Auburn University is reputed to be the most conservative college in the Bible Belt of the Deep South, which is saying something.

Inside the tiny stadium, Republican Party officials opened 18 inch × 30 inch cardboard boxes and distributed hundreds of posters with 'Bush-Quayle '92' on both sides. From a larger box, the party workers took dozens of handwritten posters of various sizes, deliberately made to look amateurish, as if they had been written individually, and passed them out over the heads of the crowd. The young people cheerfully grabbed them. They had slogans such as 'Go Back to Moscow, Bill', and 'We love Dan'.

Television crews got into position on a platform facing the podium. No other camera angles were allowed. To film the Vice-President they had to include the posters held high in front of the podium and a high terrace of supporters behind.

Then they waited. The temperature climbed into the 80s.

After what seemed an eternity, the band suddenly jumped up and blasted out 'Where's that tiger?', three parachutists descended into the baseball field trailing coloured smoke and the Vice-President at last appeared, jumping on to the podium, in shirt sleeves as if ready for a long, tough speech. He made a pistol with his thumb and finger and fired, as if greeting a top supporter.

Mr Quayle does this everywhere in front of cameras, even, as a writer for New Republic observed, if it's only to the backside of a Secret Service agent.

He took a cue card from his pocket. 'How did I do last night?' cried Mr Quayle, fresh from his debate scrap with Senator Al Gore. 'You won', they shouted back.

'Not once did Senator Gore come to Bill Clinton's defence. Bill Clinton has trouble telling the truth. Do you want a president who's going to raise your taxes? ('No!'), who has trouble telling the truth? ('No!'). Do you want a president with the integrity to make the

tough decisions?' ('Yes!').

And that was more or less it. The Vice-President and his wife, Marilyn, tossed some Frisbees and orange balls into the crowd and suddenly they were gone. A few minutes for handshakes on the way out, and they were off in the black reinforced-steel limousine to Air Force Two, leaving more than a few wondering what it had all been about.

'That wasn't a speech, it was a sound bite', said a reporter from a Montgomery newspaper on the press platform.

On television that evening, the national news showed a picture of a resolute Dan Quayle, his shirt sleeves rolled up for action, against a tableau of cheering supporters as he delivered what looked like the high point of a lengthy political speech. It was what he came to Auburn for and what he got.

The Irish Times, 17.10.1992

(a) What is your reaction to this story?

(b) What does it say to you about the ways in which television can be used to influence our opinions about people or things? Explain your thinking.

4 Read the following extract from the weekly column of a British TV critic.

On Monday night I watched the Nine O'Clock News on BBC1 and then News At Ten on ITV. The Nine O'Clock News used to be a focal point for the nation, thoughtful and authoritative. Now it's one long string of lazy clichés with pictures. Monday's news was unfortunately complex and not very visual but we got the pictures anyway. A train to go with the report on the rail strike. That old favourite, people in the street, to go with the European elections, and then, just for contrast, foreign people in the street to go with the elections in Europe. We got library film of the Lockerbie crash, presumably for those who couldn't place the words aeroplane and crash in a visual context. The only foreign reports were a brief headline about Korea and Mike Tyson appearing in court. Oh, and there was one extra-terrestrial item. The Hubble telescope was seeing stars.

News At Ten was worse. Cliché-ridden, film obsessed.

Implications were 'dramatic', there were 'margins of error', 'cushions of support', mills had 'grist', offers were 'on the table', heads perpetually 'rolled', MPs 'rallied' and agendas were 'tough'. This is writing that the junior sub on the Argus *and* Gleaner *would bin in disgust. Bits of press releases strung together with hackneyed phrases. Try watching the main evening news with your eyes shut. Without pictures it isn't nearly as incisive and illuminating as you might think.*

Adapted from *The Sunday Times*, 19.06.94.

(a) What points do you think the writer is making about the TV news?

(b) Do you agree/disagree with him? Give reasons for your answer.

5   Read the following extract and answer the questions asked.

'TUNED IN AND SWITCHED OFF'

- *Television defines what a 'whole person' is; what makes us happy; what success is; what we should buy; how we should behave.*

- *When a person spends hours in front of the TV, a whole range of leisure pursuits, social encounters, information sources are excluded. It keeps people switched off from life outside the living-room.*

- *Research at the Harvard University, USA, suggests that children who are TV addicts show poorer logical thinking and weaker imaginations than children who don't watch much TV. The former don't know how to generate their own imaginative games and are so used to TV images that they can't create their own.*

- *After parents and before school, TV is the main educator of children.*

- *Day after day viewers are exposed to a distorted portrayal of people, concentrating almost exclusively on the violent, superficial, sensational, selfish and uncaring. TV can distort our view of reality.*

- *Television's consumerism encourages a small minority of the world's population to devour a huge amount of its resources while others drown in a sea of poverty.*

- *People stay in and watch the blue flickering screen. Community living, for some, is a thing of the past. Television viewing is passive — people 'switch off' from their families and neighbours.*

117

- *Television works against an understanding and appreciation of life's spiritual and religious dimensions. The TV version of the 'good life' is one in which spirituality plays very little part. Programmes are set firmly in the here and now of immediately visible action and excitement. The qualities and goals striven for and the values held up as praiseworthy tend to be superficial, e.g. wealth, power, physical beauty.*

- *Television numbs us. It can hide from our sight the realities of our existence. We live in an enormous universe. We are all living together on one planet where many suffer because of our apathy and ignorance. Millions prefer to watch 'Coronation Street' or 'Eastenders' rather than talk to their neighbours or families about things that matter.*

Adapted from Joe Jenkin, *Contemporary Moral Issues.*

In each of the above, say whether you agree/partially agree/or completely disagree with the point made. Then explain your judgment in each case.

PREJUDICES

You have been out at the cinema to see the latest blockbuster movie with some friends. After it is over, you decide to get a takeaway. The choice is between the chip shop or the Chinese takeaway. *You* want to get the latter, but one of your friends objects to everyone buying one. He says he does not like Chinese food. When you quiz him about this, he admits that actually he has never even tasted Chinese food.

Why did he react so negatively? You discover he has some very strange ideas about the ingredients in, and taste of, Chinese food, none of which is based on fact. He is *prejudiced*, i.e. he is pre-judging the

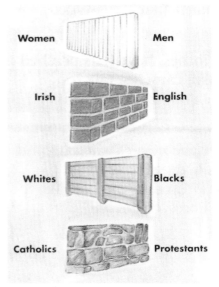

Prejudice creates barriers

situation and reacting emotionally about something without a single good reason for the opinion he has expressed. His mind is already made up *before* he has taken the opportunity to examine the evidence.

The walls of prejudice can be broken down. Nelson Mandela at his inauguration as President of South Africa with his predecessor, F.W. de Klerk

QUESTIONS

1 What do you understand by the term 'prejudice'? Give some examples.

2 The great psychologist William James once remarked: '*A great many people think they are thinking when they are merely rearranging their prejudices.*' Can you give any examples, drawn from everyday experience or from the media, of how people reveal these prejudices in the opinions they express?

STEREOTYPES

In his book, *Public Opinion* (1922), the famous American journalist Walter Lippman warned people about the way in which *stereotypes*, or pictures in the mind, can affect our opinions on many issues. He noticed that if we have a bad or unhappy experience with an individual from a particular race or social group, then there is a strong tendency in most of us to build up a picture that *labels everyone else* of his/her race or group *as being the same.*

For example, some Americans who have never visited Ireland seem to have a peculiar, stereotyped view of our country - a magical land, where tall, aggressive, hard-drinking men dance at crossroads with fiery, red-headed cailíns and raise *very* large families in tiny, thatched cottages without benefit of electricity or running water.

Question

1 From where, in your opinion, do some Americans get their idea of Irish life? Where do Irish people get their ideas of life in America?

2 Someone once said: 'Prejudice is a great time-saver; you can make up your mind without bothering with facts.' What, in your opinion, are the attractions of thinking in stereotypes? Give reasons for your answer.

The Dangers of Stereotyped Thinking

Stereotyped thinking can play a *sinister role* in human affairs when it is exploited by unscrupulous individuals to further such destructive notions as *racism*, *religious bigotry* and *sexism*. It is easy for anyone to fall into the trap of stereotyped thinking. Indeed, it is far easier than most people are usually prepared to admit.

No matter what excuse is offered, Christians believe it is wrong to discriminate against someone because of skin colour, or a physical or mental disability, or membership of a minority group, such as the travelling community.

However, it is often only when one is *personally* on the *receiving end* of discriminatory treatment that one comes to appreciate how it can cause suffering to others.

> '*The Church's teaching on this matter is clear and straightforward. Every human being is made in the image of God. We are all brothers and sisters and neighbours of each other...To love your neighbour as yourself is one of the two great, fundamental commandments. Charity, for the Christian, does not begin at home or end at home. Charity lies in what you do or in what you allow to be done*'.
>
> Catholic Hierarchy of England and Wales.

Activity

Study this cartoon from the London *Evening Standard* (p. 121).
If you were an Irish person living and working in Britain, would you consider this cartoon offensive/inoffensive? Give reasons for your answer.

QUESTIONS

1 In what ways can stereotyped thinking become destructive? Give examples.

2 Is the law of the State sufficient in itself to stop discrimination? Explain your thinking.

3 Read the Parable of The Good Samaritan in *Luke* 10. In your own words, explain what Jesus has to say about prejudice and the idea of judging others on the basis of surface appearances.

FALLACIES

We will now consider some arguments where there is an error in reasoning, called a '*fallacy*'.

Often, people unintentionally present us with advice or an argument that is unsound because they are unaware of how much their judgment is affected by the '*emotional baggage*' they carry inside their heads, i.e. past hurts, jealousies or prejudices.

These can lead them to make false assumptions which form a barrier to clear thinking.

However, as we have already seen, other people can deliberately distort words and statements to get us to do what they want us to do. A clever manipulator can be very persuasive, so we must exercise due caution.

ACTIVITY

Spot the fallacy (error) in each of the following. In each case, ask yourself if the conclusion can reasonably be said to follow from the information given.

1   Comment heard on San Francisco radio phone-in: '*Violence has no place in America. Anyone who preaches violence should be shot like a dog*'.

2   Joe and Dave are carpenters. Joe is wealthier than Dave. Therefore, Joe *must* be a better carpenter than Dave.

3   How can you say that smoking cigarettes is bad for my health and that I should give them up, while you continue to smoke them yourself?

4   Since healthy eating is essential for the good health of people in general, our government should punish people who eat junk food.

5   I know three red-haired people who have terrible tempers. Celia has red hair. I'm sure she has a terrible temper.

6   A research study showed that young children who watched '*Sesame Street*' rather than '*Barney*' did better in school. So it must be true that '*Sesame Street*' is more educational than '*Barney*'.

CONCLUSIONS

Christians believe that:

- Every human being, with the exception of the mentally ill or those with a mental disability, has to make moral decisions and, having acted upon them, accept responsibility for the consequences.

- People should have a realistic appreciation of the strengths and weaknesses of human nature. They should be aware of what is going on around them and be careful not to be manipulated into accepting the unacceptable. Further they should not try to fool themselves into believing that something is right when it is actually wrong.

- In order to make good moral decisions, people must try to think clearly and freely, without prejudice, using both the rational and emotional dimensions of their nature in a mature and constructive fashion.

- People have a responsibility to inform themselves about issues so as to make sound decisions based upon the best available evidence.

- People must be aware that no one is an island, that the life of each person touches that of another and so a person's choice and action has an effect, not just on his/her own life, but on those around him/her.

CHAPTER 17

Moral Development

THE SOURCES OF OUR VALUES

When people look back over their lives, they can see that they have never been short of those willing to offer advice or guidance on what they should or should not say or do. From the moment they are born, people begin learning, developing a sense of right and wrong, acquiring a set of values upon which they will later base important decisions in their lives. Broadly speaking, a value is:

> *something which is believed to be good or worthwhile and considered desirable or useful.*

At first, people learn most things from their immediate family; but as they grow, so too do the number and variety of influences upon them:

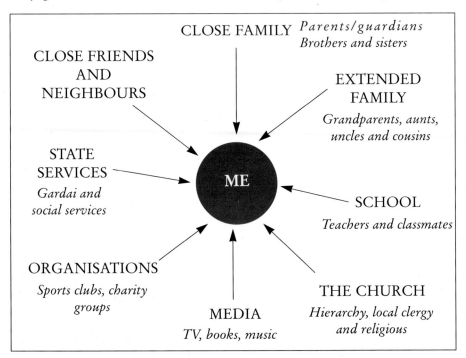

SOCIALISATION

The way people learn about the correct way to behave in their community is called *socialisation*. As they grow from infancy to adulthood, they gradually discover what is morally right as opposed to what is morally wrong by a variety of different ways:

(1) by following the example set by others;

(2) by experiencing what happens to themselves and to others when they do something;

(3) by learning from the consequences of their actions and those of others;

Learning about life in a strange new world

(4) by learning the rules laid down by their parents, their school, their religion and society in general.

A person's sense of right and wrong, of knowing how to make good moral decisions, depends on many things: the kind of upbringing he/she has had, the attitude of his/her parents, the kind of friends he/she has had, and so on. Without doubt, the most important influence on a person's moral development is the general social and economic environment in which he/she grows up.

Another influence on a person's sense of right and wrong is the human need to be wanted, to be loved and respected, to have what one does recognised as worthwhile. If such needs, especially the need to be loved, are left unfulfilled, this can have a damaging effect on the development of a person's character, and make it difficult to make the right choice when confronted with a moral decision.

QUESTIONS

1 What kind of factors can make life very hard for someone growing up, make each day an enormous struggle against giving into feelings of anger and despair, and often make it difficult to make good moral decisions? Explain your answer.

2 Do you think that people can overcome their past and learn good moral values? Why/why not? Explain your answer.

THE MORAL VALUES OF JESUS

The *Gospels* make clear that Jesus understood our human needs, limitations and hopes. He offered people a way forward, telling them that the 'Kingdom of God is among us'.

But what did he mean by these words? To begin with, it did not mean that he wished to set up some new political empire to replace Rome in the first century A.D. Rather Jesus presented it as God's free 'no strings attached' offer of his love to all, both Jews and non-Jews, and called on people to draw on him for the strength to build up a new world of greater peace and justice, where no one is ignored or left out. (Read *Mark* 12: 1–12, *Matthew* 22: 1–10.)

The *Gospels* tell us that Jesus was different from other religious figures of his day because he '*spoke with authority*'. In other words, he did not simply speak beautiful words; he *lived by them*. Jesus lived and breathed the spirit of God's commandments. He showed people that he meant what he said by putting his ideas into practice each moment of every day of his life. When Jesus told his followers that the heart of his message was to '*love God and love your neighbour as yourself*', they could see that he did not want them to 'do as I say', but rather '*do as I do*'!

When Jesus said, '*Love your neighbour as yourself*', he was not merely saying we should have nice feelings towards everyone else. It is hard to see how he could have had nice feelings in his heart when, for example, he used a whip to drive the money-changers from the temple (*Mark* 11: 15–19), or when he called the Pharisees, a large and influential group of strict religious teachers, a '*brood of vipers*' (*Matthew* 23: 33). No, he seems to have meant that if you really love someone, then you must try to act in their best interest and not simply look out for yourself. You must tell them things they may not want to hear, not to hurt but to *help* them. But good words are not enough in themselves; you must practise what you preach and lead by good

Jesus driving the money-changers from the Temple

126

example. Then, as now, this kind of message made many people uncomfortable, as it asked them to put themselves out to help other people for no personal gain.

PILE 'EM HIGH

'All talk and no action?'

The whole idea of the gospel message is to call each person to live up to his/her God-given potential. Each person is called upon to live a life of *'virtue'*. By virtue we mean *'a power of doing good'* whose growth we encourage within us by developing good living habits and which acts within us to help us do good and avoid evil. This makes tough demands on everyone. Each one of us is called to look honestly at our *selves*, to live according to the same values by which Jesus lived and ask the most discomfiting of questions:

How would Jesus act if faced with this decision?

CONCLUDING REMARKS

Christians believe that the goal of all moral development is to share the attitudes and values of Jesus and to put them into action in our daily lives.

QUESTIONS

1   What did the Gospel writers mean when they wrote that Jesus *'spoke with authority'*?

2   What is meant by *'virtue'*?

3   Read the following scripture passages: *Matthew 7: 1-5; Mark 3: 31–35*.

   What point does Jesus make in each extract about the way in which each person can play an important role in building up the kingdom of which he spoke? Explain your answer.

CHAPTER 18

Conscience

MORAL AWARENESS

'If you gotta go out and kill a guy, you gotta make yourself believe it was him or you. You justify it to yourself, but you never confess it to a priest.'

V. Teresa with T. C. Renner, *My Life in the Mafia*

These are the words of Vincent Teresa, a Mafia gangster who turned informer. He admitted that he chose a life of crime partly because it was the *'family business'*, but primarily because it was an easy way to get what he most desired — money and power.

QUESTION

Do you think Vincent Teresa's words reveal that he was aware that what he was doing was simply not right, that murder is wrong, no matter the excuse or justification offered? *Give reasons for your opinion.*

THE NATURE OF CONSCIENCE

What precisely is *conscience*? Is it the 'voice of God' in each person that tries to keep us on the right path?

Much of the confusion about conscience stems from the way people often use the word, for example: 'My conscience tells me that. . .' or 'Always let your conscience be your guide.'

Such phrases give this 'voice of conscience' the characteristics of some kind of independent entity inside each of us.

Thomas Aquinas said, however, that conscience is not some mysterious 'thing' in each person, rather conscience is basically *our ability to make practical judgments about what is the right or wrong thing to do when faced with a particular moral problem.*

Normally, our conscience operates with such computer-like speed and efficiency that we are rarely aware of how it functions. Let us take a slow-motion example to illustrate how we can apply a general moral principle to a particular moral problem:

I am tempted to make a statement that is malicious gossip.	Problem
But it is always wrong to spread malicious gossip.	Principle
Therefore, if I make this statement, I am doing something wrong.	Conclusion
A moral person would then say: I wish to help, not injure others, so I will not make such a statement.	Decision

THE TEN COMMANDMENTS

The Christian moral conscience accepts the ten commandments as its basic moral guide.

1. I, the Lord, am your God; you shall have no other gods besides me.
2. You shall not take the name of the Lord your God in vain.
3. Remember to keep holy the Sabbath day.
4. Honour your father and your mother.
5. You shall not commit murder.
6. You shall not commit adultery.
7. You shall not steal.
8. You shall not bear false witness against your neighbour.
9. You shall not covet your neighbour's wife.
10. You shall not covet anything that belongs to your neighbour.

Jesus told his followers to remember, however, that the essence of the commandments is: *'You should love God and love your fellow human being as you should love yourself.'*

QUESTIONS

1 What is meant by '*conscience*'?

2 Imagine that you are sent to the school office by your teacher to collect some photocopied material. When you get there, you find the office unattended. The door is open, so you walk in and spot the photocopies on top of the photocopying machine. As you are picking up the bundle, you notice a copy of the end of term exam paper, which you are due to sit next week, accidentally left there by your

The Devil tempting Christ, twelfth-century painting on the ceiling of a church in Switzerland

maths teacher. There is no-one around. You appear to be presented with a 'golden opportunity'.

Explore the implications of each of the following:

(a) stealing the paper and keeping it secret;

(b) photocopying it and giving copies to your friends or selling it to members of your class;

(c) refusing to steal it but looking at it;

d) refusing to either steal it or look at it.

Which of these is the correct course of action to take? *Explain your answer.*

Examine the reasons you gave. What do they tell you about your *own* set of values?

3 (a) Which of the commandments centre on our relationship with God?

(b) Which commandments centre on relationships between ourselves and other people and vice versa?

4 What do you think is the meaning and importance of the ten commandments for people today? Give reasons for your answer.

WHY BE HONEST?

An honest person is one who tries to do what is right, even when it works to his/her own disadvantage. Honesty involves being truthful with oneself and recognising one's obligation to God and to other people. Honesty has no time for self-deception, cheating and the desire for success at any cost.

Even so, dishonesty is more prevalent in our world than anyone would want it to be. We are not talking here about a 'little white lie' told to spare the feelings of a friend whose hairstyle or clothes don't match up to our particular fashion sense. We are dealing with more serious and important issues.

Frequently, people ask the question: *'Why be honest?'* Christians offer these answers:

- Because God demands it of us (Read *Exodus* 20: 15-16).

- Because it is the basis for all genuine human relationships. Without it they disintegrate.

- Because dishonesty creates situations which tempt a person to invent more lies to cover up, making a bad situation worse.

- Because dishonest acts such as shoplifting, bribery and fraudulent insurance claims lead to higher costs for everyone.

REFLECTION

Read the following questions. Think about your answers.

- Do I misuse language, describing deception as a 'white lie' or double-dealing as 'just business'?

- Do I regularly look for convenient excuses for my failures to live up to what I know to be proper moral standards?

- Do I tolerate small lapses in myself or my friends without facing up to the fact that repeated actions quickly become habits?

- Am I willing to purchase goods at suspiciously low prices without inquiring where they come from?

- Have I failed to make up for past wrong-doing?

Calvin and Hobbes on the importance of thinking about the consequences of our choices.

DEVELOPING A MATURE CONSCIENCE

Mature Christians are those who *think for themselves, honestly evaluate situations as they see them* and *determine their own course of action in accordance with their Christian values.*

But in doing so they must be wary of those things that can cloud their conscience and so make it difficult to know the right thing to do in some situations. There are four main causes of error:

(1) Where people are *ignorant* (unaware) of the true nature of the problem facing them either because they did not or could not get all the advice or information they needed.

(2) Where people allow their *emotions* to unduly influence their decision-making to the extent that they only do something because it makes them feel good. Just because something makes you feel good does not guarantee that it is the right thing to do.

People must consider both the *means* by which they do something and its *consequences* for both themselves and others.

(3) When people do something for the sake of *conformity*, to win favour

with others. Just because everyone else is either for or against something does not make it right. To be a Christian will sometimes mean having to take a stand against the crowd.

(4) If people make *a mistake in their reasoning*, e.g.

War involves killing people.	*Problem.*
It is always wrong to kill another person.	*Principle.*
Therefore, war is wrong.	*Conclusion.*

The problem here is that this principle is *not* true, for *every* situation. In some circumstances it may, regrettably, be both necessary and correct to take a life, for example in defence of yourself or your loved ones in times of extreme danger, when there is no other course of action open to you.

QUESTIONS

1 (a) Can you identify any situations where ignorance of the true nature of the problem a young person faces can have unfortunate consequences for him/her and others?

(b) In what circumstances can our emotions cloud our judgment?

(c) List the most common types of conformist behaviour or thought (i.e. going along with the crowd) among people in your age group.

2 Why do people think and behave in this way?

3 What are the consequences of this conformist behaviour for them and others?

4 In most circumstances, it would be true to say, '*It is wrong to cut another person with a knife*'.

(a) Can you identify any situations in which it would be morally correct to do so *other* than in defence of oneself or one's loved ones? Why?

(b) What does this say to you about applying general moral principles to particular moral problems? Explain your answer.

> **N.B.** One has to be careful how one uses the word '*all*'. Be aware of the tendency to make unwarranted generalisations, e.g. '*All blacks are ...*'
> '*All travellers are ...*'
> It is quite easy to slip into intolerant, stereotyped thinking.

LAW AND MORALITY

We may define Law as:

> *A rule or set of rules which is prescribed or set out by the proper authority and imposed on a society in order to protect the rights and freedom of individuals and/or the common good of the members of that society, e.g. the speed limit.*

Members of society are not only legally bound to obey the law but are also morally bound to do so — unless of course the law is unjust.

Legal systems should strive to enshrine in law and apply in practice the principles of sound reasoning and moral integrity. However, they can often fall short of the attainment of justice and in some cases can be used to deprive people of it. As a result, *what is legal may not necessarily be moral.*

History provides many examples of unjust practices which were quite legal in a particular country though clearly immoral, for instance the apartheid laws which operated in South Africa until recently, or the penal laws in 18th century Ireland. It is for this reason that the Catholic Church teaches:

> *'God's law continues to bind, no matter what the civil law says'.*
> *Love is for Life*

A Christian must remember this when forming his/her conscience.

QUESTIONS

1 What is the definition of law?
2 Are law and morality one and the same thing? Explain your answer.
3 Can you identify any forms of behaviour, past or present, which though legal are considered morally wrong in Christian teaching?

FORMING ONE'S CONSCIENCE

How can people be sure that they have properly formed their consciences so that their judgment is sound?

No one can ever be one hundred per cent certain in areas of morality. All people can do is try their best to do what is right.

Don't just blindly follow the crowd. Look before you leap!

What follows is a checklist of questions people should ask themselves before making an *important* moral decision:
- What exactly is the issue at stake? (Define the problem).
- Do I have all the relevant facts?
- What does my religion teach about this?
- What does the law of the state say?
- What can my previous experiences or those of trusted advisers tell me?
- What are my motives for doing this? What is my *intention*?
- What are the methods open to me? Remember, the thing I want to achieve (the end) never justifies the use of *every* method I want to use (the means). There are certain methods which are morally wrong and can *never* be justified.
- What are the likely effects on both myself and others?

- Is there any alternative course of action open to me? Can I take it without compromising my principles?
- Have I prayed for guidance?

Only after going through this process should a person act according to his/her conscience, because it is an *informed* conscience. However, most people only do this when faced with a *major* decision. As mentioned earlier, when faced with most minor decisions people do not consciously use this process.

N.B. While it is very important to *know* and *take seriously* the teaching of one's religion:

> '*In certain circumstances, after reflection and prayer, Catholics may have to form and follow their consciences, even if this means dissent (disagreement) from official teachers.*'
>
> R. Ekstrom, *Concise Catholic Dictionary.*

However, it is important to remember that some actions, such as murder, are *always* morally wrong. Whether a person thinks it is wrong or not makes *no difference* to the wrongness of the action. It is *objectively* wrong.

CASE STUDY: THE RIGHT TO STRIKE

'*The right to strike is a basic human right. However, certain questions must be asked by all those involved before a strike is begun:*
- *Is it certain that a real injustice is present?*
- *Is this injustice serious enough to justify the loss and the damage likely to be caused?*
- *Is there a proper proportion between the loss about to be inflicted and the lawful end pursued?*
- *Have all efforts been made to reach a settlement by negotiation, and have these efforts failed?*

A person involved in a strike decision must be able to answer 'yes' to these questions before he/she can say: "This strike is morally justified". We must not forget that a strike is a weapon of last resort *and should never be the first move in a dispute.*'

The Work of Justice.

ACTIVITY

Imagine that you are a trade union leader representing health care workers in a hospital. You have received a request for immediate strike action from members opposed to a management proposal to: (a) freeze pay at current levels for two years, and (b) make some people redundant to save money.

(1) Explain (a) how you would go about arriving at a decision as to whether you would recommend a *'yes'* or *'no'* vote in a strike ballot; and (b) the difficulties you might encounter in making your decision.
(2) What, in your opinion, would be a fair and mutually acceptable compromise agreement? Give reasons for your answer.

FACING DIFFICULT CHOICES

Sometimes it is very hard to know what is the right decision to make. After his baptism at the River Jordan, Jesus was faced with just such a problem: what kind of approach should he adopt to his people? He needed time to think and pray before coming to a decision, so he went into the wastelands of the Judean desert to be alone and choose the kind of ministry he should pursue.

Throughout his public ministry, Jesus was faced with tough choices:

(1) Should he identify the 'Kingdom of God' with material wealth and try to bribe the Jewish people with material things to win them over to him?
(2) Should he abuse his influence and authority by putting on a spectacular public miracle to convince them beyond a shadow of a doubt who he really was?
(3) Should he use violent methods to achieve his aims?

QUESTIONS

1 (a) Read *Luke* 4:1-13. What did Jesus choose to do?
   (b) What influence did his values have on his decisions?

2 Imagine you are a member of a group campaigning against the toxic emissions from a chemical plant. The evidence that it is causing damage to the health of the local people and their environment is beyond doubt. The group leader declares that swift, violent action is necessary to stop the pollution. He claims that a small explosive device, placed inside the main control room, would disable the entire plant and end the pollution. Many members of the organisation think that this kind of action is the only solution to the problem. But you wonder if it really is the best course of action. Does the stopping of pollution (the *end*) justify the use of violence (the *means*)?

Take into account the implications of such an action for:

(a) your group;

(b) the employees;

(c) the local community;

(d) the company;

(e) the local environment.

3 If the group was to go through with such an action:

(a) What would be the likelihood of preventing the same toxic emissions from ever happening again?

(b) What impact would such violent action have on the public perception of environmental protection groups? Explain your answer.

Does the end justify the means?

SUMMARY

Christians believe that:

1. Conscience is *the ability to make practical judgments about the rightness or wrongness of a particular moral action.*
2. What is legal may not necessarily be moral.
3. A Christian should develop an *informed* conscience, and when confronted with a moral problem he/she should:
   - think before acting;
   - remain faithful to his/her Christian values;
   - consider the options and their effects on both him/herself and others;
   - decide which is the best course of action to take.
4. A Christian should *follow* his/her informed conscience when confronted with a moral decision.
5. It is always wrong to go against a *properly* informed conscience.

CHAPTER 19

Original Sin

HAVING THE COURAGE OF ONE'S CONVICTIONS

A person may know where to find good advice, and even know the right thing to do. But in the end, it all comes down to having the courage of one's convictions, to actually *applying* one's values when confronted with a situation that offers a choice. Reflection must lead to *action*. Jesus said:

> *'Do unto others as you would have them do unto you.'*

But this can extract a high price and it seems that few people are willing to pay it.

The former Russian leader, Nikita Khrushchev, at the annual Communist Party Congress in 1956, made a devastating attack on his predecessor, Joseph Stalin. Khrushchev, who had been a government minister under Stalin, spoke at length about the horrors the deceased tyrant had inflicted on the Russian people. No one had dared to speak in such a fashion for many years.

Nikita Khrushchev

When he finished his speech, Khrushchev began to step down from the speaker's rostrum. The entire audience sat there in a stunned silence. Just then, a man shouted up from the middle of the packed auditorium:

> *'So, why didn't you do something at the time to stop Stalin?'*

Khrushchev looked up, scanned the audience and shouted back:

'Who said that?'

There was total silence. No one replied. After a minute or so, Khrushchev spoke into the microphone again:

'There now, you have your answer!'

It is all very well to ask someone else why he/she did not do the brave thing. Each person should look to his/her own moral courage first, before being willing to criticise others.

QUESTION

Read *Luke* 6:41–42.
(a) What does Jesus have to say about hypocrisy?
(b) Do you agree/disagree? Why?

HUMAN WEAKNESS

People often find it difficult to do the right thing. St Paul wrote about this when he said:

> *'I cannot understand my own behaviour. I fail to carry out the things I want to do, and I find myself doing the very things I hate.'*
> *(Romans 7:15–16)*

The *Gospel* accounts of St Peter's denial of Jesus powerfully illustrate this tension within the human person.

Peter had lived with Jesus, had seen him perform miracles and had witnessed him raise the dead. But none of this in any way lessened the challenge he faced. Peter felt a moral split within himself.

When confronted with a difficult moral choice, every human being experiences this pull in opposite directions: to stand one's ground and do what is right, or run away and do what is wrong. It is difficult to choose and follow the path of good; it is much easier to take the path of least resistance and give in to some desire of the moment. It takes courage to think differently from others, to choose to live by different values, to believe what others dismiss and to do the right thing.

It takes courage to take a stand against the wishes of the crowd.

QUESTIONS

Read *Matthew* 19:16-26.

(a) What is your impression of the rich young man's character? Do you think he was a sensible individual who found Jesus' request unfair? Give reasons for your opinion.

(b) What did Jesus ask of him? Was it an unreasonable request? What, do you think, was Jesus really getting at here? Explain your answer.

MODERN NOVELISTS ON THE HUMAN CONDITION

Many modern novelists have taken as their theme this dramatic tension within each human being. Reacting against theories such as Communism, which believed that people could be conditioned to live perfect lives, writers such as William Golding and George Orwell paint a distinctly unflattering portrait of human nature.

QUESTIONS

1　In *Lord of the Flies* Golding appears to offer little hope for the human race, believing that humans are vicious and murderous, driven by dark, destructive urges that quickly rise to the surface whenever people drop their guard, either individually or as a society. The ethnic strife of recent civil wars would appear to bear this out.

Do you agree/disagree with Golding's view? Is it *too pessimistic*? Explain your answer.

2　In *Animal Farm* Orwell claims that even reform movements, which seek to build a better world, inevitably lose their original idealism as they are taken over and led off course by a clever, unscrupulous minority. All the while, the majority, apparently overcome by human wickedness, just sit back sheepishly and let it all happen to them.

(a) Is Orwell correct in his assessment of *all* reform movements?

(b) Does the 'silent majority' *always* just sit back?

Explain your answers.

WHAT IS ORIGINAL SIN?

Christians acknowledge that *all people find choosing good over evil a real challenge*. It is part of the human condition. They believe that the source of this dramatic struggle within each person is what has traditionally been called '*original sin*'.

Christians do *not* believe, however, that God created human beings with some kind of built-in tendency to do bad things. Rather, they believe that God can only create what is *good*. Therefore, all people are created good. Yet experience shows that we often find it difficult to do good and avoid evil. Why?

The key to answering this question can be found in the story of the Fall as recounted in *Genesis* 2 and 3. This tells of how Adam and Eve deliberately disobeyed God and ate of the forbidden fruit. Of course we should not understand this to be an accurate historical account, yet it is an important story/parable which conveys a profound *message*. For whatever the actual details, we are told that this *first* or *original sin* was a deliberate act of disobedience by our earliest ancestors. The result of this was to create conditions of disharmony and imperfection in our world which have had a detrimental effect on all subsequent generations of human beings. This means that we are weak in our resolve to do good and avoid doing evil. Our ancestors threw away the gift of perfect happiness which Christians believe can only be found with God.

Questions

1 What do Christians believe about original sin and the human condition?

2 What is the message contained in Genesis 2 and 3 about original sin?

The Role of Jesus

A quick glance around makes it painfully obvious that Christians themselves fall far short of what Jesus expects of his followers. So what can they do?

Christians believe that God does not leave us to flounder about in hopelessness; that he sent his Son to show all people the way they were always intended to live, and to redeem all men and women by his death and resurrection. This is what is called the mystery of our redemption.

Christians believe that Jesus has shown the way by which all people can achieve peace with God, themselves and each other. He calls each of us to live to our full potential and struggle to make this world a better place, both for those living today and for all the generations yet to be born. Jesus *invites* each person to follow but does not force anyone. The choice is *ours* to make.

If we choose 'yes', there is help at hand.

'Baptism into the Christian community signifies our acceptance of, and frees us from, Original Sin; but we are still weak. We need the daily strength of the Holy Spirit to conquer that weakness, and the support of each other. That is one important reason why we need to belong to the Church, the community of believers.'

Rowanne Paxco and John Redford, *Faith Alive*.

QUESTIONS

1 What do Christians believe about the role of Jesus in their struggle to live good and worthwhile lives?

2 What is the importance of Baptism in relation to Original Sin?

3 Read the following extract:

Courage and conscience

'Courage is an inner resolution to go forward despite obstacles; cowardice is submissive surrender to circumstances.

Courage breeds creative self-affirmation; cowardice produces destructive self-abnegation.

Courage faces fear and masters it; cowardice represses fear and is mastered by it...

Cowardice asks the question, is it safe?

Expediency asks the question, is it politic?

Vanity asks the question, is it popular?

But conscience asks the question, is it right? And there comes a time when one must take a position that is neither safe, nor politic, nor popular, but one must take it because it is right.'

Dr Martin Luther King, Jr.

(a) What, in your own words, is the message of Dr King regarding courage and conscience?

(b) Do you agree/disagree with him? Give reasons for your answer.

Profile of Courage: Maximilian Kolbe

In July 1941 three prisoners escaped from the Nazi concentration camp of Auschwitz. The Nazis picked ten men in reprisal to starve to death in the underground bunker. One of the men was Franciszek Gajowniczek. When he realised his fate he cried out, 'My wife, my children, I shall never see them again.' It was then the unexpected happened. From the ranks of watching inmates, prisoner 16670 stepped out and offered himself in the other man's place. Then he was taken with the other nine condemned men to the dreaded Bunker, an airless underground cell, to die slowly without food or water.

Prisoner 16670 was a Polish Catholic priest named Maximilian Kolbe.

He was 47 years old. Before the war he had founded one of the largest monasteries in the world. He had also travelled as a missionary to the Far East and Russia. In 1939 he began helping Jewish refugees. However, in 1941 he was arrested by the Nazis and sent to prison in Warsaw and then deported to Auschwitz.

Auschwitz was a terrible place. Human beings were treated in the most inhuman ways imaginable. Thousands died every day from beatings, floggings, torture, disease, starvation and in the gas chambers. Father Kolbe dedicated his life in Auschwitz to helping his fellow prisoners. He would console them, share his food with them, organise secret church services. He tried to show others, by his own example, that even in such a hellish place God still loved and cared for them. An eye-witness of those last terrible days of Father Kolbe's life tells us what happened.

In the cell of the poor wretches there were daily prayers, and hymn singing, in which prisoners from neighbouring cells also joined. When no SS men were in the block I went to the Bunker to talk to the men and comfort them. Fervent prayers and songs resounded in all the corridors of the Bunker. I had the impression I was in a church. Fr Kolbe was leading and the prisoners responded in unison. They were often so deep in prayer that they did not hear that inspecting SS men had descended to the Bunker; and the voices fell silent only at the loud yelling of their visitors. When the cells were opened the poor wretches cried loudly and begged for a piece of bread and for water, which they did not receive. If any of the stronger ones approached the door he was immediately kicked in the stomach by the SS men, so that falling backwards on the cement floor he was instantly killed; or he was shot to death . . . Fr Kolbe bore up bravely, he did not beg and did not complain but raised the spirits of the others . . . Since they had grown very weak, prayers were now only whispered. At every inspection, when almost all the others were now lying on the floor, Fr Kolbe was seen kneeling or standing in the centre as he looked calmly in the face of the SS men. Two weeks passed in this way. Meanwhile one after another they died, until only Fr Kolbe was left. This the authorities felt was too long; the cell was needed for new victims. So one day they brought in the head of the sick-quarters, a German, a common criminal named Bock who gave Fr Kolbe an injection of carbolic acid in the vein of his left arm. Fr Kolbe, with a prayer on his lips, himself gave his arm to the executioner. Unable to watch this I left under the pretext of work to be done. Immediately after the SS men with the executioner had left I returned to the cell, where I found Fr Kolbe leaning in a sitting position against the back wall with his eyes open and his head drooping sideways. His face was calm and radiant.

Source: CTS

In 1982 Pope John Paul II declared Maximilian Kolbe a saint.

QUESTIONS

1   Who was Maximilian Kolbe?

2   What was Auschwitz? Why was it built by the Nazis?

3   How did Maximilian's Christian faith affect his response to his imprisonment and his attitude towards his fellow prisoners? Explain your answer.

4   Read *John* 15:13. Why do you think that Kolbe volunteered to take the place of a fellow prisoner in the death cell? Give reasons for your answer.

5   What do you think it means for a person to be declared a saint? Explain your answer.

CHAPTER 20

Sin and Forgiveness

WHAT IS ACTUAL SIN?

This section is concerned with what Christians call *actual sin*. We may define actual sin as:

> *any freely chosen and deliberately intended action whose consequences one desires, but which rejects Christ's law of love and inflicts harm on one's neighbours and oneself.*

Through sin, people can damage their relationship with God. The degree of damage depends on the seriousness of the sin committed.

Actual sin is different from original sin, but yet related to it. It is because human beings have to struggle within themselves to do good and avoid evil that they are prone to commit actual sin.

Catholic/Christians believe that there are two kinds of actual sin: (1) *Venial sin*, and (2) *Mortal sin*.

At the heart of Christian morality is the call of Jesus to:

> *'Love God and love your neighbour as yourself.'* (Matthew 19:19)

Venial sin is *any action a person commits that weakens his/her relationship with God*. It is a refusal to live as God intends us to live and usually stems from *pride* and *selfishness*, from a refusal to love. Venial sin can lead to a progressive movement away from God. Therefore, it can be responsible for the eventual breakdown of a person's relationship with God.

Mortal sin, on the other hand, is *any seriously wrongful act by which a person destroys his/her relationship with God*. To be guilty of mortal sin, a person must freely, deliberately and with full knowledge of its consequences, commit a very serious offence against both God and other people. It is a conscious turning away from the love of God.

Questions

1 What is meant by 'actual sin'?

2 What is the difference between mortal and venial sin? Give examples of both in your answer.

3 Read the following story, then answer the questions below.

Two men once visited a holy man to ask his advice. "We have done wrong actions, they said, and our consciences are troubled. Can you tell us what we must do so that we may be forgiven and feel clear of our guilt?"

"Tell me of your wrongdoings, my sons," said the old man.

The first man said, "I have committed a great and grievous sin."

"What about you?" the holy man asked the second.

"Oh," said he, "I have done quite a number of wrong things, but they are all quite small, and not at all important."

The holy man considered for a while. "This is what you must do," he said at last. "Each of you must go and bring me a stone for each of his misdeeds."

Off went the men: and presently the first came back staggering with an enormous boulder, so heavy that he could hardly lift it, and with a groan he let it fall in front of the holy man. Then along came the second, cheerfully carrying a bag of small pebbles. This he also laid at the feet of the saint.

"Now," said the holy man, "take all those stones and put them back where you found them."

The first man shouldered his rock again, and staggered back to the place from which he had brought it. But the second man could only remember where a few of his pebbles had lain. After some time, he came back, and said that the task was too difficult.

"You must know, my son," said the old man, "that sins are like these stones. If a man has committed a great sin, it lies like a heavy stone on his conscience; but if he is truly sorry, he is forgiven and the load is taken away. But if a man is constantly doing small things that are wrong, he does not feel any very great load of guilt, and so he is not sorry, and remains a sinner. So, you see, my son, it is as important to avoid little sins as big ones." (*Anon*)

(a) What do you think is the message of this story? Give reasons for your answer.

(b) What have you learned about the impact of our actions on the lives of both ourselves and other people? Explain your answer.

FORGIVENESS

The story of the Prodigal Son (*Luke* 15:11-32) is familiar to most people. But this familiarity can often blind people to its true significance.

Jesus wished all to know that, like the wayward son of the story, no matter what offence they commit, if people are genuinely sorry and want to reform their lives, God will forgive their sin. Though they may turn their backs on God and walk away, God remains loving and forgiving, offering them the chance to repair the damage they have done to their relationship with God and with those around them. It is never too late to repent as far as God is concerned. But if people want God to forgive them, they must show forgiveness to those who offend them (*Matthew* 18:21-35).

Love your enemies. Pope John Paul II talking in prison to Ali Agca, the man who tried to kill him in 1982.

Some people, however, cannot understand a feeling of guilt. They have so dulled their moral conscience that they apparently have no guilt feelings at all. When they are brought to court for a violent crime, they will insist either (1) they did not do it, or (2) the victim forced them to do it. Sometimes they even try to convince themselves that the victims *wanted* them to hurt them. This pattern of behaviour is quite common with violent criminals. Unlike the Prodigal Son, they cannot admit to themselves or others the responsibility for their evil deeds.

In the *Our Father*, however, Jesus tells us not only to ask God for forgiveness but to be prepared to forgive those who have hurt or offended *us*. This can often be far from easy, demanding great integrity and strength.

On November 6, 1987, at the cenotaph in Enniskillen, an IRA bomb killed eleven people, including three couples, and injured sixty.

Gordon Wilson and his daughter Marie, a nurse, were buried in the rubble. She stretched out her hand to him. 'Is that your hand, Daddy?' 'Yes, dear. Are you all right?' He repeated the question four more times before she said — her last words — 'Daddy, I love you very much.'

Interviewed the next day, he said: 'I bear no ill will . . She was a great girl. She's in heaven now. We will meet again.'

What Alf McCreary, Mr Wilson's biographer, later revealed is that originally he did not forgive his daughter's murderers. He only said he had no ill will towards them. Forgiving them took time and effort and constant prayer.

Irish Independent, 1996.

Jesus makes clear that if we want to receive God's forgiveness, we must show:

- a genuine sorrow for what we have done
- a readiness to forgive those who have offended us
- a willingness to change our way of life.

Questions

1 What do you think is the true significance of the story of the Prodigal Son?

2 What have you learned from the story of Gordon Wilson's experience of tragedy and forgiveness? Explain your answer.

THE WAYS OF COMMITTING SIN

A person can commit a sin in either of *two* ways:

(1) by *commission* — when one deliberately *does* something one knows one should not;

(2) by *omission* — when one deliberately *neglects* to do something one knows one should do.

SIN BY COMMISSION

They were known as 'the gang that couldn't shoot straight'. For two years Jack White, the boss of the Cleveland Mafia, had tried unsuccessfully to have his young rival, Danny Greene, leader of the West Side mob, killed. By May of 1977, they had tried and failed on *eight* occasions. So it was decided to recruit an *outside specialist*. His name was Raymond Ferrito, formerly a professional burglar, but more recently a killer for hire.

Ferrito was made a lucrative offer. In return for murdering Danny Greene, he would become a 'made man', that is, a member of the local Mafia hierarchy, and thus be entitled to a share in its huge profits.

For several months Ferrito followed Greene's every move. Through tapping the latter's telephone, he learned that Greene had an appointment to see his dentist on the morning of 6 October 1977. Ferrito and his Mafia 'minder' staked out the car park in front of the dentist's office from early morning. After several hours Greene arrived in a bullet-proof car and escorted by bodyguards. Ferrito waited until they had all entered the building before he drove up in a specially rigged bomb car, which he parked in the vacant space next to Greene's. Then he got out, locked it and walked to the far end of the car park, where he sat into his own car, armed the remote detonating control and waited for Greene to return.

Ferrito did not have long to wait. He let Greene walk up and open the car door before detonating his massive car bomb. Greene was killed instantly and his bodyguards were all seriously injured. A young woman and her child who happened to be passing had what the police described as a 'very near miss'. Both had to be treated for shock, but did not suffer physical injury.

Ferrito did not get away with Greene's murder. He was captured by federal agents, thanks to the action of a married couple who were driving by when the explosion took place. They saw a car driving away from the murder scene at high speed and followed it, taking down both its number-plate and the description of its driver. The car was traced to Ferrito and the couple identified him in police photographic files.

Ferrito was charged with murder. Then he discovered that his paymasters were trying to have him killed, so he offered to become a witness for the federal authorities. He was found guilty of murder but, because his testimony had helped to imprison so many senior Mafiosi, he served only three years in prison.

When interviewed in 1984, Ferrito said that he regretted having ever informed on the Mafia, claiming that *'Death would have been better.'*

When asked about how he felt about killing Greene, Ferrito replied:

'I was elated because the job was done and I was gonna become one of them and share in the profits. It was something that since I was a kid, I had dreamed of, I had wanted, and this was my chance to do it.'

Did he feel any guilt or remorse for what he had done?

'To me it was like having a glass of wine. It didn't mean a thing. I killed him and there was no remorse that I killed a man because I was brought up all through my life believing in those . . . You just have to put them out of your mind. Those were things or hurdles that you had to overcome. A man with a conscience doesn't last long on the streets . . . All I know is that I went to bed that night and I slept.'

Why did he side against the Mafia? Was it because he had seen the error of his ways?

'I decided maybe I did choose the wrong side. All my life I'd been one way and I always did what I was supposed to do and now, all of a sudden, I did them the biggest favour and they're talking about killing me! . . . I decided to flip, go to the authorities and tell them I wanted to talk, that I wanted a deal. It wasn't because I saw God or read a Bible. It was just that I thought I had to look out for me, Ray, and I thought this would be my best move.'

Dialogue extracts from: Martin Short, *Crime Incorporated.*

N.B. Having read this extract, remember that Christians believe that all people are sinners to a greater or lesser extent. No one has the right to feel superior. One may condemn the *act* but *not* the *person*. For the Christian, no one has the right to condemn another.

QUESTIONS

1   In the extract, Ray Ferrito presents himself as a 'strong man' who has a good night's sleep after committing a murder. What do you think? What kind of 'strength' does he display?

   Explain your answer with reference to his own statements.

2   Do any of his own words indicate that he knew he was doing something wrong?

3   Where does he try to justify the murder he committed?

4   Does the fact that he killed a rival gangster affect the seriousness of the act? Explain your answer.

5   How would you consider the actions of the couple whose evidence led to Ferrito's capture?

6   Would you be prepared to do what they did?

   Give reasons for your answer.

SIN BY OMISSION

On a calm night in 1964, a young New York woman named Kitty Genovese was brutally stabbed, beaten and left to die on her own doorstep. She screamed for help, but none came. Yet *thirty-eight* of her neighbours witnessed what happened. When they were questioned by both police and news reporters, they almost all gave the same reply:

   'I didn't want to get involved.'

They just decided to do nothing and allowed her to die.

In contrast, consider the story of Oskar Schindler, who risked his life on numerous occasions as he sought to save the lives of over a thousand Jewish men, women and children who worked in his factory from being murdered by Hitler's SS. Schindler used every possible trick and resource he could think of to save those people. This took enormous courage at a time in which most people around him either actively or tacitly supported the genocide of the concentration camps. Had he been discovered, he would surely have been executed. Yet he was willing to take the risk. He believed it was *worth taking*.

QUESTIONS

1 Why do you think some people are unwilling to help someone when he/she is the victim of an unprovoked assault?

2 (a) Are there any circumstances in which a person might genuinely want to help the victim of a violent attack but be *unable* to do so? Explain your answer.

  (b) In such a situation is there any action, other than personal physical intervention, that a person can take to help? If so, give examples.

3 (a) Why do you think Oskar Schindler did what he did?

  (b) Why didn't more people do the same?

  (c) What does this tell you about the nature of moral courage?

JESUS, SIN AND MORAL DECISIONS

During his earthly ministry, Jesus called on people to reform their lives. He told everyone he encountered that God had unlimited love for even the worst of us and forgave people's sins. He demonstrated this on many occasions:

- Read *John* 8:1–11, where Jesus lifted the burden of sin from a woman, enabling her to rediscover her self-respect and live her life as God intended.

- Read *John* 9:1–38, where Jesus gave sight to a man born blind, demonstrating his power to overcome all the bad effects of sin in our world, such as disease, starvation and loneliness.

  Above all, through his death and resurrection, Jesus showed that life is not pointless, that death is not the end, that it is not a waste of time trying to do good, that making good moral decisions has a great meaning and significance for both our own lives and those around us, in this world and the next.

The Christian is called to be both realistic and hopeful in the face of life's challenges, firm in the belief that God's love is more powerful than sin, accepting Christ's promise that

'with God, all things are possible.'

Each Christian is asked to put his/her trust in God, believing that as Paul wrote:

'I can do all things through Christ, who strengthens me.'
Philippians 4:13

SUMMARY

Christians believe that
- although created good, human beings experience difficulty in doing what is good (Original sin).
- it requires *courage* to do the right thing when confronted with a moral decision.
- while every person needs guidance at some stage, especially when confronted by difficult decisions, in the end it is each individual's responsibility to choose and then accept the consequences of his/her actions.
- each person is accountable for his/her *own* actions and not those of anyone else.
- no matter how grave the sin, God is always ready to forgive those who *genuinely* seek his forgiveness.
- Jesus calls his followers to get involved, to work for justice and peace, taking their inspiration and drawing their strength from their faith in him.

CHAPTER 21

Love and Sex

THE MEANING OF LOVE

Love is one of the most popular themes in western culture. Most people are in favour of love, but the word itself means different things to different people.

Christian writers identify four different kinds of love:

- A warm, general affection or fondness for a thing (e.g. a person's favourite sport) or a place (e.g. the area in which a person grew up).

- Sexual attraction to and strong desire for a member of the opposite sex.

- Love for and loyalty to family and close friends.

- Unconditional love for other people, not just those who are close to you. This was called 'agapé' by the early Christians. (Read *Mark* 12:31 and *John* 15:12–14).

One aspect of love that naturally becomes a matter of increasing interest to young people as they grow and mature into adulthood is physical love, or sex. The word '*sex*' is usually understood as the physical act of sexual intercourse. The word '*love*', however, is used to refer to the *entire* personal relationship between a man and a woman, including their sexual relations.

The Christian definition of love was best expressed by St Paul:

'*Love is always patient and kind; it is never jealous; love is never boastful or conceited; it is never rude or selfish; it does not take offence and is not resentful. Love takes no pleasure in other people's sins but delights in the truth; it is always ready to forgive, to trust, to hope and to endure whatever comes. Love does not come to an end.'*

1 *Corinthians* 13:4–8.

QUESTIONS

1 Consider the ways in which love is presented in the cinema, on television or in best-selling fiction. Do these give a realistic/unrealistic portrait of love?

Explain your answer.

2 In Morris West's novel, *The Shoes of the Fisherman*, the Russian President, Peter Kamenev, asks Archbishop Kyril Lakota, who has survived twenty years of slave labour in a Siberian penal colony, what he has learned during his long, harsh imprisonment. The Archbishop pauses a moment and then replies:

'I have learned that without some kind of loving, a person withers like a grape on a dying vine.'

(a) What do you think Lakota meant by his answer?

(b) Why do you think he came to this conclusion after his years as a prisoner in Siberia?

(c) Do you agree/disagree with him? Give reasons for your answer.

FIVE STAGES IN THE DEVELOPMENT OF A LOVING RELATIONSHIP

(1) *Attraction*

You are attracted to someone. If the attraction is strong, you will try to meet that person.

(2) *Acquaintance*

Once you become better acquainted with someone, the attraction may fade away quickly. But if the acquaintance continues, the attraction may grow and friendship blossom.

(3) *Friendship*

Becoming good friends is a special time. You may begin to see the other person in a very romantic, idealistic way. You may see him or her as 'the perfect person' — the only one for you.

(4) *Affection*

At this stage, a real caring or affection develops between a man and a woman. This true affection is based on recognising and accepting the other's faults, but still caring deeply about the other person.

(5) *Love*

Real love between a man and a woman is a growing thing. It is part of a process.

Real love is concerned with the *inner person*, not just appearances. There is no shortcut to the development of a truly loving relationship between a man and a woman. You *cannot* reach the fifth stage of the process without growing through the other four stages.

Adapted from *Learning for Adult Life*.

QUESTIONS

1   What are the qualities that you would find attractive in a member of the opposite sex?

2 (a) What factors cause the initial attraction to sometimes fade away quickly?

 (b) What factors cause the initial attraction to sometimes develop into friendship?

3 The third stage in the development of a loving relationship is sometimes called the 'starry-eyed' phase. It is a wonderful time to experience, but if people get married without having developed their relationship beyond this stage, what kind of problems can it cause after they are married to each other? Why?

4 Read the fifth stage once more. Do you think that it is possible to fall in love at first sight? *Give reasons for your answer.*

HUMAN REPRODUCTION

Human reproduction occurs when a male sex cell (the sperm) fertilises a female sex cell (the ovum) after sexual intercourse.

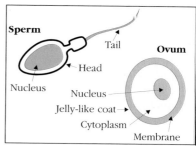

Sperm
Tail
Head
Nucleus

Ovum
Nucleus
Jelly-like coat
Cytoplasm
Membrane

Male reproductive organs

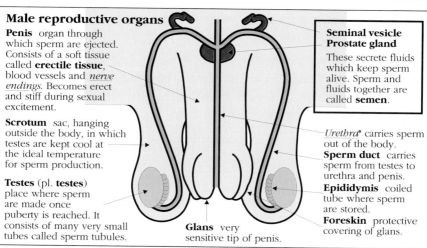

Penis organ through which sperm are ejected. Consists of a soft tissue called **erectile tissue**, blood vessels and *nerve endings*. Becomes erect and stiff during sexual excitement.

Scrotum sac, hanging outside the body, in which testes are kept cool at the ideal temperature for sperm production.

Testes (pl. **testes**) place where sperm are made once puberty is reached. It consists of many very small tubes called sperm tubules.

Seminal vesicle
Prostate gland
These secrete fluids which keep sperm alive. Sperm and fluids together are called **semen**.

Urethra carries sperm out of the body.
Sperm duct carries sperm from testes to urethra and penis.
Epididymis coiled tube where sperm are stored.
Foreskin protective covering of glans.

Glans very sensitive tip of penis.

Female reproductive organs

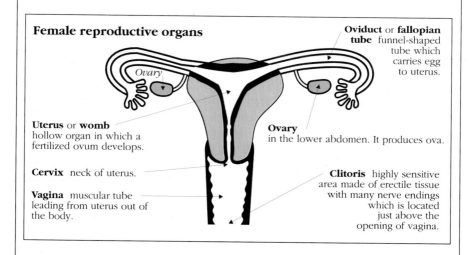

Oviduct or **fallopian tube** funnel-shaped tube which carries egg to uterus.

Ovary

Uterus or **womb** hollow organ in which a fertilized ovum develops.

Cervix neck of uterus.

Vagina muscular tube leading from uterus out of the body.

Ovary in the lower abdomen. It produces ova.

Clitoris highly sensitive area made of erectile tissue with many nerve endings which is located just above the opening of vagina.

160

Sexual Intercourse

Fertilisation takes place within the woman's body when a sperm meets an ovum in the oviduct. Sperm enter the female during **sexual intercourse** when an erect penis is inserted into the vagina. Movement of the pelvis stimulates nerve endings in the penis. This sets off a *reflex action* which results in semen being ejected into the vagina. This is called **ejaculation. Orgasm** is the name given to the intense experience of excitement and pleasure which occurs at the climax of sexual intercourse.

Fertilisation

Sperm swim from the vagina to the oviducts. If they meet an ovum, fertilisation can take place. One sperm head penetrates the ovum and the two nuclei fuse. This forms a *zygote*, the first cell of a new baby.

Sperm head
Ovum

The zygote travels to the uterus and becomes implanted in the uterus wall. After this happens it is called an **embryo.** The uterus has prepared for implantation by building up a thick lining, rich in blood vessels.

Conception

Conception includes fertilisation and the implantation of an embryo in the uterus.

Pregnancy

The time between implantation and birth is called **pregnancy,** or **gestation.** In humans it lasts about 38 weeks. The growing embryo, also called the foetus, becomes surrounded by an **amniotic sac,** a bag containing watery liquid called **amniotic fluid.** This protects the embryo from knocks.

The embryo needs food and oxygen in order to grow. At first these come directly from the blood vessels in the uterus wall. After a few weeks, however, a special plate-shaped organ develops, called the **placenta.** Capillaries from the mother and the foetus flow into the placenta and substances diffuse between them. The foetus receives food and

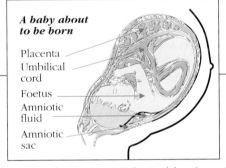

A baby about to be born

Placenta
Umbilical cord
Foetus
Amniotic fluid
Amniotic sac

oxygen from the mother's blood, and releases carbon dioxide and other waste matter into it. The baby is connected to the placenta by a cord, called the **umbilical cord.**

During the last few days of pregnancy, the baby moves so that its head is near the cervix. Finally the baby is squeezed out through the vagina by strong contractions of the muscles in the uterus. This is called **labour.**

Adapted from R. Treays, *Essential Biology*, Usborne Publications

161

LOVE AND SEX

'The Gospel says virtually nothing about sexual morality. That in itself suggests a good starting point: sex should be considered, not in isolation but as an element in the make-up of the whole person.

On the rare occasions that he uses the word love, Jesus means caring as much about the other person as about oneself, promoting other people's welfare and happiness rather than using them, serving rather than dominating or exploiting. It is this demanding vision of love that Christians firmly believe does more than anything else to promote the well-being and happiness of people. It is this that is the basis for the Christian understanding of the role of sexuality.'

B. O'Connor, *Sex, the Gospel and the Church.*

According to the teaching of the Catholic Church:

- Sex is an integral part of human nature.

- Sex should be considered within the context of love as it has a role to play in building up the kingdom of God.

- Sex is a *gift* from God that should be used in a loving and respectful way, as through the sexual act a man and a woman express their total love for and commitment to each other.

- Sex is a beautiful expression of what should be the loving, lifelong union between a man and a woman known as marriage.

- Sex can create new life and so concerns more than just the man and woman involved, bringing with it responsibility for another human life.

- Since sex is the language of *love, commitment* and *responsibility*, in which a man and a woman tell one another that each is the 'one and only love', it can only find its true expression *exclusively* within a married relationship.

- Sex outside of marriage is considered an act of 'pretend love' or deception, because those involved are *not* deliberately and unreservedly *committing* themselves to love each other both at the time and for all the years to follow.

REFLECTION

Read the following extract written by a married man on the value of *waiting* until one is married before having sexual intercourse.

My wife and I waited until we were married to have sex, which was a different decision than many people nowadays make. But I think it was a good one. Maybe if we'd had sex with other people or with each other before we were married, we'd have been more experienced or knowledgeable. But learning about sex together . . . made it that much more special. Also, we didn't have to worry if either of us was 'as good' as the other lovers either of us might have had before. . . .

By being willing to wait until we were married, I felt I was showing my wife that it wasn't just sex that I wanted from her but real, true love and lifelong commitment. And she was showing me the same thing. . . We really trusted each other, and that made us feel safe enough for us to really 'let go'. We didn't have to worry that if we did it 'wrong' or if it wasn't great the first time that it would all be over. And, really it wasn't so great the first time. It was kind of awkward and embarrassing. But I knew and she knew that we'd both be round tomorrow. . . This trusting and promising made us able to grow to be better lovers than we might have otherwise.

Adapted from J. Ahlers, *Growing in Christian Morality*.

QUESTIONS

1 What is the Christian understanding of love and sex?
2 What does the author identify as the benefits to a couple's relationship if they wait until after marrying before having sex?
3 Do you agree/disagree with his point of view? Explain your answer.
4 Read the following extracts from *Love is for Life*:
- *'A way of life that involves casual sex in relationships makes for instability. The casual partner tends to ask "What's in this for me?" rather than "What can I do to promote the happiness of this person?" Such an attitude can make it impossible to form a serious, stable relationship.'*

(a) What is meant by 'casual sex'?

(b) Why is it claimed that the attitude at the heart of casual sex can undermine the chance of building a lasting loving relationship?

(c) Do you agree/disagree? Why?

- *'Group pressure to conform is a tremendous force. Once young people become sexually aware, they hear their friends tell them of their exploits, tales that may or may not be true. At a later age, couples pair off and make no secret of "having sex" together. It is the done thing. Those not wishing to conform to this practice may find themselves regarded as curiosities, suggestions being made that they are not quite normal, not capable.'*

(a) What is meant by 'group pressure'?

(b) Why do many young people experience a considerable pressure to conform?

(c) Are those who do not wish to conform regarded, in your experience, as 'curiosities' or 'not quite normal'? Why/why not?

PORNOGRAPHY

Pornography comes from the Greek word *'porne'* meaning 'prostitute'. In pornography a person uses photographs, videos, etc. for sexual stimulation. This involves a rejection of genuine relationships between people, because other persons are used as *objects* for sexual arousal.

> *'Pornography is an assault on the dignity of the human person. It presents human beings, chiefly women and children, as little more than collections of body parts and hormones to be abused and exploited. Life is portrayed as nothing more than an endless series of conquests and seductions, occasionally interrupted by rage at the opposite sex. Pornography degrades both its providers and its consumers through its advocacy of loveless and violent sex. Pornography is the theory, rape is the practice.'*
>
> Love is for Life.

(a) Why is pornography described as 'an assault on the dignity of the human person'?

(b) What attitude towards sex does pornography encourage?

(c) Re-read the final sentence of the extract. Do you agree/disagree with it? Explain your answer.

HOMOSEXUALITY

The majority of people are *heterosexual*, i.e. sexually attracted to members of the opposite sex. Some people are *homosexual*, i.e. sexually attracted to members of the same sex; while others are *bisexual*, i.e. sexually attracted to both men and women. Female homosexuals are more commonly known as *'lesbians'*.

Psychologists are divided as to the causes of homosexuality. Some think it is due to biological inheritance, some say that it is due instead to upbringing and environment, while others hold that a person becomes a homosexual due to a combination of both factors. There is some disagreement among social commentators as to the exact proportion of homosexuals in the national population, with figures ranging from one to five per cent.

The traditional Catholic Christian teaching is that the most desirable result of a person's psychological development is the ability to enjoy a full *heterosexual* relationship. It states that homosexuality is a *disorder*, but adds:

> *It is not Christian to despise homosexuals and exclude them from society. It is unchristian to look on homosexuals with disgust or disdain because they are of a particular personality type.'*
>
> Love is for Life.

The Church recognises that homosexual tendencies

> '. . . *can be innate and irreversible. They can cause drives and temptations which are difficult to control and resist.'*

Note the use of the word 'tendencies'. Catholic teaching makes a distinction between homosexual *tendencies* and homosexual *acts*. This is because moral choices are what people *do* with their sexual feelings, *not* with the feelings themselves.

165

'Being a homosexual person is neither morally good nor morally bad; it is homosexual genital acts that are morally wrong.'

Cardinal Basil Hume, *The Tablet*, 5 February 1994.

The Church considers marriage between a man and a woman as being the *only* true context within which two people should express their mutual love of one another through sexual intercourse. Furthermore, it adds:

'Between persons of the same sex there cannot be sexual intercourse as God designed it.'

Love is for Life.

The Catholic Church teaches, therefore that homosexual acts are

'intrinsically and gravely immoral'.

A homosexual person is asked to abstain from homosexual acts and to practise self-denial, admittedly a demanding and difficult way of life. The Church teaches that freedom and human dignity are to be found in the *control* of a person's passions and instincts, whether he/she is heterosexual, bisexual or homosexual. A person's sexual tendencies *are controllable* and self-denial need *not* stunt his/her personality.

We are all of equal value in the sight of God in virtue of our common humanity. God expects homosexual people, as indeed he does heterosexual people, to keep his law and to work towards achieving a difficult ideal, even if this will only be achieved gradually. God has a love for every person which is greater than any love which one human being could have for another. In all the circumstances and situations of life, God calls each person, whatever his or her sexual orientation, to fulfil that part of God's created design which only that person can fulfil.'

Cardinal Basil Hume

Questions

1 Why is it 'unchristian' to despise or seek to exclude homosexuals from society?

2 What is the distinction between homosexual *tendencies* and homosexual *acts*?

3 Why does the Catholic Church consider homosexual acts to be immoral?

4 What does the Catholic Church teach about human dignity, freedom and sexuality?

CHAPTER 22

Marriage

THE MEANING OF MARRIAGE

A couple planning their wedding usually find that, immersed in the exciting but hectic preparations for their 'big day', it is easy to lose sight of the other aspects of their wedding.

According to the law of the state,

> *'Marriage is the voluntary union for life of one man and one woman to the exclusion of all others.'*
>
> Brian Doolan, *Principles of Irish Law.*

Marriage, then, is a legally binding *contract*, though one entered into in a spirit of love, which grants certain rights and imposes certain responsibilities on both partners in the relationship. In the Catholic Christian tradition, however, marriage is *more* than a contract; it is believed to be a *sacrament*, i.e. a visible sign of God's love.

> *'In the Old Testament, God often calls his people his "bride". Jesus too spoke of himself as the bridegroom . . The relationship of sacramental marriage should show forth the love of God that binds him to humankind as husband and wife are united. The fidelity unto death of husband and wife reflects the eternal faithfulness of God to his promises. The family which begins with marriage is a great sign of the great family of God.'*

from *The Rite of Marriage.*

QUESTIONS

1 Read *Mark* 10:6–9. Write out in your own words what Jesus said about marriage.

2 What does the Catholic Church mean when it says that marriage is '*a sacrament*'?

WHY MARRY?

Traditionally marriage has been considered a good thing in western culture because it was accepted as providing the ideal context in which people could:

* freely commit themselves to love and care for each other for the rest of their lives;

* bring up children in what should be a secure and loving home;

* direct the sex instinct towards the most constructive purpose, i.e. to show mutual love and build a happy home;

* give and receive companionship and love both in good times and in bad.

> *'Married people tend to be healthier people. At every age, as a recent study of Britain by One plus One records, men and women are more*

likely to die prematurely if they are single, divorced or widowed than if they are married. These differences partly reflect the lower incomes of those who are not married. But whatever adjustments are made, it is clear that people suffer physically from not being married — and, incidentally, men suffer more than women.'

The Economist, January 1993.

It is advisable for couples intending to marry to attend marriage preparation courses such as those offered by *ACCORD*. It is important for a couple to know if they have what it takes to sustain a relationship.

QUESTIONS

1 (a) Arrange these four reasons for getting married in what you consider to be their order of importance. Give reasons for your priorities.

(b) Do you agree/disagree with all/some of the reasons set out above? Why?

(c) Can you suggest any other reasons for getting married?

2 Read the following extract:

'Cohabitation is the practice of "living together" without marriage. These relationships are make-believe situations. The couple live as if they were finally committed to each other. They live as if they loved each other for life, yet each retains the freedom to walk out on the other. They are, in effect, saying to each other: 'I want your body but I don't want you' or 'I want you now but I may want someone else after a while.' You can't build a relationship on hesitation like that.'

Love is for Life

(a) Why is cohabitation described as 'a make-believe situation'?

(b) According to a report in the American journal *Psychology Today*, studies of couples who lived together *before* marriage showed that cohabitation did *not* improve their chances for marital happiness but did point to a higher incidence of infidelity *after* marriage.

Why do you think this is the case? Give reasons for your answer.

THE MARRIAGE VOWS

The following is an extract from the *Rite of Marriage* in the Roman Catholic tradition:

> *'I take you as my husband/wife, for better, for worse, for richer, for poorer, in sickness and in health, until death do us part.'*
>
> (First Forum)

Following this exchange of *vows* (i.e. solemn promises), the priest blesses both wedding rings. Then, in turn, each partner places a ring on the third finger of the other's left hand and says:

> *'Wear this ring as a sign of our love and fidelity. In the name of the Father, and of the Son, and of the Holy Spirit.'*

QUESTIONS

1 (a) In your own words, explain the meaning of the marriage vows.

(b) Do you think a person should be asked to make such a binding commitment? Give reasons for your opinion.

2 Guidance counsellors state that for a marriage to succeed, *both* partners must:

• appreciate and understand the kind of pressures they will have to face, and

• be prepared to support each other through whatever crisis they may face.

(a) What are the kinds of *pressures* a married couple is likely to face?

(b) What are the kinds of *crises* a married couple may have to face?

(c) How important do you think it is for both partners to enter into marriage *'with their eyes open'*? Give reasons for your answer.

Remember:

Behind the headlines and the statistics on divorce, a great reality is overlooked.

> *Most marriages succeed.* And they succeed even though married couples today face challenges quite different from those faced by earlier generations, including:
>
> * Greater acceptance of divorce as a way of solving marital problems.
> * The relatively new but unrealistic expectation that marriage will bring constant and lasting happiness.
> * Stresses stemming from longevity or the failure to plan for retirement.
> * Isolation from traditional family supports due to work-related moves.
> * Financial problems stemming from life in a consumer society.
> * Changing husband-wife roles.
>
> John Catoir

THE LEGAL ASPECTS OF MARRIAGE

• *Minimum Age*

The minimum age of marriage is 18 (Family Law Act, 1995). If either party to a marriage ceremony is under 18, that marriage is not valid in law.

• *Exemption from Minimum Age*

The High Court can exempt parties to a marriage from the minimum age requirement. An exemption order can only be granted if '*the applicant shows that its grant is justified by serious reasons and is in the interests of the parties to the intended marriage.*' (Family Law Act, 33.2.3.1995).

• *Age Limits on Sexual Relations*

It is an offence for a male to have sexual relations with a girl under the age of seventeen. S.1 (1) of the Criminal Law Amendment Act., 1935 provides that any person who unlawfully and carnally knows any girl under the age of fifteen years should be guilty of an offence. The maximum penalty is life imprisonment. S.1 (2) of the same Act provides that an attempt to commit such an offence is also an offence carrying a maximum penalty of five years imprisonment and for a second conviction a maximum penalty of ten years imprisonment. S.2 (1) of the same Act provides that any person who unlawfully and carnally knows any girl who is under the age of seventeen years shall be guilty of an offence. There is a maximum penalty of five years imprisonment and ten years imprisonment for a second conviction. S.2 (2) of the same Act provides that an attempt to commit such an offence is an offence carrying a maximum penalty of two years imprisonment and for a second conviction a maximum penalty of five years imprisonment.

The only lawful way for a male to have sexual relations with a girl under 17 is to be married to her, having been given legal exemption.

BUILDING A STRONG MARRIAGE

Marriage is not the end of a loving relationship but the *beginning* of one. For it to succeed, it requires both partners to *continually work at their relationship*.

According to experienced marriage counsellors, *both* partners must show:

- genuine commitment
- willingness to communicate
- close friendship
- respect for each other's privacy
- shared basic values and life goals
- readiness to put their relationship ahead of everything else
- sensitivity in resolving conflict
- willingness to seek and offer forgiveness
- consideration towards each other in practical ways
- realistic expectations regarding sex.

ACTIVITY

Examine carefully the list of qualities necessary for a marriage to succeed. In each case, say whether or not you think it is truly essential. Give reasons for your answers.

CHAPTER 23

Family Planning

WHAT IS FAMILY PLANNING?

Family planning may be described as:

> *any method by which married couples plan the number of children they will have, and decide the length of time between the conception of each child.*

The subject of family planning has, over the years, given rise to considerable controversy, especially in regard to the morality of certain methods of family planning.

Basically there are two forms of family planning:

(1) *Artificial methods*

(2) *Natural methods.*

WHAT ARE ARTIFICIAL METHODS OF FAMILY PLANNING?

Artificial methods of family planning use a drug or a device to alter or interfere with the normal processes of the human reproductive system in order to prevent a woman becoming pregnant. Sometimes they are called '*contraceptives*' (meaning: 'against conception').

THE DIFFERENT ARTIFICIAL METHODS OF FAMILY PLANNING*

1. The Pill

There are many different types of contraceptive pills (also called oral contraceptives). They control ovulation by acting on those hormones which cause the egg to mature in the woman's ovaries.

---

* Source of statistics on effectiveness: Consultant physician and endocrinologist Dr Bob Ryder, *The Tablet*, 18.12.93.

Effectiveness
- Progestogen-only pill failure rate: 1.2% to 23%

  Combined oestrogen-progestogen pill failure rate: 0.18% to 28%

  Figures dependent on degree of commitment to the method.

Advantages
- Easy to use.
- Lighter, more regular periods.
- May reduce menstrual symptoms such as cramps, backache and premenstrual tension (PMT).

Disadvantages
- Fertility is delayed once pill is stopped.
- Remembering to take it at the same time, every day.
- Relatively expensive.
- Can have harmful side-effects: nausea; breast discomfort; weight increase; gum inflammation; mood swings, depression; thrombosis (clotting); loss of sex drive or 'libido'; headaches; skin problems (acne, eczema); increased body hair; increased possibility of problems in childbirth; increased possibility of circulatory disorders, especially in a smoker; increased risk of breast cancer; no protection against sexually transmitted diseases (STDs).
- The man does not share any of the responsibility with this method of contraception.

A full medical examination is necessary before a woman starts taking the pill. The woman should return to her doctor *every six months* to have a follow-up examination before the pill is prescribed further.

N.B. The term contraceptive pill (meaning: to prevent conception) is in some cases a misnomer. Conception is *not always* prevented and fertilisation sometimes takes place. The drug then acts to disturb the wall of the uterus, preventing implantation of the human embryo. As a result, some forms of the pill can have the effect of producing an *abortion*, without the woman even being aware of it.

2. The Diaphragm or Cap ('Dutch Cap')

The diaphragm is a dome-shaped rubber cap. The woman inserts it into her vagina before sexual intercourse. It acts as a barrier to sperm. It is usually used with a spermicide (a gel or foam which kills sperm). A woman is measured for a diaphragm by her doctor.

Effectiveness

- Failure rate: 1.9% to 23%

  Figures dependent on degree of commitment to and extent of knowledge of the method.

Advantages

- Few side-effects (unless the woman is allergic to the rubber cap or to the spermicides).
- Inexpensive.
- Easy to use.
- Does not affect fertility.

Disadvantages

- Individual fitting is needed.
- The woman must always remember to insert it.
- Must be checked for fit if there is an increase or decrease in weight.
- Doesn't last indefinitely.
- May be displaced during intercourse if not inserted correctly, or if it is the wrong size.
- The man does not share any responsibility.

3. The Condom

A condom is a thin piece of rubber which is unrolled on to the erect penis during sexual intercourse.

Effectiveness

- Failure rate: 3.6% to 21-22%.

  Figures dependent on degree of commitment to the method.

Advantages

- No health risk or side-effects (unless one partner suffers from rubber allergy).
- Decreases risk of contracting a sexually transmitted disease.

- The man has a direct responsibility with this method of contraception.
- Inexpensive.
- Easy to use.
- No drugs involved.
- Does not affect either male or female fertility.

Disadvantages
- Unreliable if used carelessly or incorrectly.
- Awkward to use, because of having to put it on during lovemaking.
- Some men complain that it reduces sensation.

4. Spermicides
Spermicides are chemicals which are used to kill sperm. They are usually used along with a cap or a condom. They are inserted high in the vagina in the form of a foam or gel before intercourse.

Advantages
- Easy to obtain.
- Easy to use.

Disadvantages
- Inconvenient.
- Messy.
- Can cause allergic reactions.
- High failure rate if used on their own, without a cap or condom.

Information adapted from: *Learning for Adult Life* and *The Tablet*.

EXERCISE

In each case, identify the artificial method of family planning from the description given:

(1) *'Chemicals which are used to kill sperm.'*
(2) *'They control ovulation by acting on those hormones which cause the egg to mature in the ovaries.'*

(3) *'A dome-shaped rubber cap. The woman inserts it into her vagina before sexual intercourse. It acts as a barrier to sperm.'*

(4) *'A thin piece of rubber which is unrolled on to the erect penis during sexual intercourse.'*

QUESTIONS

Read the following statements about the moral and social consequences of the widespread availability of artificial methods of family planning:

- *'They make it easier to separate sex from love and marriage. There's no need to be really committed to the other person.'*

- *'They put women, especially teenage girls, under a lot of pressure to have sexual intercourse outside marriage.'*

- *'Their widespread availability will discourage people from controlling their sex drive, contribute to sexual permissiveness and a lowering of moral standards.'*

Love is for Life

1   Rewrite each statement in your own words.

2   Why do you think the authors of these statements hold these views?

3   Do you agree with some/all/none of these statements?

Give reasons for your answer.

THE INTRA-UTERINE DEVICE (IUD)

An IUD is a small loop or coil made of copper or plastic. It is inserted into the womb by a doctor. The IUD changes the structure of the wall of the womb, so a fertilised egg cannot implant itself.

> *'IUDs do not prohibit fertilisation or conception; only implantation is prevented, so that any ovum which becomes fertilised is simply expelled during the next menstrual period.*
>
> *That the use of an IUD does not prevent fertilisation is verified by studies which have revealed the presence of the hormone HCG in women fitted with IUDs. This hormone is one which is detected in the urine of pregnant women. Thus, the conclusion seems unavoidable: women wearing IUDs do conceive, but the*

implantation of the fertilised egg is prevented. The IUD should therefore be viewed as an abortifacient, not as a contraceptive device. The majority of moralists judge the IUD to be a morally unacceptable method of family planning.'

Vincent Genovesi, In Pursuit of Love.

Further, there is some concern as to the medical safety of the IUD, as Genovesi has written:

'It is known that IUDs do sometimes produce discomforting side-effects like uterine cramps or a heavy menstrual flow; they are also associated with an increased risk of pelvic inflammatory disease (PID) which can result in such damage to the fallopian tubes that sterility ensues.'

QUESTIONS

1 What is the function of an IUD?
2 Why is the IUD described by Genovesi as an abortifacient rather than a contraceptive device? Explain your answer.

THE CATHOLIC CHURCH AND ARTIFICIAL METHODS OF FAMILY PLANNING

According to the Catholic Church, sexual intercourse between a married couple has *two* purposes:

(1) to express the mutual love between a husband and wife — called the *unitive* aspect; and

(2) to express their willingness to conceive children with whom they share their love — called the *procreative* aspect.

According to the Catholic Church, these two aspects of sexual intercourse are *inseparable*. As a result, Pope Paul VI condemned

'any action which either before, at the moment of, or after sexual intercourse, is specifically intended to prevent procreation'.

Humanae Vitae

The Catholic Church teaches that artificial methods of family planning are morally wrong because, in its view, such methods interfere with God's intention that sex within marriage should be an act of mutual love and generosity open to the creation of new life.

THE CATHOLIC CHURCH AND RESPONSIBLE PARENTHOOD

Some couples may be convinced that artificial methods are their only option when planning the size of their family. Consequently, they may consider Catholic teaching on the subject to be naive and unfair. However, the Church recognises that:

> *'Those who, for serious reasons, choose to have no more children for the time being or even for an indeterminate period, are considered to exercise responsible parenthood.'*

Limiting and spacing the number of children in a family is both an important responsibility and a practical necessity for a married couple. The Catholic Church argues, however, that both their *intention* in planning the size of their family and the *means* by which the couple choose to achieve this are of moral concern. It teaches that they should *plan* their family *for loving and unselfish motives*, according to methods it deems morally acceptable.

QUESTIONS

1 What are the factors that influence married couples' decisions as to the size of their family and the space between the birth of their children?
2 Why does the Catholic Church argue that the intentions behind a couple's decision to plan their family are important and of moral concern?

NATURAL METHODS OF FAMILY PLANNING

Some people believe that a married couple's only alternative to having an unlimited number of children is to either:

(a) totally abstain from sex; or

(b) use artificial methods of family planning.

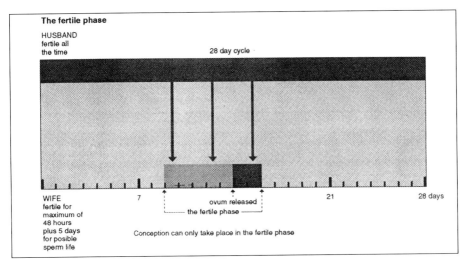

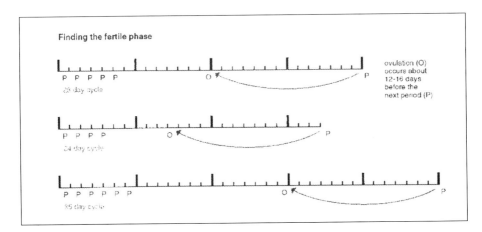

However, there is another option.

Nature itself has provided a built-in system to limit the number of children that a woman can conceive. Generally speaking, a woman can become pregnant between the ages of 15 and 47 years. However, she can only become pregnant during a certain number of days during her menstrual cycle.

'Natural Family Planning (NFP) is a simple way of planning for pregnancy or preventing pregnancy by observing the natural signs and symptoms of fertility which a woman experiences during her menstrual cycle. Her body provides a whole series of signals around the fertile time, some more reliable than others. Charting the more precise symptoms allows a couple to decide whether they will abstain from intercourse during the fertile time in order to avoid pregnancy.'

Jean Johnson, *Natural Family Planning.*

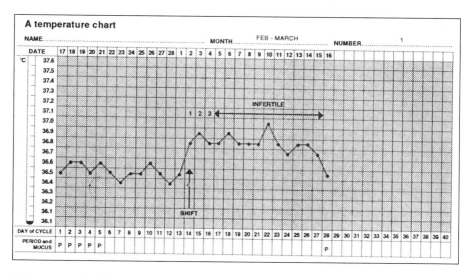

The most highly recommended form of NFP has been the Symptothermal method. This is based on

> *the observation of the mucus discharge from the cervix which varies during the menstrual cycle and can therefore indicate the most fertile days of the month;*

and

> *the measurement of body temperature, which rises when the ovum (egg) has been released from the ovary.*

The Sympto-thermal method is the one considered the most reliable by ACCORD, an organisation which provides qualified instructors to help couples understand and use natural methods, and by the World Health Organisation.

QUESTIONS

1   What is the difference between natural and artificial methods of family planning?
2   According to NFP, why should the woman chart certain symptoms provided by her body around the fertile time?

THE BENEFITS OF NFP

'Through natural methods of family planning, couples can be offered not just a set of rules for achieving or avoiding conception, but a real understanding of the natural processes within their own bodies which result in these phases of fertility and infertility. This means that the decisions they make about intercourse are informed ones. They are not relying on any appliance or drug but on their own careful day-to-day observations. This offers the couple a high degree of control over their reproductive potential.

Couples agree that NFP does require personal control and co-operation between husband and wife. NFP is not his method or her method but a shared method. The understanding and discussion this involves can benefit the couple in a wider sense. It encourages them to talk over decisions affecting other areas of family life, promotes co-operation and so enriches the marriage.'

Jean Johnson

QUESTIONS

1   Why does the author of this extract claim that NFP helps couples to make '*informed*' decisions about sexual intercourse?
2   (a) List the advantages she claims NFP can offer a married couple.

(b) Do you agree/disagree with her estimation of the value of NFP? *Give reasons for your opinion.*

THE EFFECTIVENESS OF NFP

A study conducted by the World Health Organisation concluded that the Sympto-thermal method compares favourably with artificial means for effectiveness in preventing conception. However, there is some disagreement as to NFP's degree of effectiveness. Dr Derek Llewellyn-Jones, author of the best-selling *Everywoman*, states that it has a 75 per cent success rate, while advocates of NFP rate its effectiveness between 85 per cent and 98 per cent *depending on the degree of care taken by its users*. The pregnancy rate among NFP users depends on the quality of their instruction, the extent of their knowledge of the method, the strength of their motivation and the degree of their commitment.

In his articles in the *British Medical Journal* (1993) and *The Lancet* (1995), Dr Bob Ryder maintains that when properly used, the ovulation method of family planning can achieve the effectiveness of the pill but *without* either the latter's cost or its side-effects.

It is sometimes claimed that few agencies are willing to either promote or explain NFP and that any attempts to promote it are:

> '*often frustrated by indifference or opposition by international agencies and governments. A conference in Bangkok, which included both WHO and the United Nations, examined the ethics and human values in family planning. Vatican officials were not allowed to speak officially, but they did submit a withering attack on the "contraceptive imperialism" of agencies and companies that impose IUDs, pills, antifertility vaccines and other products on illiterate women without warning them of the potential medical dangers.*'
>
> *Time* Magazine, 19.9.1988.

Despite claims to the contrary, NFP is *not* an exclusively 'Catholic' method of family planning. It is used by Muslims, Hindus and people who are not members of any religion.

THE CATHOLIC CHURCH AND NFP

The Catholic Church has advocated that married couples use NFP because, in its opinion, NFP respects

'God's plan for human fertility'.

However, it is sympathetic to couples who

'find it (NFP) is not effective for them and feel driven to use artificial methods'.

It encourages those couples who are using artificial methods to

'do all in their power to avoid or terminate this practice, relying on God's help to make possible what seems humanly impossible'.

Extracts from: *Love is for Life.*

QUESTIONS

1 Why does the Catholic Church advocate the use of NFP?
2 Is NFP an *exclusively* Catholic method of family planning as is sometimes alleged? Explain your answer.
3 What is its response to couples who do use artificial methods instead of NFP?

FURTHER READING

1 C. and E. Balsam, *Family Planning: A Guide for Exploring Issues.*
2 T.W. Hilgers, *NFP: A Doctor Answers Questions.*
   Both are available from Ligouri Publications.

CHAPTER 24

Marital Breakdown

FOUR KINDS OF MARITAL RELATIONSHIP

Most married couples aim for and many achieve happy, stable, loving relationships. Others, sadly, do not succeed. Most families enjoy a happy home life, but those who do not know only too well the problems and tensions it can create.

Dr Jack Dominion, a leading psychiatrist and marriage counsellor in the UK, argues on the basis of his research that there are basically *four* different kinds of marital relationship in western society:

- Happy, deeply committed and loving marriages which are strong enough to weather the stormy times that strike any relationship.
- Those that are 'moderately workable', where the couple settle for a friendly relationship and create a home with an acceptable level of happiness and comfort.
- Those where the couple no longer love each other but, for a variety of reasons, choose to stay together in barely concealed misery.
- Those that completely break down and where the family is dispersed.

It is a matter of unverifiable speculation how many Irish marriages belong to the first three categories. However, figures are available for those belonging to the *fourth* category.

> *'There are some 75,000 people in broken marriages'.*
> Government Information Services, 1995.

WHY MARITAL BREAKDOWN?

'Why the acceleration of marital breakdown? Most observers would attribute it, above all, to the recent and tremendous change in the relationship of the sexes. Until relatively few years ago, most marriages were based on a patriarchal structure, in which the man was deemed superior. The wife was expected to submit in most matters to the husband.

There were exceptions, of course, but even where the wife was dominant, she held sway only within the home. Outside, the man reigned supreme. Moreover, there were many social and economic factors that might keep a woman from seeking a separation or divorce.

The movement for female equality, however, has made large strides in the past few decades, and many women today will no longer accept a subordinate role. They also have a much better chance of gaining financial independence by going to work. They are no longer willing to grant the privileges men have to come to view as their right. In brief, their expectations no longer match their husbands', and they find communication in this regard very difficult.

The various methods of family planning have given the woman much greater freedom, since she no longer need be constantly pregnant. Families generally are smaller and many women find it possible to combine domestic responsibilities with outside jobs.

This has been described as a change from the patriarchal *to the* companionship *model of marriage. Its psychological consequences are many. The companionship model of marriage requires the couple to relate at a deeper level of their personalities. This deeper intimacy makes greater demands, and it is often the frustration of these demands that causes marital breakdown. For a variety of reasons, a spouse may come to a marriage burdened with potentially crippling emotional problems, which, perhaps unconsciously, he or she expects the partner to solve. One of the most common of these is the* anxious attachment *syndrome, which often later surfaces in a marriage. Such a one, who is anxiously attached to the spouse, has a great need to be loved but a low tolerance of criticism and will deny responsibility, or project blame onto the partner, or (for instance) display bad feelings about the boss by taking them out on the spouse or children, or rationalise bad behaviour and refuse to admit the consequences of actions or omissions.*

Since a greater amount of emotional maturity is demanded by marriage today, those who marry young run a much greater risk of ending in divorce. Statistics show that the rate of divorce is at least double for those who marry under twenty.

Studies of more specific causes of divorce have disclosed many factors that tend to move couples toward divorce:

- *premarital pregnancy*
- *poor housing and financial conditions*

- *disparity in educational and religious backgrounds*
- *lack of any religious commitment*
- *unwillingness of the husband to share in household tasks*
- *jealousy of each other's friends*
- *feeling of being confined on the part of a wife who gives up her job for housekeeping and children*
- *sexual maladjustment especially since people have come to expect more from sexual relations, etc.*

Adapted from: T. Bokenkotter, *Essential Catholicism*.

QUESTIONS

1 What does Bokenkotter mean when he says that until recently '*most marriages were based on a patriarchal structure*'?

2 Do you agree that '*the movement for female equality has made large strides*' in recent years? Explain your answer with reference to the points made in the extract above.

3 What do you think the '*companionship model of marriage*' means?

4 What does Bokenkotter claim are the psychological consequences of the '*change from the patriarchal to the companionship model of marriage*'? Explain your answer with reference to the points made in the extract.

5 List the factors identified as important contributors to a couple seeking a divorce. In each case say why you think they are considered to contribute to marital breakdown.

6 Read the following statements. In each case identify the problem(s) eating away at the couple's relationship.

'The first thing my husband does when he walks in the front door each evening is to ask: "When will the tea be ready?" He never says hello or asks, "How did you get on today?" He just eats his meal, heads off to train with his football club and afterwards goes to the pub with his pals. He treats me like I'm part of the furniture."

(Susan, aged 27).

'My wife has some nerve! Imagine telling me that she wants to wait a while before having any children. Sure didn't she know what I wanted before we got married? OK we never actually discussed the issue when we were going together, but it's obvious. Isn't it?'

(Dave, aged 26).

'When Kevin comes home from the labour exchange he's always in foul humour. He won't talk about it, but I can see that it's eating away at him. He doesn't know what to do with himself since he was made redundant. He's started drinking heavily. I can't pay our bills anymore.'

(Carol, aged 37).

'My wife is unreal! She says that since she's earning a wage, she's entitled to an equal say in the way things are run in the home. It was never like that between my parents. I just don't understand her.'

(Kieran, aged 25).

'I got married at 18, I'd never gone out with anyone other than Joe beforehand. Recently I've met a really nice man at the local sports club. He's kind and attentive to me, just like Joe was before we got married. I'm really having second thoughts about this marriage.'

(Ashling, aged 21).

'Eddy had to give up his studies to look for a job when I got pregnant. Now we're married but he's working in a dead-end job. We're forced to live with his parents and while he adores our baby, I think he resents me. But I never set out to trap him.'

(Deirdre, aged 19).

Can you suggest any possible ways in which these relationships could be repaired and a breakdown of their marriages avoided?

N.B. ACCORD offers an effective and confidential marriage counselling service to enable couples to resolve conflicts and difficulties in their relationships, and help them to live more rewarding and satisfactory lives. Contact numbers can be found in your local phone directory.

OPTIONS FACING COUPLES WHEN A MARRIAGE BREAKS DOWN

Some couples try to work through their problems with the help of a sympathetic clergyman or a marriage guidance counsellor. Others, for a variety of reasons, do not.

If a couple believe it is impossible to live together, there are four possible solutions:

(1) *Desertion* — one partner simply chooses to leave the family home to live somewhere else.

(2) *Judicial Separation* — a judge grants a separation order which means the couple agree not to interfere in any way in each other's lives, settle custody of children, decide maintenance, and set out how the family's property will be dealt with. However, the couple are *still* married to each other.

(3) *Decree of Nullity* — a court declares that the marriage is invalid, i.e. *never existed*, due to some fundamental defect in either the form of the marriage ceremony itself or the state of mind of either party at the time they got married.

> *'Nullity is a civil remedy. If you are granted a Decree of Nullity by the court, either party is usually free to remarry in the eyes of the State. However, your religion may not permit remarriage. For example, if you are a Catholic you are still married in the eyes of the Church, and unless you are granted a Canonical Annulment by the Church (which is an entirely different process), you are not allowed to remarry in a Catholic Church.'*
>
> Olive Brennan, *Laying Down the Law.*

(4) *Divorce* — which may be defined as:

> *'the termination of a valid marriage other than by death or annulment'.*
>
> Brian Doolan, *Principles of Irish Law.*

Divorce grants both partners a legal right to remarry.

The grounds for divorce as written into the *Irish Constitution* are as follows:

'A Court designated by law may grant a dissolution of marriage where, but only where, it is satisfied that:

i. *at the date of the institution of the proceedings, the spouses have lived apart from one another for a period of, or periods amounting to, at least four years during the previous five years,*

ii. *there is no reasonable prospect of a reconciliation between the spouses,*

iii. *such provision as the Court considers proper having regard to the circumstances exists or will be made for the spouses, any children of either or both of them and any other person prescribed by law, and*

iv. *any further conditions prescribed by law are complied with.'*

QUESTIONS

1 What is a *divorce*?
2 What are the legal grounds for obtaining a divorce?
3 What is the difference between:
   (a) a divorce and a judicial separation, and
   (b) a divorce and a decree of nullity?

THE CATHOLIC CHURCH AND DIVORCE

Divorce is available in most countries. However, it is not a recent phenomenon. It was permitted by Jewish law in the time of Christ (see *Deuteronomy* 24:1), but Jesus opposed this idea of divorce (see *Mark* 10:9-12). Ever since, Catholic Christian teaching has consistently opposed divorce, not because it lacks compassion for those whose marriages have broken down, but because it understands marriage as a *sacrament*, which if entered into by *two baptised people*, cannot be dissolved. Marriage is a commitment *for life*.

QUESTIONS

(1) Why does the Catholic Church oppose divorce?

(2) Read the marriage vows again. Then re-write them to take into account the idea of marriage that underlies divorce. Does this in any way affect your views on divorce? Explain your answer.

FOREIGN EXPERIENCE OF THE IMPACT OF DIVORCE

Since divorce has only recently been introduced into Irish law, it is instructive to consider its impact on countries which have had it on their statute books for a longer period.

> *'By far the highest divorce rate in the industrial world is that of the United States. On current rates, about half of all American marriages will be dissolved. In Europe, if present rates continue, two out of every five marriages in Britain, Denmark and Sweden will end in divorce. In the US, half of all children are likely to witness the break-up of their parents' marriage; in Britain, a quarter; in Norway, a third.'*
>
> *The Economist*, December 1992–January 1993.

Studies reveal that:
- Those who divorce and remain unattached are:

  more likely to contract chronic illness (e.g. cancer or heart disease) and die at an earlier age than people who remain married.

  more likely to commit suicide, as the rate of suicide among unattached divorcees is higher than for the general population.

- *'Ironically many divorced women who have been given custody of their children find that they are even more emotionally and economically tied to the home than ever before. Research shows that many of these one-parent families are seriously economically handicapped, and that the mother (it is usually the mother) is under stress, over-tired, harassed and unable to give due time and attention to children, work and personal life.'*

  Jack Dominion, *Passionate and Compassionate Love.*

N.B. In fairness, it must be said that some single parent families are happy, stable and secure. However,

> *'The predictable upshot is that women and children are poorer. A study of American families who have been interviewed each year since 1968 finds that separated and divorced women suffer an average fall of about 30% in their incomes the year after their marriage breaks up. Worst hurt are middle-class wives who have stayed at home. But 31% of all wives whose incomes were above average when they were married found that their living standards fell by more than half in the first year after their marriages collapsed.'*
>
> The Economist, December 1992–January 1993.

- Though a high percentage of divorced people remarry,

> *'Research in some countries indicates that second marriages tend to be of shorter duration, especially if there are children from the first marriage. The evidence from the UK is that second marriages there are more likely to end in divorce than first marriages. Data from the USA tends to support this view. Glick and Norton indicated a 44 per cent divorce rate among second marriages.'*
>
> Marital Breakdown: A Review and Proposed Changes.

In theory, a second marriage should succeed because a person should have learned the lessons from the first marriage. But in practice a substantial number *repeat* their mistakes because they have not learned that for a marriage to succeed it needs mutual commitment and sustained effort.

- When men and women are abandoned, sometimes for another person, they usually feel deeply hurt and resentful, and often wish to strike back. Children can become the innocent battleground if one parent tries to turn them against the other. Frequently, divorced couples forget that they have a duty to form some kind of tolerant relationship with each other and to act as parents to their children, no matter how difficult that may be.

- Research available on the long-term effects of divorce on children shows that divorce has a detrimental effect on their lives. However,

'Many of these effects may be the result not of the divorce, which is easy to record, but of the thunderous atmosphere of a rocky marriage. An important study of children on both sides of the Atlantic appeared in Science in June 1991, by Mr Cherlin, Ms Kiernan and five other authors. It argued that "a substantial portion of what is usually considered the effect of divorce on children is visible before the parents separate". For boys in particular, most of the effects usually ascribed to divorce seem to appear before the parents actually break up.'

The Economist, December 1992 – January 1993.

Further, other legal remedies such as judicial separation and a decree of nullity can also have a traumatic effect on those involved.

QUESTIONS

1 ' *There is no denying that every divorce is a nail in the coffin of human love. A divorce is a betrayal of some of the deepest aspirations of the human spirit.'*

Dr Jack Dominion

(a) What point is Dominion making?

(b) Do you agree/disagree that there is evidence to support his claim? Give reasons for your answer.

2 A consistent finding in surveys conducted in both the UK and the USA is that more than half those people who opted for divorce now *regret* their choice.

What are your reflections on this finding?

ANNULMENT

As stated earlier, the Catholic Church opposes divorce. It does, however, grant an annulment in certain circumstances. We may define annulment as

'a declaration that the marriage bond did not exist'.

This is different from divorce, since the latter seeks to dissolve a bond that *did* exist.

According to the Catholic Church's *Code of Canon Law*, a marriage may be annulled if it can be proven that *before* the marriage occurred, or *at the time* it was celebrated, some essential element for a valid (correct) marriage contract did not exist, namely where one or other partner:

- was underage;
- suffered from mental instability;
- suffered from an inability to have sexual relations;
- was not fully aware of what marriage entails;
- lacked the necessary maturity required for entering into marriage.

However, any events or experiences *after* the couple have married

> *'are relevant only if they can be shown to point to defects which were already present at the time of the marriage'.*
>
> *Love is for Life*

The *most recent* figures available state that in 1990 there were 216 annulments granted by the Catholic Church in Ireland (32 counties).

> *'In about 75% of cases ending with a nullity decree, a prohibition on marriage in the Church is imposed on one or both parties. This is because the defect which caused the nullity is judged to be serious enough to put at risk the validity of a future marriage. This prohibition may be lifted by the local bishop only if he is satisfied, after investigation, of the person's fitness for marriage in all essential respects. The purpose of the prohibition is to prevent the sacrament of marriage being brought into disrepute and to protect the genuine interest of any future spouse.'*
>
> *Marital Breakdown: A Review and Proposed Changes*, Appendix 3.8.

QUESTIONS

1 What is an *annulment*?

2 Explain the difference between an annulment and a divorce.

3 In what circumstances will the Church grant an annulment?

4 Why does the Church sometimes impose a prohibition on marriage once an annulment has been granted?

CHAPTER 25

Sexually Transmissible Diseases

CHANGING ATTITUDES TO SEX

In modern Irish society, people are generally more relaxed and open when discussing sex and matters related to it than in times past. This is a positive, healthy development. But the downside to this has been a more relaxed attitude as to when and why people should engage in sexual relations. The causes of these changes are complex and the subject of much controversy among social commentators. Whatever the cause, the results of this change in attitudes to sexual relations have been serious:

- More young people are having sex at an earlier age. For example: a total of 259 girls under 17 years of age gave birth in 1995, compared to 229 in 1992.
- There has been a sharp increase in the number of children born outside of marriage, e.g.

  In 1983 there were 4,517 births outside marriage, equivalent to 6.8 per cent of all births registered.

  In 1995 there were 10,507 births outside marriage, equivalent to 22 per cent of all births registered.

  Irish Times, 29.5.1996
- The number of those suffering from sexually transmissible diseases has risen significantly.

In this chapter we will examine the nature and consequences of sexually transmissible diseases. But the aim is not to scare people into moral sexual behaviour. That would be a poor approach to morality, saying in effect,

> *'Don't have sex outside marriage because you might get ill or maybe even die.'*

Christian belief is that sex should be respected out of *love, not fear.* But it is important to know the facts.

SEXUALLY TRANSMISSIBLE DISEASES

AIDS is by far the most publicised and well-known health risk of promiscuous sexual behaviour (i.e. having sexual relations without love and commitment, with a number of different partners). However, although there can be no doubting the danger of AIDS, it is only one, even if the most deadly, of a whole series of diseases that can be contracted through sexual intercourse with a person infected with an STD.

STDs can be transmitted through sexual intercourse and oral-genital contact, as the chart indicates.

NAME	CAUSE	SYMPTOMS	TREATMENT
AIDS/HIV	Human Immuno Deficiency Virus	People with HIV may have no visible symptoms	No cure. Treatment with drugs may delay the onset of AIDS.
Genital Warts	A virus similar to that which causes ordinary skin warts	Fleshy growths on genitals	A special ointment may be applied. There may be a link between genital warts and cancer of the neck of the womb. It is advisable for women to have an annual smear test following infection.
Gonorrhoea	Bacteria	*In women*: Unusual discharge from vagina. Pain when passing urine, fever, chill, abdominal pain and pains in the joints—sometimes no symptoms. *In men*: Pain when passing urine. Yellow discharge from penis.	Antibiotics cure the disease. Early detection and treatment are essential to avoid sterility.
Hepatitis B	A virus	Two stages. (1) 1 to 6 months after contact— flu-like symptoms, tiredness, pain in the joints; (2) jaundice, brown urine, soreness in the abdominal area.	No satisfactory cure. Healthy diet and rest may help recovery.

Herpes	Herpes simplex (similar to common cold sore)	Small painful sores or blisters or itching in the genital area. Flu-like symptoms. Pain or burning sensation when passing urine.	No specific cure. A number of remedies ease pain and ward off further infections.
Non-Specific Urethritis	Various micro-organisms e.g. Chlamydia	May vary. A few days to 6 weeks after infection — abnormal discharge from the vagina, urethra, penis or back passage. Inflammation of genital area, pain or burning sensation when passing urine.	Specific treatments are available in most cases. Early treatment is essential to prevent infertility or the occurrence of pelvic inflammatory disease — a disease of the fallopian tubes.
Pubic Lice	Lice living in pubic hair	Severe itching. Eggs (nits) on the pubic hair or underwear.	Special lotions.
Syphilis	Bacteria	Three stages: (1) Sores appear in genital area within 1 to 12 weeks after infection, (2) 2 to 6 months later — a rash may develop with other flu-like symptoms; (3) Damage to heart, brain and vital organs.	Antibiotics.
Thrush	Yeast called Candida Albicans	*Men*: Inflammation of penis. *Women*: Thick white discharge from vagina. Soreness and pain on urination. Itching in vaginal area.	*Men*: Cream to administer to affected areas. *Women*: A course of pessaries (soft tablets which are inserted directly into the vagina) and cream to prevent itching.
Trichomonas	A small parasite	Often no symptoms in men. Frothy vaginal discharge, itching in the vaginal area and burning feeling during urination.	Special Tablets.

Department of Health

ACTIVITY

Identify the STD from the following symptoms:

(a) Severe itching. Eggs (nits) on the pubic hair or underwear.

(b) *In women*: Unusual discharge from vagina. Pain when passing urine, fever, chill, abdominal pain and pains in the joints.

In men: Pain when passing urine. Yellow discharge from penis.

(c) Small painful sores or blisters or itching in the genital area. Flu-like symptoms. Pain or burning sensation when passing urine.

(d) Fleshy growths on genitals.

(e) Three stages: (1) Sores appear in genital area within 1 to 12 weeks after infection; (2) 2 to 6 months later — a rash may develop with other flu-like symptoms; (3) Damage to heart, brain and vital organs.

(f) Two stages: (1) 1 to 6 months after contact — flu-like symptoms, tiredness, pain in the joints; (2) Jaundice, brown urine, soreness in the abdominal area.

(g) *Men*: Inflammation of penis. *Women*: Thick white discharge from vagina. Soreness and pain on urination. Itching in vaginal area.

QUESTION

Read the chart on STDs and identify:

(a) Those STDs for which there is a cure.

(b) Those STDs for which there is no known satisfactory/specific cure.

(c) Those for which there is no known cure.

AIDS

(1) What is AIDS?

First identified in 1982. 'AIDS' stands for 'Acquired Immune Deficiency Syndrome'.

Acquired means a person gets it from another person.
Immune Deficiency means a person's body is unable to defend itself against certain illnesses.

Syndrome means a collection of signs and symptoms which may indicate that a person is infected with AIDS, e.g. pneumonia, skin cancer or fungal infections.

The World Health Organisation estimates that over one million people world-wide have developed full-blown AIDS. However, it believes that more than thirty million adults and children may actually carry the virus.

Source: CNN, 29.11.97

(2) What causes AIDS?

AIDS is caused by the *Human Immuno-Deficiency Virus* (HIV) which weakens the body's immune system by destroying its white blood cells. HIV strips away the body's ability to resist disease and leaves it vulnerable to infection.

Usually the disease with which a person becomes infected, and not the virus itself, causes death. However, many people who get HIV do not immediately become ill. They may continue to enjoy good health, but during this phase they can infect other people with the virus. It is not known for sure exactly what percentage of those discovered to be HIV positive will go on to develop full-blown AIDS.

(3) How is HIV transmitted?

HIV is usually passed on in one of the following four ways of exchanging bodily fluids:

- Through intimate sexual contact:

  HIV is transmitted when a bodily fluid containing it (e.g. semen, vaginal fluids or blood itself) enters the bloodstream of another person. In most kinds of intimate sexual contact that is easily done. The linings of body openings frequently have tiny cuts or tears which a person is not even aware of. They are not big enough to cause pain or noticeable bleeding. But even the tiniest provides access for HIV to enter the bloodstream.

- By sharing an intravenous needle that has been used by an HIV infected person.

- From a pregnant woman to the child in her womb.

- By blood transfusion from an infected donor.

EFFECTS OF AIDS

Central Nervous System

Widespread damage to the central nervous system

Pregnancy

HIV can be transmitted during the birth, putting both mother and baby at risk of developing full-blown AIDS

Skin

Skin cancer occurs in AIDS in a highly malignant form. Other skin conditions include rashes and eczema

Brain

AIDS increases the risk of encephalitis, tumours and dementia

Digestive Tract

Severe thrush affects the mouth and the oesophagus, making eating difficult

Lungs

Lung diseases such as tuberculosis are characteristic of AIDS

A Cure?

Drugs are being developed to treat HIV, but concerns remain about side-effects and so far they do not actually cure AIDS.

Further, the cost of such drugs may exclude many AIDS sufferers in less developed regions, e.g. Africa, Asia, etc.

N.B. The Department of Health assures us that there is now virtually no risk of being infected with HIV by receiving a blood transfusion in Ireland and the UK. Every unit of blood is screened for antibodies to HIV. Nor is there any danger of exposure to HIV by donating blood. However, unfortunately, some people were unintentionally infected by contaminated blood products before health agencies became aware, in the early 1980s, of the dangers of HIV.

HIV is not transmitted by:
- Hugging.
- Shaking hands.
- Sharing a cup.
- Sitting beside someone in class.
- Using the same toilet seat.
- Breathing the same air.
- Swimming in swimming pools.

What about kissing?

HIV is present in saliva, although not in such concentrated amounts as it is in blood, semen and vaginal secretions. Until 1997 there had been no recorded case of HIV being transmitted solely by kissing. However, the US Centre for Disease Control and Prevention has indicated just such an extraordinarily rare and unusual case. A woman apparently became infected with HIV '*through deep kisses with her sexual partner, whose saliva was contaminated because his gums bled after he had brushed and flossed his teeth. Researchers ruled out other possible paths of infection*'.

Source: *Irish Times*, 11.7.97

(4) Is there a test for HIV?

Yes. It can detect antibodies to HIV in the bloodstream. A positive test result means that a person has been infected with the virus but he/she may not have or ever develop full-blown AIDS.

(5) Is there any cure for AIDS?

As yet, there is *no known cure* for AIDS once a person is infected, nor is there any vaccine available to prevent infection occurring.

(6) What precautions can be taken against infection?

- Do not abuse drugs, especially those taken intravenously (i.e. by injection).

- Never share any object that punctures the skin unless it has been properly sterilised, e.g. razors, toothbrushes, tattooing needles, etc. The Department of Health recommends soaking such a device at 56°C for not less than ten minutes.

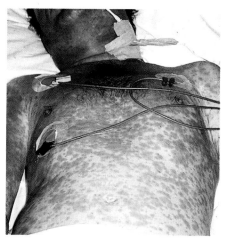

AIDS victim

(7) Can condoms prevent infection?

The Department of Health advises that the proper use of a condom will substantially reduce the risk of contracting HIV, but it does *not* guarantee one hundred per cent protection. There is still a risk of infection.

However, regardless of the debate over the effectiveness of the condom to prevent HIV infection, the Catholic Church opposes the use of such contraceptive devices on *moral* grounds:

> *'Sexual intercourse expresses the total, unconditional self-giving of husband and wife, with openness to the procreation of new life. The use of contraceptives contradicts this truth and is, therefore, morally wrong.'*

Further, it advises people:

> *'The only safeguard against the AIDS virus by sexual means is through fidelity and good living — faithfulness to one's partner in marriage and self-denial and self-restraint outside of marriage.'*
>
> Paul Lavelle, *Understanding AIDS.*

Also, the Church calls on all Christians to show:

> *'a compassionate and caring attitude towards those who are victims of AIDS. We must strive to carry on Christ's work of caring and healing. To people with AIDS we should respond as we would to*

anyone suffering from serious or terminal illness. The Christian community must be a sign of Christ's love, especially for the marginalised and the suffering.'

Statement on AIDS.

QUESTIONS

1 What is AIDS?

2 What is HIV?

3 What are the four ways of getting infected with HIV?

4 Read the following extract:

> *'The whole condom propaganda encourages sexual promiscuity — the very behaviour which is most conducive to the spread of the disease. This campaign threatens to weaken public morality. By making "safe sex" respectable it undermines people's willingness to be moral and maintains those very attitudes and behaviour patterns which have contributed so much to the spread of the AIDS virus. The truth is that the risk of HIV infection can be eliminated completely if men and women can be persuaded to practise faithful, exclusive sexual relationships. Risk elimination is possible, whereas risk reduction simply perpetuates the problem.'*
>
> Maurice Reidy, *AIDS Education and Sexual Morality.*

(a) Why does the author of this extract argue against the use of condoms in AIDS prevention?

(b) What does he propose as a strategy of *'risk elimination'*?

(c) Why does he claim that *'risk reduction simply perpetuates the problem'*?

(d) Do you agree/disagree with this argument?

Give reasons for your answer.

5 (a) What attitude is a Christian expected to adopt towards AIDS sufferers?

(b) What kind of facilities and care should be provided for those in the terminal phase of their illness?

CHAPTER 26

Human Rights

INTRODUCTION

To fully appreciate the importance of human rights we must first be clear about what it means to be *human*.

It is said that because men and women are descended from ape-like ancestors, we should no longer think that we have a privileged place in creation. Since humans do not have an origin different from other animals, it is claimed that we are in no way different from other animals. Human beings are just another kind of animal, and nothing more. We are nothing special. In the following extract, David Jones, OP challenges this view.

'ARE PEOPLE MERE APES?'

'The first thing to notice is that the descent of humans from ape-like creatures does not imply that people are really, or merely, or nothing but apes; or for that matter anything but people. As a matter of fact there are quite clear and striking differences between people and all other animals. The ability of people to talk to each other, to tell stories and jokes, to paint pictures and make tools is quite unparalleled in the rest of the animal kingdom. The instincts and behaviour of animals are, for the most part, passed on genetically (though in higher animals learning from others occurs). The behaviour of people is dominated by culture, by the language and habits, the customs and stories they grow up with. This language does not come from anyone's genes but from a tradition.

It is because of this cultural inheritance that people are free from the dominance of genetically conditioned behaviour. The making of free informed choices and the possibility of understanding the world spring from our having a language which is given to us with a tradition. Further, no other animal has the freedom to rise above its own immediate interests and contemplate the good of the larger community. People are both the only animals which can really know themselves and the only animals that can really forget themselves. The human power of understanding and the ability to act justly permits that religious understanding which truly differentiates people from other animals.

If it were shown that chimps spent their time talking of God, while resting and while walking by the way, and that this perhaps spurred them on to acts of justice towards their fellow chimps, then it would be reasonable to claim that the differences between chimps and people were minor. The differences between people and other animals are not accidental, as their height is. The human passion for communication, the existence of culture, reason, creativity, freedom and religion mark human life off as a different kind of thing from mere animal life.

Only people can be citizens. A dog may be cleverer than a human baby, but so long as the child is treated justly and allowed to grow up, it can enter a way of life unlike that of any other animal. We treat both pets and babies as pretend people. The difference is that with babies we pretend so they may become mature people, whereas with pets we just pretend.

Presenting a resumé of all that it is to be human is a hopeless task. Yet it should be clear that there are significant differences between people and other animals. Also it is clear that these differences bear on those aspects of humanity with which religion is most concerned, speculative knowledge (i.e. knowledge for its own sake), mythology and morality for instance.'

Extract from *Can Catholics Believe in Evolution?*

Christians do not see human beings as merely 'naked apes' but as completely unique creatures, possessing the capacity to *reason* and *make free choices*. They believe that human beings have not evolved this way by blind chance, but as the deliberate result of God's creative action. Women and men are made in God's *'image and likeness'* (*Genesis*, 1:26). We are God's children. As such we have both a unique *dignity* which should be *respected* and *protected*, as well as a *responsibility* to care for the world we have been given to share. Human life is *sacred*.

QUESTIONS

1 What characteristics set human beings apart from other creatures on the earth?

2 Why do Christians believe that human beings possess a unique dignity which should be respected and protected?

3 What do Christians mean when they say that *'human life is sacred'*? Do you agree/disagree? Explain your answer.

WHAT ARE HUMAN RIGHTS?

Human Rights may be defined as:

Those basic entitlements each person needs to promote and defend his/her freedom and dignity in relation to the state.

The United Nations Declaration of Human Rights (1948) states that each human being is entitled to:

- Life
- Liberty and security of person
- Not be made a slave
- Not be physically, psychologically or sexually abused
- Protection of the law
- A fair and public hearing in the courts
- Be presumed innocent until proved guilty
- Freedom of movement and residence
- Marry and found a family
- Own property
- Freedom of conscience and religion
- Freedom of opinion and expression
- Freedom of peaceful assembly and of association
- Seek and receive information and ideas
- Education
- Take part in politics
- Work
- Fair wages and equal pay for equal work
- Social security

- A decent standard of living
- Join a trade union
- Rest and leisure

All these rights are to be upheld, irrespective of any differences of race, colour, sex, language, religion, political opinion, social origin, property, birth.

COMMENT

The provisions of the *UN Declaration of Human Rights* are *not* legally binding, but their frequent contraventions are monitored by human rights organisations such as Amnesty International, which has over half a million volunteers world-wide. Its annual report on human rights violations makes chastening reading. By failing to make endorsement of the *Declaration* an obligatory condition of membership, the UN has left many people at the mercy of governments not of their own choosing.

QUESTIONS

1 Examine each of the human rights listed above. Then explain why each is important.

2 '*Human rights are fundamental to our nature. Without them we cannot live as human beings.*'

What do you think this statement means? Do you agree/disagree? Why?

3 Can you justify defending the 'rights' of animals if you ignore the denial of human rights? Explain your answer.

CHRISTIANS AND THE DEFENCE OF HUMAN RIGHTS

At the Second Vatican Council, the assembled leaders of Catholic Christianity declared:

'*In our times, a special obligation binds us to make ourselves the neighbour of every person . . . whether he be an old person abandoned by all, a foreign labourer unjustly looked upon, a refugee, a child born of an unlawful union and wrongly suffering for a sin he/she did not commit, or a hungry person who disturbs our conscience by recalling the voice of the Lord, "As long as you did it for one of the least of my brethren, you did it for me."'*

During his earthly ministry, Jesus always showed concern or respect for others:

- Jesus noticed the widow giving coins in the temple [*Mark* 12:41–44].
- Jesus cured the woman who touched the hem of his robe [*Mark* 5:25–34].
- Jesus was kind to the sinful woman who anointed his feet [*Luke* 7:36–50].
- Jesus cured the disturbed man who had been forced to live among the tombs [*Mark* 5:1–20].
- Jesus cured Bartimaeus who had been forced to beg because he was blind [*Mark* 10:46–52].

The Christian must get involved — faith involves *action*. This is a real challenge, as too many people find it easier to say 'It's none of my business'. Jesus made it clear that people show their love of God by loving their fellow human beings. Christians should champion the cause of social injustice and resist the violation of human rights. They must always remember, however, that:

> *'The first right of the human person is to his or her life. He or she has other goods and some are more precious, but this one is fundamental —the pre-condition of all others. Hence, it must be protected above all others.'*

Sacred Congregation for the Doctrine of the Faith.

Catholic Christians are called upon to protect human rights from the moment of conception onwards.

QUESTIONS

1 Read *Matthew* 25:35-40.

What is the Christian attitude to the struggle for human rights in today's world?

Explain your answer.

2 Why is the right to life the most precious right of all?

3 *'I disapprove of what you say, but I will defend to the death your right to say it.'*

Voltaire, eighteenth-century French philosopher.

(a) What point was Voltaire making about freedom of speech?

(b) Do you agree/partly agree/disagree? Why?

4 The law of the Irish Republic places certain limits on personal rights in such areas as freedom of speech (e.g. laws of libel and slander) and freedom of association (e.g. laws prohibiting membership of subversive organisations).

(a) Why is this the case? Give reasons for your answer.

(b) Do you think such limits on personal rights are necessary for the preservation of a democratic society? Explain your answer.

SECTARIAN VIOLENCE IN NORTHERN IRELAND

'Somebody they had never met tried to burn a family to death.'

Sectarian attacks on homes in religiously mixed areas sadly constitute a serious ongoing problem in Northern Ireland. Suzanne Breen spoke to one County Derry family who narrowly escaped death.

It was 12.25 a.m. when Odessa Kealey crept downstairs for a glass of water. Her husband Colum, exhausted after a hard day's work, was in a deep sleep, as were two of her three sons. The house was in darkness. Suddenly, a brick came crashing through the glass front door of their home in Coleraine, Co. Derry, followed by a petrol bomb. Odessa started screaming.

'I went to pick the bomb up,' she says, 'but it exploded.' It consisted of a green bottle filled with petrol and a burning rag. Odessa yelled at Colum and the boys — Ryan (10), Eunan (15) and Fergal (17) — to get out. She escaped through the back door. They scrambled to safety through a bedroom window and jumped on to the boiler roof. A neighbour rescued them with a ladder.

'We just made it and no more,' says Colum. 'The flames were hitting the ceiling when I climbed out — they scorched the back of my head. Seconds later, they were shooting through the roof.'

Struggling to take in what was happening, the Kealeys watched as their home was consumed by flames. Neighbours wrapped blankets and coats around the family.

'We lost everything in the fire,' says Odessa. 'All that we had worked so hard for. We were left with just the nightclothes we were standing in.'

Odessa Kealey (48) and her husband Colum (52) were born in the nearby predominantly Catholic towns of Dungiven and Claudy. They moved to Coleraine to find work 14 years ago. They bought a three-bedroom semi-detached house on the Portrush Road. It was a quiet, middle-class area, mainly Protestant but with a few Catholic families.

'There was never any trouble from the neighbours or anything like that,' says Colum. 'We kept ourselves to ourselves and they did the same. Although, we never liked being at home around the Twelfth. We usually headed down South.'

The family stayed with relations for two days after the attack and then moved into accommodation arranged by a local priest. They plan to live in the home of a local man who is working abroad for six months while their own house is being rebuilt. Their insurance company is footing the bill. It will be reimbursed by the Northern Ireland Office.

'We'll probably not move back into our old house,' says Colum, 'it would be better to buy something else.' He feels like 'packing up and leaving Coleraine for good', but there is a better chance of his sons finding jobs there than in other County Derry towns.

A middle-aged man and a youth were seen running away after the attack but no paramilitary organisation has claimed responsibility. 'We'd feel better if they did,' says Odessa, 'and if they told us why. We feel sad, not bitter. We're not members of the SDLP or Sinn Féin. We're not interested in politics at all.'

The Kealeys believe that they were targeted because a photograph

211

of their son Fergal returning from the GAA All-Ireland football final in Dublin had appeared in two local papers a few days earlier.

'It seems they attack you now for watching a football match,' says Colum. 'It's difficult to come to terms with the fact that somebody you have never met tried to burn your family to death. You could bump into them on the street, in a shop, on the bus, and they'd just be a face in the crowd, you wouldn't even know them.'

The family's nerves have been destroyed by the incident. Odessa lies awake for hours at night - 'I'm frightened to close my eyes' — Colum manages to sleep but wakes at the slightest noise.

Catholics in the Portrush Road area now fear for their safety, while Protestants are concerned that the attack will lower house prices, Colum says. However, people from both sides of the community have rallied around the family, he adds. Boxes of food, clothes, pots and pans, crockery, cutlery, towels and toiletries piled up on the floor are testimony to that.

There have also been numerous gifts of money and a letter of sympathy from Coleraine Borough Council.

Starting over again and building a new home will be difficult, Odessa says. She lost things in the fire which money can't replace — her wedding album, photographs of the children's First Communion and Confirmation, presents they brought back from holidays, ornaments her mother left her when she died.

'I get very upset when I think that all those bits and pieces are gone forever,' she says. 'But then I thank God that it was only possessions, and not people, that were taken from me and that my family is still in one piece.'

The Irish Times, 20.10.1993.

QUESTIONS

1 What is meant by a *'sectarian attack'*?

2 (a) What was the relationship between the Kealeys and most of their Protestant neighbours both before and after the attack on their home?

(b) How does this relationship contrast, if at all, with the stereotyped image of relations between the two sections of the northern community?

212

3 Why, in their opinion, was the Kealey family singled out for a sectarian attack?

4 Re-read the UN Declaration of Human Rights. Identify those human rights of which both the Kealey family and so many other families (both Catholic and Protestant) have been deprived by sectarian violence, both republican and loyalist in origin.

ARGUMENTS FOR AND AGAINST TORTURE

Torture may be defined as:

'the infliction of severe bodily pain, especially as a punishment or means of persuasion.'

Concise Oxford Dictionary.

Very few people openly support the use of torture, yet many governments allow it to be used.

Torture is prohibited by all international human rights treaties, yet reports show that it is used by the security forces of over eighty countries (Source: *Irish Times* 3.4.97).

QUESTIONS

1   Read each of the statements on torture set out here. Then divide your page into two columns: one column for those with which you agree and another for those with which you disagree.

(a) Choose those statements with which you agree and those with which you disagree and write them into the appropriate column.

(b) Give reasons for your choice.

2   Governments and security forces sometimes argue that the use of torture can be justified for certain purposes in special circumstances.

Do you agree/disagree? Why?

3   Read the following:

First they came for the Jews
and I did not speak out —
because I was not a Jew.
Then they came for the communists
and I did not speak out —
because I was not a communist.
Then they came for the trade unionists
and I did not speak out —
because I was not a trade unionist.
Then they came for me —
and there was no one left
to speak out for me.

A survivor of the Nazi concentration camps.

(a) What point does the author make about the importance of protecting the human rights of all political, racial and religious groups in both one's own society and those elsewhere?

(b) Do you agree/disagree? Why?

ATTITUDES TO TORTURE

Torture: for or against?

• *Torture degrades the torturer as well as the victim.*

• *It's not really torture — just intensive interrogation. We need to find out about enemy agents and their friends.*

• *You can make anyone confess if you hurt them enough. As a result you are bound to hurt innocent people.*

• *A terrorist is not an ordinary soldier or criminal. If he gives information quickly, OK — if not, his secret must be forced from him. He must face suffering as part of his job.*

• *Torture is inhumane and is always wrong. It can never be justified.*

• *Torture may be useful in the short term. But some short-term methods must be forbidden in order to save the more important values of civilisation. Torture is never limited to 'just once'. Once we start to use it it spreads to more and more cases.*

• *Torture is a regrettable act, but it is necessary for the good of everyone. If we are threatened by evil people, we have to use ruthless methods too.*

• *We must use torture to keep people afraid. If they don't fear us they won't obey us.*

Source: J. Jenkins, *Religious Studies.*

215

THE FOUR PILLARS OF PEACE

'World religions should in a special way represent the moral conscience of the world, and condemn anything which degrades and destroys human life, dignity and freedom. We recognise that anything which offends our common humanity is itself a threat to world peace.

Today's roll-call of repression would include many countries and minorities. We recall not only the oppressed people of Iraq but the plight of the Palestinians, the long agony of Lebanon, the occupation of Tibet. There are many others, too, whose anguish should be ours.

Much of the secular world is seemingly content with a partial and self-interested response to injustice and aggression. We who are engaged in a common search for values which extend beyond and above those of secular society should seek a fairer, a more peaceful, a more united world. Pope John XXIII spoke of "the four pillars of peace": truth, justice, freedom and charity. Where one of these is lacking there is no true peace. These are values to be prized in every society, of whatever religious faith, ethnic origin or cultural background. Surely the religions of the world can come together in the defence and promotion of these four fundamental values.'

Cardinal Basil Hume, *The Month*, May 1991.

QUESTIONS

1 Why should people of all religions condemn abuses of human rights?

2 What are the *'four pillars of peace'*?

3 Why is the promotion and defence of these four fundamental values important?

A SUMMARY OF CATHOLIC CHRISTIAN TEACHING ON THE SACREDNESS OF HUMAN LIFE

- The Christian principle of respect for human life at every stage of its existence is founded on God's commandment, 'You shall not commit

216

murder', which unconditionally forbids all taking of innocent human life from its beginnings in the womb onwards.

- Certain behaviour is good or evil in itself, such as giving food and shelter to the homeless, or the deliberate murder of an innocent person.

- No motive or intention, however good and sincere, can change what is wrong into what is right.

- Throughout history, a wide range of brutal acts have been justified in the name of patriotism, defence, freedom or religion — but this does not serve in the slightest degree to make them any less wrong.

- No good intention will ever justify murder or torture or cruelty or racial or religious discrimination.

Source: *Love is for Life*

CHAPTER *27*

Abortion

LIFE BEFORE BIRTH — THE MEDICAL FACTS

DAY 1: Sperm and ovum meet in fertilisation. Genetic make-up complete. Colour of eyes, hair, sex and even build are determined. A unique individual is created.

DAY 23: Heart starts to beat.

DAY 28: Legs, arms have started to form, eyes and ears too.

WEEK 6: Skeleton complete and reflexes present. Liver, kidneys and lungs formed. Electrical brain wave patterns can be recorded.

WEEK 8: All organs functioning. Milk teeth formed as are fingers, thumbs, ankles and toes.

WEEK 10: Sensitive to touch. Can turn head, frown, bend elbow and wrist independently.

WEEK 12: Capable of swallowing. Fingernails commence. Vocal chords complete. Inherited physical features can be discerned.

WEEK 16: Baby is half birth length; heart pumps fifty pints of blood a day.

WEEK 20: Hair, eyebrows, eyelashes appear. Can turn, suck and kick.

WEEK 28: Eyes open. Can hear mother's digestive processes and heartbeat.

WEEK 36–40: Approaches birth. Another stage of a well-advanced process.

Sources: *CARE* and *LIFE*

'It is scientifically correct to say that an individual human life begins at conception, when the egg and sperm join to form the zygote, and that this developing human always is a member of our species in all stages of its life.'

Dr Micheline Matthews Roth,
Harvard University Medical School, USA.

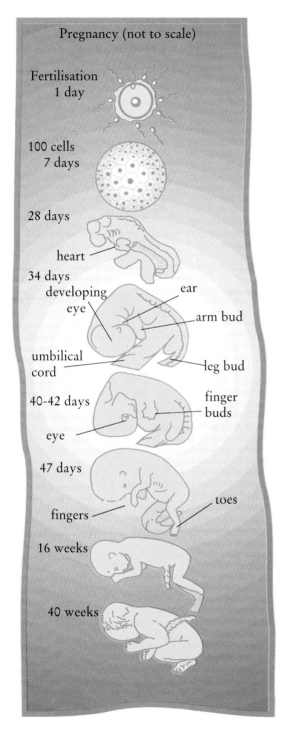

Pregnancy (not to scale)

Fertilisation
1 day

100 cells
7 days

28 days

heart

34 days
developing
eye

ear

arm bud

umbilical
cord

leg bud

40-42 days

finger
buds

eye

47 days

fingers

toes

16 weeks

40 weeks

How a baby grows before birth

The egg and sperm unite to form a cell called a *zygote*. The zygote divides into two, then these cells divide again, and so on. As the cells increase in number, they differentiate — that is they form the many different kinds of cells that make up the human body. Gradually, the bundle of cells takes on a recognisably human shape. In its early stage, the developing baby is called an *embryo*. At later stages, it is called a *foetus*.

There is ample evidence that each human embryo:

'*is more than a potential human being, it is already a human being with potential, complete with every genetic detail, unique, individual, unrepeatable*'.

Dr Ian MacDonald,
Regius Professor of
Midwifery
at Glasgow University.

Furthermore, one should be clear that:

'.. The difference between the day-old or hour-old embryo and the human adult is one of degree of maturity only, not of essential nature; the adult is a mature member of the species, whereas the embryo is a human person whose characteristic human powers and potentialities have only just begun to be developed and actualised'.

Agneta Sutton, Linacre Centre.

WHAT IS ABORTION?

Abortion* may be defined as

'any procedure the direct purpose of which is to prevent the implantation of the embryo or to remove it from the womb before it is viable; in other words the direct and intentional destruction of an unborn life'.

CPIS, *The Catholic Church and Abortion*.

Abortion statistics

Ireland
The most recently available figures for the number of women giving Irish addresses who have had abortions in Britain, released by the UK Office for National Statistics, show that 4,894 women of all ages had abortions in 1996. The largest number of abortions occur among women in the 20-34 age group, followed by those under 20 years and then those over 35 years.
Elsewhere
UK: 1967–1997 — over 4 million legal abortions performed.
USA: An estimated one-third of all pregnancies are aborted.

SOME QUESTIONABLE ASSUMPTIONS MADE IN THE ABORTION DEBATE

Thomas Bokenkotter offers the following analysis:

---

*Also referred to as 'direct abortion' or 'therapeutic abortion' or 'contragestion'.

(1) *An abortion will often save the pregnant teenage woman from disastrous long-range consequences such as economic distress and other life disadvantages.* But social science researchers who have studied the negative impact of early or unwed parenthood have found this impact less severe than is often asserted.

2) *Children who are aborted are unwanted.* Actually, evidence is sorely lacking that unwanted children are really unwanted in a sense that would be injurious to their chance of a happy life. A major study of Czech children published in 1975 showed no major differences in outcomes between children whose mothers were denied abortions and children who were 'wanted'.

Also, a study exploring the effects on children having very young parents showed similar results. It would be difficult to conclude that these children of younger mothers suffer such disabilities that they would be better off not born.

(3) *Legal abortion is necessary to reduce abortion deaths.* It is a fact that the maternal death rate from abortionists in the UK and USA has taken a dramatic plunge since abortion was legalised. But how much of this decline is simply due to the legalisation and how much is part of a long-term decline in such deaths is difficult to establish. Moreover, *a number of studies do indicate some risk of reproductive complications following abortion*, especially in the case of repeated abortions (e.g. ectopic pregnancies), and *serious psychological distress* in some cases.

Adapted from: *Essential Catholicism*

CAN ABORTION BE JUSTIFIED ON MEDICAL GROUNDS?

Study I

In the decade 1970 - 1979, there were 74,317 births and 28 maternal deaths recorded at the National Maternity Hospital Holles Street, Dublin. Dr K. Driscoll and Dr J.F. Murphy examined every case in which the mother died. Their findings were as follows:

(1) While (a) assuming that an expectant mother is willing to accept appropriate medical care, and

(b) not offering an opinion as to the subsequent physical and/or mental health of the mother beyond six weeks after the birth of the child, they stated:

> 'Women do not die because therapeutic abortion is not practised in Ireland.'

(2) There was no recorded case of suicide committed by a pregnant woman.

> 'The finding in regard to suicide is not peculiar to Ireland. A study in 1963 of 294 Swedish women who were refused abortion did not find a single case of suicide or attempted suicide, though one in ten had made a threat of suicide during the period that their application for abortion was being considered.'

CPIS

(3) Only one of the twenty-eight women who died was a single mother.

> 'One can but speculate as to the likelihood of finding no case of suicide in a representative sample of 74,317 women in similar age who are not pregnant, but there is surely no support here for the growing emphasis on emotional stress as an indication for termination of pregnancy. Nor do the facts support the contention that unmarried mothers are especially vulnerable.'

Irish Medical Journal, August 1982.

QUESTION

In your own words, explain why Dr Driscoll and Dr Murphy concluded that 'women do not die because therapeutic abortion is not practised in Ireland'.

Study II

> 'In each of the three large Dublin maternity hospitals, an audit of obstetric practice and performance takes place each year. These reports are subjected to external scrutiny by a distinguished member of the speciality at a meeting convened by the Royal Academy of Medicine in Ireland held in either the College of Physicians or the College of Surgeons.
>
> A recent report on a seven-year review at the Coombe Hospital, Dublin, shows that there were 51,343 mothers delivered at the

hospital between 1985 and 1991 inclusive. No death could be attributed to the withholding of medical treatment for any reason. During that period 134 cardiac cases and 979 cases of essential hypertension were successfully delivered at the hospital, again without any maternal death.

During the same period, 52,331 mothers were delivered at the National Maternity Hospital, Holles Street, and 45, 619 at the Rotunda Hospital. There was no death associated with essential hypertension at either hospital during that period, nor was there 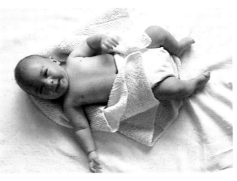 *any death associated with cardiac disease at the Rotunda. There was one cardiac death at Holles Street, but this was due to an extremely unusual event, the rupture of a patent ductus arteriosus, which could not have been predicted.*

The care and dedication of Irish obstetricians and our consultant colleagues in related disciplines whose expertise has enabled us to bring babies into the world in difficult circumstances is widely acknowledged. In the most recent seven-year period for which figures are available, 1984-1990, the maternal mortality rate in Ireland has been consistently lower than that reported in England and Wales.'

Extract from letter signed by 31 leading members of the
medical profession, in *The Irish Times*, 16.11.1992.

In 1993 a UNICEF survey concluded that Ireland was the safest country in the world for women giving birth. This is a remarkable testimony to the skill and care found in Irish maternity hospitals.

Irish Medical News, 11.7.1994

QUESTION

According to this letter and the recent UNICEF report, would the availability of therapeutic abortion have had an effect on the maternal mortality rate in the three large Dublin maternity hospitals during the period for which the latest figures are available?

Give reasons for your answer.

WHY DO SOME IRISH WOMEN CHOOSE TO HAVE AN ABORTION?

- For some women it seems to offer the best solution to a distressing personal problem, especially in cases of pregnancy due to rape or incest.

- Sometimes economic hardship and/or pregnancy late in married life may lead some women to believe that abortion provides the only solution to their problems.

- In some cases powerful pressure is applied to the pregnant women by another interested party. This can be the father of the unborn child, her relatives, or perhaps those from whom she may seek advice.

- The single pregnant women is often fearful of the future. She is frequently abandoned by the father of the unborn child or rejected by her own family. She is vulnerable. Her decision to have an abortion is often taken in desperation and against her own moral beliefs. It is a decision which can be bitterly regretted later.

THE MORALITY OF ABORTION

Abortion is not simply a 'Catholic issue', though it is sometimes presented as such. It concerns people of all religions and those who do not belong to any religion. Why? Because abortion is fundamentally a *human rights issue.*

The Catholic Church has always officially condemned any directly willed and procured abortion as an objective, serious sin.

> *'An embryo or foetus is actually a living human being, and therefore no other human being has the right to terminate this life. In the United States, Great Britain, and in many other countries, abortions are allowed by law. Nevertheless the Church teaches that abortion is wrong because it takes away a defenceless human being's right to life. Abortion violates the fifth commandment.'*
>
> R. Ekstrom, *Concise Catholic Dictionary.*

QUESTION

Why does the Catholic Church condemn any directly willed or procured abortion?

CATHOLIC ACTION ON ABORTION

In April 1972, the Catholic Bishop of the diocese of Shrewsbury, England, made the following offer of help to women faced with the abortion choice:

> *'We recognise that, for one reason or another, a pregnancy can cause a problem, distress, shame, despair to some mothers. Perhaps in our concern to uphold the sanctity of life, we have failed to show sufficient practical concern for the mother-to-be who feels herself to be in an intolerable situation. That is all over.*
>
> *This Diocese publicly declares its solemn guarantee. It is this: any mother-to-be, Catholic or non-Catholic, is guaranteed immediate and practical help, confidentially and at no expense to herself if, faced with the dilemma of an unwanted pregnancy, she is prepared to allow the baby to be born and not aborted.*
>
> *This help includes, if she wishes, the care for her baby after birth. All the resources of the diocese are placed behind this pledge.'*

Established by the Irish Catholic hierarchy, *CURA* offers all that the Shrewsbury diocese offers. *CURA* is a national network of support funded largely by Church resources with a grant from the Department of Health. *CURA* offers information, advice and counselling to any woman, married or single, with an unwanted pregnancy. The confidential telephone service is staffed by people experienced in handling situations of this kind and works in close liaison with other services throughout the country. It also offers help to women who have had an abortion but who later regret doing so.

Telephone contact numbers can be found in your local directory and on posters displayed in your local parish church.

QUESTIONS

1 What services does *CURA* offer to all women faced with an unplanned pregnancy?

2 Why is there a moral obligation on Catholic Christians to offer such help?

DIFFICULT CASES AND ISSUES

(a) Where a woman is the victim of rape:

'Rape is a horrendous crime. It is difficult to express adequately the deep feeling of shock and hurt experienced by the victims and their families. Rape is a brutal assault on the dignity of women and because it totally separates sex from love. Sex is a language which of its nature speaks of love. If instead it speaks of violence and humiliation, as it does in the case of rape, it becomes perverse.

Because it is an act of violence the victim has a right to seek medical help with a view to preventing conception. Immediate intervention to remove the semen and prevent fertilisation is morally right. They are part of a woman's legitimate resistance to the rapist's attack and the medical procedure used is not an abortion; conception has not yet taken place. It is only in extremely rare cases, in fact, that conception does result from rape. If it does, however, a new human being then exists whose right to life must be protected. This innocent human being cannot rightly be made to pay the penalty of death for a man's crime in violating the woman.

The situation of a woman violently placed in such a cruel dilemma demands great understanding; but it would be no service to her, nor to truth and justice, to destroy the new life within her on the plea of allaying her anguish. An act of violence is not appeased by a second act of violence.'

Adapted from: *The Catholic Church and Abortion* (CPIO)

(b) Where there is danger of death of the mother:

'The abortion that must be judged always unacceptable to the upright moral conscience is the direct abortion, i.e. those procedures and techniques that are intended to stop the unborn child's continuing development. We are not speaking of cases where the interference with the unborn child is in fact an unintended, though foreseen, side-effect of

procedures necessary to save the mother from some condition that threatens her life. For example, a treatment for cancer of the uterus can be justified even if it also causes a miscarriage. Even in such cases, however, it is the doctor's duty to regard both the mother and the unborn child as his patients, and to try to sustain the pregnancy so long as there is any reasonable prospect of saving both of them.'

Abortion and the Right to Life,
Catholic Archbishops of Great Britain.

QUESTIONS

1   What medical assistance is a rape victim morally entitled to and should be given as soon as possible after suffering such a horrific assault?

2   (a) Why does Catholic Christian teaching oppose abortion in the case of rape?

   (b) Do you agree/disagree? Why?

3   (a) Why does Catholic Christian teaching state that medical intervention in a case of cancer of the uterus, for example, is morally justified?

   (b) Do you agree/disagree? Why?

ABORTION AND THE LAW IN IRELAND

(The law on abortion in Ireland is stated as at date of publication.)

Illegal abortion
The destruction of an unborn child by means of an unlawful miscarriage is a serious offence under the Offences against the Person Act, 1861, and is punishable by penal servitude for life.

Legal abortion
Where there is a real and substantial risk to the life of a mother which can only be avoided by the termination of a pregnancy then such termination is permissible. The Supreme Court has so ruled arising out of the *Attorney General v 'X'* and other cases.

Constitution, Article 40, s.3
Under the Constitution the State acknowledges:

(i) the right to life of the unborn child, with due regard to the equal right to life of the mother;

(ii) a woman is free to travel abroad for an abortion;

(iii) the freedom to receive and impart information on abortion subject to such conditions as may be laid down by law.

ACTIVITY

Choices and their consequences:

1 In each case below, state the consequences of each choice for: (a) the woman, and (b) her child.

2 Then assess the implications of these consequences for both of them.

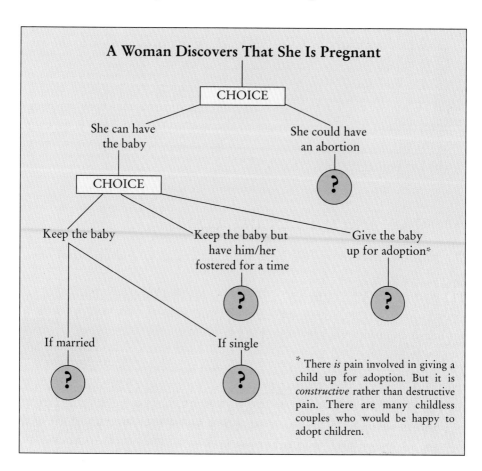

A Woman Discovers That She Is Pregnant

CHOICE

She can have the baby

She could have an abortion ?

CHOICE

Keep the baby

Keep the baby but have him/her fostered for a time ?

Give the baby up for adoption* ?

If married ?

If single ?

* There *is* pain involved in giving a child up for adoption. But it is *constructive* rather than destructive pain. There are many childless couples who would be happy to adopt children.

'ABORTION CULTURE': THE BRITISH EXPERIENCE

In 1967, the British Parliament passed an act permitting abortion. Thirty years later, the editor of the *Daily Mail* newspaper made the following comment:

'Consider. When the Abortion Act was being debated, Parliament was assured that it would apply only in the agonising circumstances of rape, incest, severe disability or a serious threat to the mother's health.

So much for assurances. Since 1967, more than four million terminations have been carried out in this country, a figure which suggests that abortion on demand is now the norm. Some 3,000 women submit to the operation every week. In the overwhelming majority of cases — 98 per cent — abortions are done on "social" grounds.

An abortion culture now holds sway. Indeed it is extending its grip, as advances in genetics mean that the slightest foetal "imperfections" can be spotted early, adding to the pressure for a supposedly easy way out.'

Daily Mail, 10.3.1997.

QUESTIONS

1 What does the editor say was the original intention of the 1967 Abortion Act?

2 What percentage of abortions are claimed to be conducted now for these reasons?

3 (a) Why does the editor maintain that '*an abortion culture now holds sway*'?

(b) Why do you think that this has happened?

THE ARGUMENTS FOR AND AGAINST ABORTION

For:

(1) The rights of the mother. Her right to choose. Medically and legally the embryo and foetus are parts of the mother's body. Since it is her body it is also her choice.

Against:

(1) The right of the defenceless unborn child to live. God is the only giver, sustainer and taker away of life (*Acts* 17:25,28). *Only God* can decide matters of life and death. Mother's right to her body

not denied. Biologically, the foetus is someone else's body.

(2) More a woman's issue than a man's. It is the woman who has been made pregnant, perhaps without her consent.

(2) The fundamental issue at stake is the life of the unborn child. The responsibility of defending human life devolves *equally* on men and women.

(3) Compassion towards mother and/or rest of family.

(3) Compassion on one person's distress cannot justify the taking of another person's life.

(4) Rape and incest are tragedies enough in themselves, without adding an unwanted child.

(4) The fact that an illegal, unwanted, sexual act has taken place is *not* sufficient ground for taking a life. One action that is wrong should not lead to another that is also wrong.

(5) The loss of 'quality of life' in the case of a severely handicapped child. The pressure on parents.

(5) If admitted, this argument could equally be used to justify infanticide, euthanasia and suicide. The 'defective' child is *no less a human being*. Who has the right to eliminate his/her life?

Adapted from CARE and LIFE

QUESTIONS

1 List the above arguments for and against abortion in what you consider to be their order of importance. Then give reasons for your choice.

2 Examine the arguments for and against abortion in the light of the evidence presented.

   Which argument do you find the most convincing, the argument for abortion or that against it?

   Give reasons for your choice.

CHAPTER 28

Sexism

WHAT IS SEXISM?

Sexism may be defined as

> 'belief in the superiority of one's own sex, often accompanied by a stereotype or preconceived idea about the opposite sex. Sexism may also be accompanied by discrimination on the basis of sex, generally as practised by men against women.'
>
> Webster's New World Encyclopaedia.

The term sexism was first used in the 1960s by feminist writers to describe any language or behaviour that implied women were inferior to men, for example the use of a male pronoun to describe both men and women, and the assumption that some jobs should be typically performed only by one sex.

QUESTIONS

Read the following quotations taken from the writings of influential men over the last two and a half thousand years:

• *'The female is a female by virtue of a certain lack of qualities.'*

Aristotle

• *'Women should remain at home, keep house, bear and bring up children.'*

Martin Luther.

• *'A man neither consults women about, nor trusts them with, serious matters.'*

The Earl of Chesterfield.

• *'What a misfortune it is to be a woman.'*

Soren Kierkegaard.

In your opinion,

(1) What view of women is conveyed by these statements?

(2) What, do you think, was the intention behind such comments? Explain your answer.

THE GLOBAL SITUATION

Women are half of the earth's population, and yet:

- Two out of every three illiterate people are women, because of their lack of educational opportunities.

- Women work two-thirds of the world's working-hours, receive one-tenth of the income and own one-hundredth of the property.

- While women everywhere are overburdened in the home, in poor countries they are also the main food producers.

> '*If woman's work were accurately reflected in national statistics it would shatter the myth that men are the main breadwinners in the world...*'
> **Mr Muhbub ul Haq**, *leader of a team which conducted a UN Human Development Report*, (1996).

But most of the technology, finance and training in agriculture is given to men.

- Even in Third World primary schools there are only five girls for every seven boys.

So lack of education and heavy responsibilities keep women isolated and weak — unable to get together to take their rightful share.

- Violations of the human rights of women and girl children are extensive and severe. Many women are targeted because they are leaders in the struggle for freedom and justice. Others are victimised because they are seen to be vulnerable, because they can be used to put pressure on male relatives, or because of the inferior status of women in their societies. Some are imprisoned, tortured and killed simply because they were in the wrong place at the wrong time.

- The Catholic Bishops of Korea, for example, have condemned the killing of unborn female babies due to South Koreans' preference for male children. About 22,400 female babies are reportedly killed yearly by abortion following gender testing. The bishops have called for an end to this culture of death.

CASE STUDY: THE STATUS OF WOMEN IN HINDUISM

Women are *not* accepted as the equals of men in the Hindu religion, although it does insist that women *should* be treated with love and respect. An example of this inequality is that:

> '*Only a son can perform the funeral rites which provide the soul of his dead father with a new spiritual body with which to pass on to the next life.*'

Myrtle Langley, World Religions.

Due to the influence of Islam in the twelfth century, Muslim women in Northern India have had to veil their faces and have had numerous restrictions placed upon their movements.

Although modern India has raised the status of Hindu women, many of the 'village Hindus' still retain traditional beliefs and downgrade the role of women. Initiation into the Hindu religion and the stages of life are often applied only to males. Among the guidelines for women's behaviour, traditional Hindu beliefs state that:

(1) A female must always be *submissive*, as a daughter to her father, as a wife to her husband, as a widow to her sons.

(2) A good wife is one who is always cheerful, efficient, willing to do her husband's bidding and never does anything which might offend him.

(3) After her husband dies, a good woman will *never re-marry* or even mention the name of another man.

(4) A wife has *no right to her husband's property*; anything she might acquire automatically belongs to *him* and once he dies, all his property passes on to his *male heirs*.

QUESTIONS

1 In your own words, describe the Hindu view of women.

2 What, do you think, are the *consequences* of this view for Hindu women? Explain your answer.

THE STATUS OF WOMEN IN IRELAND

Under Irish law:

Women demanding the right to vote in England in 1914

- women over 18 years are entitled to vote;

- women may stand for election to the Dáil and Seanad;

- women are entitled to equal pay for work of equal value;

- women have equal employment opportunities and cannot be discriminated against on the basis of gender.

QUESTIONS

1 Identify those women who are currently playing important roles in the economic, political, religious and social life of the state.

2 In your opinion, does this indicate an improvement in the status of women generally in Irish society? Before answering, read the following extracts:

(a) *'The hard sociological reality, however, is that the vast majority of positions in the middle and top ranks of business and public administration are held by men. Moreover, there are still parts of the country where "herself" thinks it best to say nothing.'*

Jim O'Donnell, *Wordgloss*

(b) *'After 20 years of equality legislation, the number of women in top jobs is abysmal. There is no political will to support the return of women to the workforce or even encourage married women to stay there. All the talk about equality is lip service. The evidence is that, today, we are no closer to providing childcare facilities than we were 20 years ago.'*

Dr Eileen Drew, *Sunday Tribune*, 1994.

3   In recent years, several leading campaigners for women's rights have described pornography as an assault on human dignity, especially that of women, and have called either for an outright ban or greater restrictions on its availability.

Do you agree/disagree that much of pornography is *anti-women*? Give reasons for your answer.

4   *'I do not wish women to have power over men; but over themselves.'*

Mary Wollstonecraft, *A Vindication of the Rights of Women*.

What, in your opinion, does women having 'power over themselves' mean? Explain your answer.

JESUS AND WOMEN IN THE NEW TESTAMENT

Jesus lived in a very sexist society where women were treated as second-class citizens. Yet, consider what the novelist Dorothy L. Sayers has to say about Jesus. She believes that no one can read through the *Gospels* without realising what a deep appreciation Jesus had for women.

Jesus and the Woman at the Well (John 4)

'They had never known a man like this Man — there never has been such another. A prophet and teacher who never nagged at them, never flattered or coaxed or patronised; who never made jokes about them; who rebuked without querulousness and praised without condescension; who took their questions and arguments seriously; who never mapped out their sphere for them, never urged them to be feminine or jeered at them for being

female; who had no axe to grind and no uneasy dignity to defend; who took them as he found them and was completely unselfconscious. There is no act, no sermon, no parable in the whole Gospel that could possibly lead one to guess from the words and deeds of Jesus that there was anything "funny" about woman's nature.'

Are Women Human?

QUESTION

Read the following scripture passages:

Mark 12:41–44.

Luke 8:1–3, and 10:38–42.

John 4:4–30, and 11:5 and 25–27.

Do you agree/disagree with Sayers' opinion? Give reasons for your answer.

CHRISTIAN TEACHING ON SEXISM

- 'The state of submission and oppression to which women are subjected in the world constitutes a sinful situation, something to correct. The Church must, in fidelity to the word of God, recognise the modern feminist movement as a positive reality. We are dealing on the whole, with an advance in civilisation; and it's a forward step in the establishment of the Kingdom.' **Canadian Hierarchy**, 1984.

- 'The feminist movement is one of the most significant in our time. In the phrase used by the Vatican Council, it must be seen as one of the *signs of the times* which the Church must read in our age. Indeed the equality of the sexes is basic Christian teaching. One of the important challenges facing the Church today is to develop a truly Christian feminism; and this task must fall primarily on women themselves, filled with the love of Christ and anxious to play their full part in the life of the Church.' **Irish Hierarchy**, 1985.

- 'It is a profound sin to label women as the source of evil in the world, as intellectually inferior, psychologically unstable and inclined to sensuality. Yet sexism does just that. When our actions do not conform to our ideals, all suffer. We therefore regret and confess our individual and collective failures to respond to women as they deserve. We call the People of God to join us in personal and corporate contrition for the sins of sexism that violate the basic tenets of our faith.' **Statement by the American Bishops**, 1988.

QUESTIONS

1 Why does the Catholic Church teach that sexism is '*a profound sin*'?
2 What role do you think the Catholic Church could play in combatting sexism in Irish society? Give examples.

CHAPTER 29

Ageism

WHAT IS AGEISM?

Since more than half the population of the Republic of Ireland is aged 29 years or younger, much public attention has understandably been focused on the needs and concerns of this age group. Unfortunately and inexcusably, far less attention has been focused on the needs of our *senior* citizens (i.e. those over 65 years).

Our society is tending, increasingly, to push our senior citizens aside. Many of them live alone, while many more reside in private or publicly funded homes for the elderly. All too often they are forgotten by their relatives. Some people treat them with contempt, considering them to be nuisances with nothing to contribute. This prejudice against our senior citizens is called *Ageism*.

Read the following poem. It was written by Kate. She spent her last two years in a hospital ward. She couldn't speak but, on occasions, she was noticed writing on a notepad. After she died, this poem was discovered in her bedside locker.

What Do You See?

What do you see nurses, what do you see?
Are you thinking, when you are looking at me:
A crabbit old woman, not very wise,
Uncertain of habit, with far-away eyes,
Who dribbles her food and makes no reply
When you say in a loud voice, 'I do wish you'd try.'
Who seems not to notice the things that you do

And forever is losing a stocking or shoe.
Who, unresisting or not, lets you do as you will,
With bathing and feeding the long day to fill.
Is that what you're thinking, is that what you see?
Then open your eyes, nurse, you're not looking at me.
I'll tell you who I am as I sit here so still,
As I use at your bidding, as I eat at your will.
I'm a small child of ten with a father and mother,
Brothers and sisters who love one another.
A young girl of sixteen with wings at her feet,
Dreaming that soon now a lover she'll meet.
A bride soon at twenty, my heart gives a leap,
Remembering the vows that I'd promised to keep.
At twenty-five now, I have young of my own,
Who need me to build a secure, happy home.
A young woman of thirty, my young now grow fast,
Bound to each other with ties that should last.
At forty my young ones now grown, will soon be gone,
But my man stays beside me to see I don't mourn.
At fifty once more babies play round my knee,
Again we know children, my loved one and me.
Dark days are upon me, my husband is dead,
I look at the future, I shudder with dread.
For my young are all busy rearing young of their own,
I think of the years and the love I have known.
I'm an old woman now, but nature is cruel,
'Tis her jest to make old age look like a fool.
The body it crumbles, grace and vigour depart,
There now is a stone, where I once had a heart,
But inside this old carcass, a young girl still dwells,
And now and again my battered heart swells.
I remember the joys, I remember the pain,
And I'm loving and living life over again.
I think of the years, all too few — gone too fast,
And accept the stark fact that nothing can last.
So open your eyes nurse, open and see,
Not a crabbit old woman, look closer — see ME.

QUESTIONS

1   What is 'ageism'?

2   What did Kate believe the nurses thought about her? Do you think they saw her as a person like them? Give reasons for your answer.

3   (a) What were the events in Kate's later life that caused those years to be dark days?

    (b) What kind of help should she have received during that time?

PROBLEMS ASSOCIATED WITH BEING ELDERLY

1. **Physical ageing**: There are no diseases that affect only people above a certain age, but there are some conditions which become increasingly common with advancing age. Both the major forms of arthritis are common — rheumatoid and osteoarthritis — and about half the strokes that occur happen in people over 75 years of age. Other ailments which occur include deafness, difficulty in understanding speech, poor memory and reduced mobility. The end result may often be complete dependence on other people.

2. **Hypothermia**: In the elderly, the part of the brain that controls body temperature is often less efficient than in younger people. In cold weather, body temperature can fall to dangerously low levels, and hypothermia is responsible for several premature deaths of elderly people each winter.

3. **Inadequate diet**: Old people are often malnourished, whether due to poor co-ordination, digestive problems, shopping difficulties or lack of money. Diet-related disorders, e.g. anaemia, osteoporosis, bowel disorders and scurvy, can occur if the diet is unbalanced.

4. **Reduced income**: If, as is often the case, no provision has been made for retirement or old age, the elderly must survive on the old age pension. Their standard of living may well therefore become lower than they have been accustomed to.

5. **Inadequate housing**: Accommodation for the elderly is often sub-standard, without even a private bathroom or kitchen, heating or telephone. It may be damp and in need of repair, and too often is located away from where the elderly person has lived all his/her life.

6. **Loneliness and social isolation**: While some old people remain alone by choice, others are forced to live alone because their families have emigrated, their spouse has died or they are unable to leave their homes for some reason. Loneliness may lead to depression and apathy.

7. **Fear**: Old people who live alone are vulnerable to attack, as they are not able to defend themselves. Some, especially in inner city or isolated areas, live in fear of being robbed and assaulted.

Information adapted from *School and College Magazine*.

QUESTIONS

1 The fourth commandment calls on people to '*Honour your father and your mother*'. What kind of response does this commandment call on people to make in the case of their aged relatives and neighbours? For example, in what ways might sheltered accommodation, which provides separate housing but has support and services on call if necessary, be one way forward?

2 '*The strain of caring for someone who needs help with feeding, washing and going to the toilet, who may sleep badly and need attention during the night as well as in the daytime can bring even a loving relative to the point of violence.*'

F. van Zwanenberg, *Caring for the Aged*.

What kind of support services should be made available to help those caring for an elderly relative?

3 What kind of quality of life do you hope for in your old age?

REFLECTION

Mother Teresa is credited with saying the great disease of our time is loneliness. She tells a story:

'*One day I visited a house where our sisters shelter the aged. This is one of the nicest houses in England, filled with beautiful and precious things. Yet there was not one smile on the faces of the people. All of them were looking towards the door.*

'*I asked the sister in charge: "Why are they like that?"*

241

'She answered: "They are always waiting for someone to come and visit them. Loneliness eats them up and day after day they do not stop looking. Nobody comes. Abandonment is an awful poverty."'

Colm Kilcoyne.

PROJECT

Find out more about the work of organisations involved in caring for the elderly such as: *ALONE, AOSTA, Friends of the Elderly* and *SHARE*.

CHAPTER 30

Drug Abuse

DYING FOR A 'FIX'

'*If you can imagine a young man, any age from twelve upwards, in a public toilet cubicle sharpening a hypodermic needle with a matchbox, and then drawing water from the toilet bowl, you have an idea of his lifestyle. He may even witness the death of a companion through overdosing. His first reaction will be almost certainly to search the dead person's pockets for money or drugs. It is important to understand that this is the level on which the addict operates. He has no scruples and is totally self-absorbed. His compulsion drives him on and that is all that matters. Witnessing the death of a friend does not frighten or deter him. His sole preoccupation is getting his next fix.*'

James Cumberton, *Drugs and Young People*.

WHAT IS A DRUG?

We may define a drug as:

'*any chemical which alters how the body works, or how a person behaves or feels.*'

WHAT IS DRUG ADDICTION?

When a person becomes either physically or mentally *dependent* on some chemical substance, it is said that he/she is a drug addict.

Drug abuse, whether it is of a *legal* substance (e.g. tobacco) or of an *illegal* substance (e.g. ecstasy), occurs in *all* social classes and age groups.

Drug addiction *is* a moral issue. Generally speaking, a person does not simply *become* an addict; he/she normally *chooses*, for a variety of reasons, to take drugs, sometimes out of ignorance but more often in spite of knowing the dangers involved. When faced with an offer designed to lead him/her into abusing drugs, a person must choose to either accept or reject the offer. It is true, however, that a person's upbringing and circumstances can have a serious effect on his/her ability to make a good moral decision about drugs. If a person accepts and begins to abuse drugs, his/her physical or psychological dependence on them makes any attempt to break free of their hold very difficult, though *not* impossible.

DRUG USE AND DRUG ABUSE

Drugs are of positive value when they are prescribed by a doctor to help someone recover from an illness or to cope with severe pain due to an injury or terminal illness. A problem arises, however, when a person decides to '*prescribe*' a drug for him/herself and engages in drug abuse.

WHY ABUSE DRUGS?

Despite all the recent publicity about the hazards of drug abuse, of how it can lead to a nightmarish existence for both the addict and those who love him/her, too many people are still prepared to put their lives in jeopardy. When questioned by a reporter about his drug abuse, a young Dubliner in his early twenties replied:

'Taking ecstasy was the best thing I've ever done in my life. For the first time it doesn't matter that I haven't got a job and don't have any money. It's heaven on earth for five hours.'
Irish Independent, 18.3.1992.

QUESTIONS

1 Read the young man's statement carefully once more. What, in your view, are his reasons for abusing drugs? Explain your answer.

2 Do you think that his abuse of the drug known as 'ecstasy' brings him *any nearer* a solution to his problems? Give reasons for your answer.

3 Examine the following chart.

Which of the reasons given (p. 245) do *you* think provide the strongest reason for entry into the drugs scene? Give reasons for your answer.

Database

The reasons young people use drugs

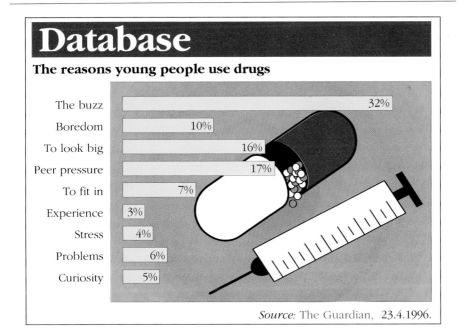

Reason	Percentage
The buzz	32%
Boredom	10%
To look big	16%
Peer pressure	17%
To fit in	7%
Experience	3%
Stress	4%
Problems	6%
Curiosity	5%

Source: The Guardian, 23.4.1996.

Common Drugs

Stimulants	Sedatives
Effects of Use	*Effects of Use*
Produce an increase in physical and mental activity. They range from mild stimulants such as nicotine and caffeine to strong stimulants such as cocaine and amphetamines. Weight-reducing drugs are also part of this group.	Reduce feelings of anxiety and tension, e.g. alcohol, sleeping tablets, tranquillisers, anti-depressants. A person on prescribed medication should consult his/her doctor before altering the dose.
Effects of Abuse	*Effects of Abuse*
Physical and mental hyperactivity. Feelings of confidence and superiority. Effects depend on user's mood and amount taken.	Slurred speech, staggering, lack of co-ordination.
Risks	*Risks*
Anxiety, panic attacks, depression, fatigue, dependence and overdose.	Overdose with risk of death, particularly if combined with alcohol. Dependence may occur with regular use.

Hallucinogens	Opiates
Effects of Use	*Effects of Use*
May distort reality and cause hallucinations, e.g. LSD, inhalants/ solvents, magic mushrooms. N.B. Even one experiment with solvents may be be fatal.	Pain-relieving drugs derived from the opium poppy. They include heroin, opium, morphine, codeine, as well as the synthetic opiates. Of value in the medical treatment of severe pain.
Effects of Abuse	*Effects of Abuse*
Hallucinations, paranoia, confusion of time and distance, disturbance of reality.	Drowsiness, slowing down of mental and physical activity, detachment from reality.
Risks	*Risks*
Personality change, psychosis, memory loss, accidental injury, death.	Physical and psychological dependence. Physical debilitation due to neglect of health. Infection from using and sharing unclean needles, e.g. Hepatitis B, HIV/AIDS. Risk of overdose and death.

CANNABIS, derived from the cannabis sativa plant, has both sedative and hallucinogenic properties. Its effects depend on the strength of the drug, as well as the mood and personality of the user and the frequency of use.

It comes in three forms: (1) Marijuana (grass) — the leaves and fruiting tops of the plant; (2) Hashish (hash) — resin extracted from the plant; (3) Hashish oil — a further concentration extract. The active ingredient in cannabis is THC (tetrahydrocannabinol). THC remains in the fatty tissue of the brain and reproductive organs for up to several weeks.

Effects of Abuse

Intoxication, impaired judgment and concentration, risk of accidents, fatigue, mood swings, loss of interest in school or work, impairment of memory and learning ability.

Risks

- Increased risk of mental disturbance.
- Increased risk of cancer.
- Adverse effect on male and female reproductive systems.
- Maternal cannabis use during pregnancy may affect the foetus.
- Psychological dependence.

ECSTASY is a manufactured drug which can produce effects similar to both stimulant drugs and hallucinogenic drugs like LSD. Users take the drug in expectation of pleasurable effects.

Effects of abuse

The effects of ecstasy are unpredictable and may result in mental disturbance, confusion, anxiety, panic and depression lasting for several weeks.

Risks

- Ecstasy may cause brain damage and even death.
- Dependence may occur with regular use.

Department of Health

Case One

'The Hug Drug'

Ten years ago doctors in Dublin hospitals' accident and emergency units had never even seen an Ecstasy tablet, let alone tried to resuscitate a teenager suffering from a heart attack after swallowing one of the tiny pills at a disco. Now Ecstasy-induced emergencies make up over 10% of all overdose patients rushed to the city's hospitals.

According to Dr Eamon Keenan, who has co-written a report for the National Drug Treatment Centre based on a study of patients being brought into Dublin accident and emergency departments for drug misuse, those who recover from the physical side-effects — heatstroke, cardiac and respiratory failure and kidney damage — are in danger of developing psychiatric problems at a later stage. In fact, some adolescent Ecstasy patients treated by Dr Keenan are already faced with having to undergo psychiatric treatment or remain in rehabilitation centres for years to come.

A non-addictive synthetic stimulant and hallucinogenic amphetamine, Ecstasy is fast becoming the most popular recreational drug, after cannabis, among the under-30s. But Ecstasy is unpredictable, dangerous and, according to American neuroscientists, can do lasting damage to the brain by reducing the level of at least one neurotransmitter.

Its use is most prevalent among those aged between 15 and 22 and has already led to fatalities. However, while gardai have made numerous Ecstasy seizures recently, doctors are anxious that youngsters be educated about the dangers of the so-called 'hug drug'.

All over the country, Dr Keenan warns, young people are ingesting the small white, brown or black and red capsules. And he says some users, concerned about having to return home to their parents in a state of artificial excitement, have now begun to smoke heroin in order to 'come down'.

'Ecstasy is available everywhere,' Dr Keenan says, 'its use has spread all over the country. Initially it was associated with acid house parties and rave parties in inner city Dublin but it's quite quickly spread right throughout the whole country. It's not just confined to raves or discos, it's in colleges, schools and nightclubs.'

Scottish authorities held an official inquiry after the Ecstasy-related deaths of three young men who attended the Hangar 13 rave club in Ayr, Strathclyde. It concluded in February 1995 that Ecstasy is 'a dangerous, unpredictable stimulant' *capable of leading young people into a* 'dance with death'.

A doctor who had tried to save one of those who died in Ayr, an 18-year-old, discovered that the young man's heartbeat was three times the normal rate and his brain was not functioning normally. His bodily functions had entirely collapsed. Another died from respiratory failure and pulmonary oedema (fluid in the lungs) while the other died from pulmonary oedema and kidney failure. The same thing is happening and will continue to happen, according to Dr Keenan, and yet 'some people believe that it is a safe drug.'

The detrimental physical side-effects of taking the drug occur when the body temperature rockets to up to 107 degrees Fahrenheit. In the stifling conditions of a rave or nightclub, particularly given the increased desire to dance, this causes life-threatening heatstroke, dehydration and renal failure. Users are being admitted to hospitals around the country with acute renal failure. But there are also psychiatric problems.

'We do know you don't have to be a heavy user of Ecstasy over a long time to get adverse consequences: you may get it only after using it a few times. People are coming in with anxiety states, panic attacks, depressive illnesses and with psychoses, where the person shows a loss of touch with reality, or is paranoid after Ecstasy or having visual or auditory hallucinations,' says Dr Keenan.

Now senior registrar in psychiatry at Cork University Hospital, he previously treated one 17-year-old who had taken one to two Ecstasy tablets a week over five months. He was admitted to hospital complaining of cold sweats, vomiting, palpitations and disturbing thoughts. He exhibited paranoid delusions about his family, whom he claimed were watching him and bugging his room, and suggested that they may be putting unknown substances in his food. It was diagnosed as a paranoid psychosis.

'*When these psychoses become chronic it is very worrying. That person will be attending psychiatric services over a long period of time and will require medication. They will lose their job and end up in a long-term psychiatric unit.*'

For as many as five days afterwards, a young person who has taken just one Ecstasy tablet can experience adverse consequences such as inability to sleep or eat and a deep depressed mood. But what the naive young ravers don't know is that US neuroscientists at John Hopkins University in Baltimore have discovered that Ecstasy selectively damages brain cells that contain the neurotransmitter serotonin, which is associated with mood. By analysing fluid drained by spinal taps, they found lower levels of serotonin in Ecstasy users (the subjects had taken Ecstasy on average only nine times over five years). These changes do not seem to be reversible.

Helen Callanan, *The Sunday Tribune*, April 1995.

Questions

1 What is the scientific name for '*Ecstasy*'?

2 What are the detrimental side-effects of Ecstasy noted by Dr Keenan?

3 What have neuro-scientists at John Hopkins University discovered about the effects of Ecstasy use?

Case Two

Marijuana: The 'Safe' Drug?

Some people believe that the use of marijuana is 'no big deal', that it is safer to use than one of the more sinister drugs — ecstasy, heroin or cocaine.

It is well documented that heavy smoking of cannabis can cause lung cancer, but it is now apparently accepted that, in moderation, this is a harmless drug. Nothing could be further from the truth.

Jessie Hawkins is just 17, but she has been a psychiatric patient in a Manchester hospital for the past four months, detained under section three of the UK's Mental Health Act. To the horror of her middle-class parents, she has been diagnosed as suffering from 'marijuana-induced psychosis'.

Her mother, Margaret — devastated by the fate of her daughter — admits that although she has never tried cannabis herself, she believed it to be the lesser of many evils.

When she first discovered her daughter (then 14) and friends using it, Margaret took the view that if this was going to happen, it was better for them to be smoking somewhere safe rather than on the streets. She did what some parents would be tempted to do and turned a blind eye, which she now regrets.

'Jessie's breakdown happened very suddenly,' says Margaret. 'Within 24 hours, she began to speak in a confused, disordered way. She was having terrible hallucinations, and it was as though she could see demons all around her.'

When Jessie showed no signs of improvement, Margaret called in the family doctor, who confirmed she had been smoking cannabis. He said no other drugs were involved and told her parents she would soon calm down. Instead, they went through three days of hell.

'It was extremely distressing and frightening for my two younger daughters,' says Margaret. 'Jessie was becoming increasingly aggressive and had alarming paranoia. My husband and I were beside ourselves with worry.'

Finally, they decided that their GP had got it wrong and contacted psychiatric services. They were given an urgent referral and Jessie ended up in hospital under an observation order. Her psychiatrist told her parents that her breakdown was due to marijuana-induced psychosis. Now, four months on, she is still taking anti-psychotic medication.

'The doctors cannot give us any realistic prognosis, but they say it won't be a matter of months; it is going to take a long time for her to get better,' says Margaret.

Christopher Luke, consultant in the accident and emergency department at the Royal Liverpool University hospital, confirms that Jessie's reaction to this so-called 'soft' drug is not unusual.

'Cannabis is certainly not the benign drug it is perceived to be and it is not infrequent to see cases of psychosis in youngsters. In the late teens, any tendencies towards mental-health problems such as schizophrenia or

mania are likely to surface, so one can never be sure if a mental illness was already there, waiting to be triggered or whether this psychosis is due solely to drugs.

'I am totally against legalising marijuana for recreational use. Believe me, it is a very dangerous drug. Even when smoked on a weekend-only, recreational basis it can impair your natural biological drives in every way: job prospects, social communication and ambition can all be hampered, and people who are vulnerable to its properties may become profoundly ill.'

Luke, like 70% of doctors, remains adamant that the use of cannabis in medicine is still justified, but stresses that smoking a joint is not the same as taking a prescribed tablet. The difference is subtle but significant: when used in medicine, the drug acts more as a muscle relaxant. The key constituent is the chemical tetrahydrocannabinol, which is distilled from the cannabis plant. Although it has a therapeutic effect, it is certainly not the same as smoking a joint.

Ben Empson, 22, a psychology student who lives in Nottingham, says his reaction to the drug was so bad he thought there was something seriously askew with his mind. At his lowest point, he even tried to commit suicide.

'When my psychiatrist first suggested my problems could stem from smoking dope, I didn't believe him. I had never been psychotic as such, but I was incredibly depressed. I stopped smoking dope and one day, after a few months, I woke up and felt as though a fog had lifted.'

Empson says he no longer has anything to do with any drugs. His story will strike a chord with William Staccy, now 29, who also dropped out of university after only a year. He, too, says the drug made it almost impossible to study or work. 'I'd smoke a joint as soon as I woke up, have my cornflakes and switch on the television to find that I'd missed most of the day.'

Staccy, who is now a carpenter, had a breakdown in 1989 when, over a period of three weeks, he became delusional and hyperactive. 'I couldn't sleep and I didn't eat. My whole mind was animated and everything took on untold significance. Finally, I just couldn't handle it. I flipped and was sectioned, because, apparently, I was becoming threatening to others.'

After a week in hospital, Staccy was sent home — with no aftercare. He went straight back to his habit of smoking cannabis until his parents, baffled by his condition, sent him to see a private psychiatrist who diagnosed cannabis-induced psychosis.

The Institute for the Study of Drug Dependence says that 'skunk' — a relatively new strain of cannabis which is as hallucinogenic as LSD — has flooded the market and could be responsible for some cases of psychosis.

Detective Inspector Barry Cooper, head of the UK's National Criminal Intelligence Service Drugs Unit, says: 'By using certain horticultural techniques, the strength of cannabis can be increased. You have a product that is certainly two or three times the strength of ordinary herbal cannabis.'

Smart dealers are now said to be cashing in on people's fear of impure ecstasy, and are offering high-purity cannabis instead.

'Any drug, including alcohol, has potentially negative psychological effects,' says Michael Farrell. 'We know that the use of cannabis is addictive, because many do go on to use it habitually.'

Margaret Hawkins says she is utterly convinced that her daughter's illness is solely due to her drug use: 'There is no history of mental health problems whatsoever in our family and, since this has happened, I have talked to many others who have been through the same thing with their children.'

The Sunday Times, 27.4.1997.

QUESTIONS

1   What is marijuana? (See Department of Health diagram.)

2   What do you understand by the expression *'marijuana-induced psychosis'*? Give examples drawn from the text.

3   What is *'skunk'*?

4   Why does Michael Farrell describe marijuana as *addictive*?

5   (a) What reasons does Dr Christopher Luke advance for opposing the legalisation of marijuana?

    (b) Do you agree/disagree with him? Explain your answer.

Case Three

Crack comes to the nursery
'When reports surfaced in the early 1980s that cocaine use by pregnant

women could cause serious physical and mental damage to their unborn babies, it was another warning that the snowy white drug was not as harmless as some believed. Doctors found that cocaine, like heroin and alcohol, could be passed from the user-mother to the foetus with disastrous results. Since then the epidemic of cocaine-addicted babies has only become worse. The main reason: growing numbers of women are using "crack", the cheap and readily available purified form of cocaine.

Snorting cocaine

A study of 36 US hospitals found that at least 11 per cent of the 155,000 pregnant women surveyed had exposed their unborn babies to illegal drugs. In 1988, one inner-city hospital recorded that 20 per cent of all babies born had been afflicted by crack.

As doctors see more and more crack-damaged infants, many of them premature, a clearer picture of the effects of the drug on the child in the mother's womb is emerging. It is not a pretty one. Because a mother's crack binge triggers spasms in the baby's blood vessels, the vital flow of oxygen and nutrients can be severely restricted for long periods. Foetal growth, including head and brain size, may be impaired, strokes and seizures may occur, and malformations of the kidneys, genitals and spinal cord may develop. If the cocaine dose is large enough, the blood supply can be cut so sharply that the placenta may tear away from the uterus, putting the mother in danger of killing the foetus. The horrid litany is not just the result of binges. Even one 'hit' of crack can irreparably damage a baby.

At birth the babies display obvious signs of crack exposure — tremors, irritability and lethargy. These symptoms may disappear in a week or more, but the underlying damage remains. These children have lower than normal IQs and are prone to long bouts of inconsolable crying.

Crack mothers who show up at hospitals have often smoked up to the last stages of labour. Many are so high that they do not notice when labour begins. As one doctor put it:

"The crack cocaine mothers are the sickest you're going to see. They come in right when they're ready to deliver, and you just hold your breath waiting to see what you're going to get."'

Adapted from *Time* Magazine, 19.9.1988.

QUESTIONS

1 When asked by a *Time* reporter why she had taken the drug and caused her unborn child to be brain-damaged, one young woman broke down in tears and replied:

'In the back of my mind I knew I was hurting my baby, but in the front of it I needed more of the drug.'

Again, when questioned by an *Irish Independent* reporter who had discovered that pure ecstasy is often mixed with other drugs like heroin and LSD, and even substances such as embalming fluids, detergents and rat poison, before being sold in tablet form, one drug pusher admitted:

'Half the time I don't know exactly what I am selling, so the kids sure as hell don't have a clue what they are buying. The majority of people at raves are so young and eager to get high that they don't care how.'

Report dated 18.3.1992.

What have you learned about the power and impact of drug abuse?

Give reasons for your answer.

2 Why, in your opinion, are so many people prepared to place their trust in the 'product' a drug pusher offers them? Explain your answer.

'Don't Be Afraid To Say No'

From my experience as State Solicitor conducting criminal prosecutions I am satisfied that over 80 per cent of crime, particularly juvenile crime, is in some way connected with alcohol abuse or drug abuse. Young people are getting involved in crime under the influence of drugs as well as having to steal and deal in drugs to feed their own habits.

It is a complete fallacy to say that drugs (even drugs such as cannabis, or so called 'designer' drugs such as ecstasy) are harmless, or can be justified. All drugs become habit forming either chemically or psychologically. Much publicity is being given to people who are trying to justify or legitimise drug-taking, but these are either users or dealers trying to justify their operation, or people otherwise making a profit from drugs.

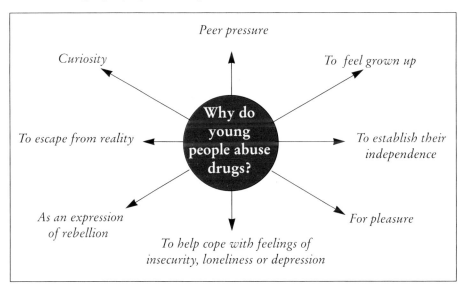

Throughout Ireland now, more particularly in the big cities, there is a huge drug culture, and drugs are being offered widely to younger and younger age groups. I have conducted prosecutions against people selling in school yards and outside schools, even primary schools. I have seen instances of 12-year-old children calling to drug dealers' houses to collect 'deals' and using 3 and 4-year-old brothers and sisters to actually carry the drugs to escape Garda detection.

Don't be afraid to say no when offered drugs.

The person offering you the drugs is either trying to make money for himself, trying to take advantage of you, or on the basis that 'misery loves company', trying to drag you into his stupefied circle.

Don't be afraid to say no if you are being pressurised to sell drugs, even one or two deals or tabs.

The maximum sentence for drug dealing is life imprisonment. In most areas even first-time dealers get jail sentences. If you are convicted of drugs offences you can never get a visa to go abroad to America or anywhere else.

Don't be afraid to say no if you are already involved.

Get out of the vicious circle. Go to your parents. Go to the Gardaí. If you go voluntarily to the Gardaí and explain your problems and help them to prevent further drug dealing, you will almost certainly not be prosecuted and you will get every help and assistance.

Don't be afraid to say no to drug dealing in your presence, in your school or in your club.

More particularly never act as a courier. It may sound like easy money — £1,000, £2,000, £5,000 is more money than you could ever imagine yourself getting lawfully. The personal dangers are enormous. There have been a number of deaths, including a young man from the outskirts of Cork whose young life was tragically ended when drugs he was carrying inside him burst in their packages. It is almost certain that drugs barons or 'minders' were on the plane with him. If they had not been so cowardly

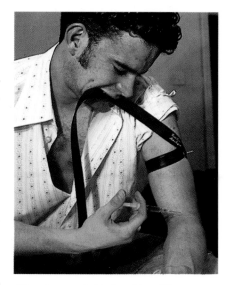

Heroin user injecting himself

and stayed quiet at the time when he became suddenly ill, the cause of his illness might have been found earlier and his life might have been saved. If you are approached tell the dealer to 'get lost'.

If it's happening in your presence.

If it's in school, advise the teachers who will deal with it. If it's in a public house or club in your area, inform the Gardai. After all, if you saw someone abusing a child or young person you would immediately have no fear of protecting that person. Have you not a much higher duty to intervene and help persons, young and old, if their whole lives are threatened by drug-taking?

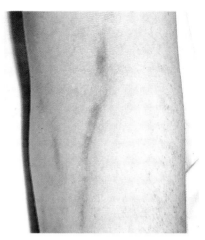

'Track marks' on the forearm of a drug abuser, caused by repeated insertion of needles

Don't be afraid of threats.

Drugs barons and lower dealers are protected by the aura of fear that they create for themselves. Anyone who knows what is involved will be able to tell you that this is a complete fiction. There have been incidents of violence, but this is mainly low life fighting with low life over money and drugs territories. What these people really fear is for the ordinary citizens to stand up to them and the fear that they will lose their ill-gotten gains and evil trade. Anyone who deals in drugs to spread such misery for profit is, by definition, a selfish parasitic coward. In my experience in dealing with cases it appears that most drug-taking arises from peer pressure, boredom and idleness. Young people need to get out and work off their energy in sport, particularly those who are unfortunate enough not to have regular education or employment. There are very many opportunities available if you only look for them. There are school facilities, community facilities, and for people who feel really threatened or disadvantaged, social welfare and garda-based facilities. Everyone will be delighted to help, but you must start to help yourself. Act now.

Stop the onslaught of misery for yourself, your friends and your family.

Source: Barry Galvin, *Alert News* 1993.

QUESTIONS

1 What is the connection between drug abuse and crime?

2 Why does Galvin state that it is 'a complete fallacy to say that drugs are harmless'?

3 What kind of people seek to justify illegal drug-taking?

4 What response should a person give if offered drugs? Why?

5 What are the legal consequences of being found guilty of drug offences?

6 What are the dangers of acting as a drugs courier?

7 What does Galvin consider to be the moral duty of every person if he/she is aware of drug-dealing in his/her school or locality?

8 What does he propose as a better alternative to a drug-centred lifestyle?

THE PROBLEMS CAUSED BY DRUGS

Personal

- Destroys relationships with one's family and friends.

- Does not solve any problems, merely adds to them.

- Can cause serious injury, mental illness and even death (especially by an overdose or poisoning).

- Risk of contracting HIV and of developing full-blown AIDS.

- Habit is very expensive, often leads to criminal activity to raise money for each fix, e.g. prostitution or theft. High likelihood of imprisonment.

- Even if drug abuse ends with help of prison detoxification treatment, prison record will seriously affect future employment prospects.

Social

- Hurts family and friends. Addicts will steal and use violence to obtain the price of his/her next fix.

- Addict prepared to deal drugs to anyone or any age group to fund his/her habit.

- Baby born to an addicted mother born an addict.

- Addict is totally self-absorbed and capable of extreme violence in commission of a crime.

QUESTIONS

1   In his book, *On Liberty*, John Stuart Mill argued that a person should be free to do whatever he/she wishes so long as it does not harm anyone else. Having read the above, would you agree/disagree that drug abuse is a matter for each individual and nobody else? Why?

2   Read 1 *Corinthians* 6:19-20 and *Romans* 6:19.

(a) What is the Christian attitude to drug abuse?

(b) Can someone who is obsessed with and addicted to drugs love either him/herself or others?

If a person needs help with a drug problem, there are many places to which he/she can turn for help:

- Drug Treatment Centre Board

- Cross Care
  Catholic Social Service Conference
  Drug Awareness Programme

- Garda Drug Squad (Dublin, Cork, Limerick)

Please consult the telephone directory for their current contact numbers.

CHAPTER 31

Alcohol Abuse

ALCOHOLISM — DYING FOR A DRINK

There are more drug addicts in today's Ireland than is generally realised. Yet these men and women would not consider themselves addicts. Why? Because, they might reply: *'We don't inject ourselves with syringes full of heroin, smoke crack or swallow Ecstasy tablets'.* But they *are* addicts none the less. They are dependent on the legally available and socially acceptable drug, ethyl alcohol, which is present in all alcoholic beverages. They are *alcoholics.*

> *'Alcoholism is the major drug of abuse in Ireland and the western world. It is a major public health problem and causes many medical problems such as brain damage, liver disease, and it affects every body organ and system.'*
> Dr Art O'Connor, interviewed in the *Irish Independent*, 1997.

Many people start consuming alcohol in their teenage years, usually through their families and circle of friends, but sometimes they begin by drinking alone. Of course, not everyone who takes an alcoholic drink becomes dependent on it. Many *moderate* drinkers harm neither themselves nor others. This said, however, a person does not have to be an alcoholic to have problems with alcohol. Serious health problems can and do occur before the drinker reaches the stage of addiction or chronic abuse.

THE ALCOHOLIC CONTENT OF DIFFERENT BEVERAGES

Beer, cider and stout = 4 to 7%

Table wine = 10 to 12%

Fortified wine (e.g. port, sherry) = 15 to 22%

Spirits (e.g. gin, vodka, whiskey) = 40 to 55%

N.B. The consumption of spirits has risen more sharply than the consumption of beer in recent years.

The consumption of alcohol generally has more than doubled since 1960.

THE LAW AND ALCOHOL

Age

Eighteen is the minimum age at which you may legally be served or legally purchase drink in a licensed premises or off-licence.

It is an offence to allow people under 15 years of age in a bar during business hours, unless accompanied by a parent or guardian.

A person aged between 16-18 years is allowed into a public house during normal opening hours but is not allowed into a premises during the time that an exemption order is in force.

To work in a licensed premises you must be 18 years of age, unless related to the licencee, or apprenticed.

Drunkenness

It is an offence to be drunk in a public place. Even a small amount of alcoholic drink can release inhibitions and contribute to bad judgment.

Uncontrolled drunken behaviour can lead to a police record which could affect you all your life and limit your schooling and your career potential.

Source: Department of Health.

PROJECT

Make a study of television advertisements which promote the sale of alcoholic drink.
Note the following:
(1) The total number of different advertisements which promote alcoholic beverages shown between 7 pm and 9 pm.

(2) The types of drink advertised.

(3) The number of times each particular advertisement is shown in one evening's viewing.

(4) The kind of message the advertisements transmit about alcoholic drink and the people who drink it.

(5) The advertisement which, in your opinion, is the most effective. Give reasons for your choice.

QUESTIONS

1 In your view, do advertisements present a fair and balanced presentation of the reality of drinking alcoholic beverages? Do they make unrealistic claims about the value of alcoholic drinks?

2 Do advertisements give any hint of the darker, tragic side of alcohol abuse?

Give reasons for your answers.

ONE MAN'S STORY

Joe woke up in hospital with a blinding headache and a doctor standing by his bed asking if he knew where he was. He didn't. His memory of the night before was very vague. He could just about recall going into a pub alone and downing one drink after another until he lost count of how many. Joe hadn't a clue as to what happened later. The doctor informed him that shortly after leaving the pub he had tried to hail a passing taxi, but had ended up on its bonnet instead of its back seat, and was rewarded with a fractured skull and considerable bruising.

Yet it took Joe another two years to admit that he was an alcoholic and to ask for help - two years of hell for both himself and his family. It had all started out innocently enough. He would stop off in his local pub on his way home after work for a few quick drinks and a chat with his pals. After a while he developed a capacity to consume quite a lot of drink. He would spend his lunch-hour in a pub near his workplace. But this lunchtime drinking made him anxious during the afternoon, so he would be on tenterhooks waiting to get back to the pub in the evening after work.

Sometimes Joe had no idea how he had managed to get from one place to the next. His memory had started to black out for several hours at a time. He wasn't unconscious during this time; on the contrary, he was wide awake. But *his excessive drinking had affected the areas of his brain associated with memory*. As time went on, these blackouts became more frequent.

To Joe's wife, Sarah, and their two young children, it was glaringly obvious that he had a problem. Initially she would downplay the matter and joke with friends about his 'fondness for the bottle'. But the situation quickly lost any humorous gloss. Joe was spending most of his weekly wage on drink. She got a part-time job, but she couldn't earn enough to pay essential bills, never mind buy clothes for herself and the children.

Joe's behaviour at home steadily deteriorated. At times he acted like a wild animal, kicking down doors and smashing furniture. It was only when he began to physically abuse both his wife and their children that Sarah decided it was time to separate. She obtained a court order barring him from the home and applied for a judicial separation.

By now Joe was drinking at work. Even threats of losing his job failed to frighten him enough to admit his alcoholism. Then the firm announced job cuts due to the economic slump. Joe was among the *first* to be made redundant.

Some mornings he would wake up shocked at his own behaviour, or at least whatever he could remember through a mist of alcohol. But he had become a master of denial. He didn't *need* to drink, he just *liked* to drink. *He* didn't have a problem, *other* people did. He wasn't an alcoholic. Surely everyone knew that an alcoholic was an old wino who sat in rags in a backstreet drinking meths. He wouldn't listen to advice.

Eventually something snapped inside him. He was sitting alone in the kitchen of his flat one Monday morning when he had his first bout of the 'DTs' (*delirium tremens*). His hands shook so violently that he couldn't hold a cup. A wave of panic and shame washed over him. Joe finally realised he was in terrible trouble. At last, he was willing to look for help.

QUESTIONS

1   What is the cost of alcoholism for (a) Joe; (b) his family; (c) his employer; and (d) public safety?

2 Did alcohol reduce Joe's anxiety or solve his personal problems? *Explain your answer.*

3 What does Joe's story tell you about the power and consequences of alcohol abuse. *Give reasons for the opinions you express.*

4 Read the following extract:

> *'Ireland has the doubtful distinction of topping the European and possibly the world league table for proportion of disposable income spent on alcoholic drink, at 11.6 per cent. This cannot be good news, in particular for the families of the many Irish who live below the poverty line.'*
>
> Prof. Tom Fahy, *Mental Health in Ireland*

(a) Why do you think Ireland has achieved this *'doubtful distinction'*? Explain your answer.

(b) Why does Prof. Fahy say that this *'cannot be good news'*? Give reasons for your answer.

Alcoholism is usually caused by the following combination of factors:

(1) *The Person*

The physical and psychological make-up of the individual. Although alcoholism seems to run in certain families, experts are divided as to whether it is inherited or due to the way in which the person was brought up.

(2) *The Environment*

Ready access to alcohol where he/she lives and works.

(3) *The Drug*

Sufficient funds must be available for him/her to be able to purchase and consume alcohol in sufficient quantities each day.

Widely held but mistaken ideas about alcohol abuse:

(1) *You cannot become an alcoholic if you only drink beer.*

Wrong: All alcoholic drinks contain ethyl alcohol. A person can become an alcoholic by drinking any such beverage.

(2) *Alcohol is great for boosting your spirit when you're feeling unhappy.*

Wrong: Alcohol is a *depressant* drug, but because it removes people's inhibitions it gives them the *impression* that it is a stimulant. Once its initial effects wear off, it only serves to *deepen* a person's depression.

(3) *Alcohol can help a shy, tense person become more outgoing and relaxed.*

Wrong: Alcohol does remove inhibitions, but too much can lead to careless and foolish behaviour, and often a complete lack of discretion, where a person says and does things he/she would never ordinarily do. Not surprisingly, he/she is usually very embarrassed afterwards. It does nothing to promote lasting self-confidence; instead it does the opposite.

(4) *You can control your drinking behaviour by will-power.*

Wrong: A person cannot stop the effects of alcohol on his/her body if he/she drinks heavily. This is because alcohol acts as a *depressant* on the nervous system and dulls the frontal area of the brain, which is associated with the critical faculties. It effectively anaesthetises a person's capacity to judge rationally. This is usually evident from his/her slurred speech and poorly co-ordinated actions. This is why a person who has consumed alcoholic beverages should not drive a motor vehicle afterwards.

(5) *All alcoholics are 'down and outs'.*

Wrong: Anyone, from any age-group or social class, can become an alcoholic.

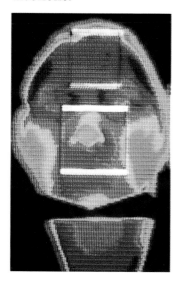 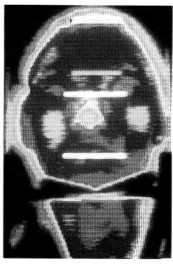

Heat pictures of a person's face before (left) and after (right) drinking alcohol show a big rise in temperature. Red indicates warm, blue is for cold and yellow/white is for hot.

QUESTION

Some people believe that getting drunk is an essential part of 'having a good time'. Consider the role that alcohol plays at such social events as birthday parties and weddings. Then read *Proverbs* 20:1.

Do you agree/disagree with their point of view? Give reasons for your opinion.

PROBLEMS CAUSED BY ALCOHOL ABUSE

Alcohol makes people less inhibited. This can cause them to say and do things they might *not* do when sober. Studies reveal that:

- One in three road accidents involves alcohol intoxication.
- Alcohol abuse is a major contributor to marital disharmony and is very often associated with domestic violence and sexual abuse.
- Very frequently, violent crime involves an intoxicated individual assaulting another person. About 40% of the prison population have an alcohol abuse problem.

DO YOU HAVE A DRINK PROBLEM?

The Department of Health asks people to consider their alcohol-drinking habits and answer the following questions truthfully:

(1) Do you drink to help you cope with problems or stressful situations at home or in school?

(2) Do you drink because you want others to think of you as grown-up?

(3) Do you prefer to drink alone rather than with others?

(4) Do you feel the need to drink in the morning before going to school or work?

(5) Do you drink quickly in large gulps as if trying to quench a great thirst?

(6) Do you drink after having a row with others?

(7) Do you get drunk frequently, even when you don't intend it?

(8) After you drink, do you ever find it hard to remember what you have done while 'under the influence'?

(9) Has your drinking ever got you into trouble of any kind?

(10) Do you tell lies when challenged about how much you drink?

(11) Does your drinking ever affect the way you perform in school or in work?

(12) Have you tried unsuccessfully to either stop drinking altogether or to reduce the volume you consume?

Source: Alcohol and You.

Someone answering '*Yes*' to any of these questions should seek help immediately.

Remember: Alcoholism is a treatable disease. However, a person cannot be 'cured' as such. He/she must choose to abstain from drinking any alcoholic beverage and then *stick to that commitment*. Organisations such as Alcoholics Anonymous provide support for those who struggle daily to live free from the drug ethyl alcohol.

Alcoholics Anonymous (AA) is a worldwide fellowship of people who meet together to attain and maintain sobriety. It began in 1935 when Bill W., a New York stockbroker, and Dr Bob S., a surgeon, met in Akron, Ohio, and started helping each other to stay sober. From that modest beginning, AA has grown to an estimated 87,000 groups in more than 130 countries, with a total membership of more than 2 million.

All those who feel they have a drinking problem are welcome to attend any AA meeting. The only requirement for membership is a desire to stop drinking. A member's privacy is respected, and he/she is anonymous at the public level. No fees are required. All contributions are entirely voluntary. The AA programme is one of total abstinence, in which members are encouraged to stay away from '*one drink, one day at a time*'. Their sobriety is maintained by sharing their experience, strength and hope at group meetings, and following the suggested Twelve Steps to recovery.

If one member of a family has a drink problem, it can place an enormous strain on all concerned. They need help to cope with the situation. *Al-Anon* provides support for one whose marriage partner is an alcoholic, while *Alateen* offers help for those with an alcoholic parent or parents.

Please consult your local doctor or telephone directory if you require their assistance. Remember, *there are people willing to help*.

Chapter 32

The Environment

'Me Save the Environment?'

'Environment! That's for highbrows,' I said. 'Me preserve and improve the environment?' I said. You must be joking,' I said. 'What's the environment got to do with me?' I said.

'Listen, friend,' he answered, 'you are the environment, or part of it, and you're certainly a product of it, just as I am. The environment is the room, the flat, the house where you live; the factory, the office, the shop where you work; your road, your parish, your village, town or city; Ireland, Europe, the world — even the space the world sails through.

'It's the street where your children play, the park they take the dog in, the flowers, the trees, the animals and birds, the fields, the crops, the streams, the waterfalls. It's the fish, the cliffs, the seashore, the sea itself, the hills and the mountains, the pubs, the bingo halls, the lanes, the motorways, the highways and byways, the farms, the rows of shops and houses, the dustbins, the historical buildings, the trains and buses and cars.

'It's the music and dancing and peaches and cream. It's the insects, an empty tin can, aeroplanes, pictures, pollen, and the leaves that fall from the trees. It's the smoke from a fire, a wormcast on the lawn, a cigarette end in the gutter, books, papers, greenfly on the roses, the paint on your front door, unbreakable plastic, the rain on the roof, an empty beer bottle, the heather and the bracken and the butterflies. It's the air you breathe, the blue sky, peace and quiet, the clouds and the sun.

'Through ignorance, thoughtlessness, stupidity or greed, people have done, and go on doing, an unbelievable amount of damage to their world. As new processes and new products are developed, and as the pace of what we call "technological advance" speeds up, so the danger to the environment (and to you and me) increases faster and

faster. But it doesn't only snowball; there's a chain-reaction too, because nowhere will you find it so inescapable that one thing leads to another.

'So, if you enjoy some of the millions of things that make up the environment, and if you want your children and their children and their children's children to enjoy them too, now is the time to act. The crisis is on us already. The detergent in this week's washing-up water can mean no fish in the river next week.'

'Well, I'll be damned!' I said, 'I —'

He stopped me with a wave of his hand, and looked me squarely in the eyes.

'If you sit on your backside and do nothing to help,' he said, 'we all will be.'

J. Barr (ed.), *The Environmental Handbook.*

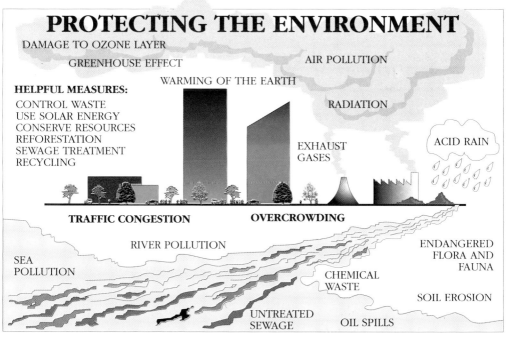

PROTECTING THE ENVIRONMENT

DAMAGE TO OZONE LAYER

GREENHOUSE EFFECT

AIR POLLUTION

WARMING OF THE EARTH

HELPFUL MEASURES:
CONTROL WASTE
USE SOLAR ENERGY
CONSERVE RESOURCES
REFORESTATION
SEWAGE TREATMENT
RECYCLING

RADIATION

EXHAUST GASES

ACID RAIN

TRAFFIC CONGESTION

OVERCROWDING

RIVER POLLUTION

SEA POLLUTION

ENDANGERED FLORA AND FAUNA

CHEMICAL WASTE

SOIL EROSION

UNTREATED SEWAGE

OIL SPILLS

WHAT CAN YOU DO PERSONALLY TO LESSEN POLLUTION?

QUESTIONS

1 What do you understand by the word *'environment'*?

2 What does the author identify as the main threats to a healthy environment?

3 Why should people be concerned about the state of the environment?

4 Read the following story:

> *In 1309, an Aztec Indian inhabitant of what is now Mexico City was found guilty of burning charcoal in the city and polluting the air. He was ordered to be hanged for the offence!*
>
> *Today, Mexico City has a carbon-monoxide level greater than metropolitan New York, a sulphur-dioxide level greater than that of London, and ten times the industrial contaminants of the industrialised Rhine-River valley.*

What has changed in people's attitudes to capital punishment and the environment since? Are many people inconsistent in the values they claim to hold? Explain your answer.

THE NATURE OF OUR WORLD

The dominant world-view since the scientific revolution of the 1600s tended to see all material reality as a vast machine operating blindly, without a purpose of its own. From this many scientists concluded that the only meaning the material world has is the meaning human beings give it. This left it ripe for commercial exploitation. The 17th century philosopher Descartes regarded animals as merely complicated biological machines. Experimenters of the time were able to convince themselves that the screams of animals in their laboratories were of no more significance than the click of a switch when you turn on a room light.

Over the past century, this view has been challenged by environmentalists—and this challenge is now becoming a popular cause. A new era has begun, one in which people are now questioning the assumptions of this mechanistic world-view. Today, we are trying to see the universe as an *integrated whole* again, in which *everything* has its part to play. There is now a greater sense of there being a pre-existing order of things in our world, a meaning which is already there, waiting to be discovered and acknowledged by us.

The environment in which we live, then, is being seen more and more as a *gift* to be cherished.

For human beings, the environment is located in what is called the '*biosphere*', namely,

> '*the narrow zone that harbours life on our planet. It is limited to the waters of the earth, a fraction of its crust, and the lower regions of its atmosphere.*'

Within the biosphere there exist a number of interconnected ecosystems. By an '*ecosystem*' we mean:

> '*an integrated unit consisting of the community of living organisms and the physical environment in a particular area. The relationships among species in an ecosystem are usually complex and finely balanced, and the removal of any one species may be disastrous.*'

> Webster's New World Encyclopaedia

To illustrate, consider the sad tale of the Dodo's extinction and the impact it had on the local ecosystem.

CASE STUDY I: THE DODO'S DISAPPEARANCE

- Physical description: The dodo was a most improbable-looking bird. Standing 3 ft tall, it was larger than a turkey and primarily ash grey in colour. Its 50 lb body was fat and lumpy, with a ridiculous tuft of curly feathers serving as a tail. It was flightless but still retained stubby wings from which three or four black feathers protruded. Its huge beak, which ended in a hook, was sometimes as long as 9 in. Its legs and heavy feet were large and yellow, and most of its face lacked feathers.

- Where and how they lived: The dodo and its relative, the solitaire, lived on the three Mascarene Islands in the Indian Ocean. The dodo called volcanic Mauritius home and was content to waddle along undisturbed by predators, snacking on native fruits and vegetation. It nested on the ground, and the female laid one big white egg per year.

- How and when destroyed: The Portuguese discovered Mauritius in 1507, but the explorers were soon off in search of other new lands, and their records fail to mention a large, clumsy bird. The discovery of the dodo fell to a Dutch admiral, Jacob van Neck, who landed on the island in 1598. Fascinated by the huge flocks of odd birds, one of the admiral's colleagues walked through the dodos' nesting grounds to investigate and was *'pecked mighty hard'* for his interest. Undaunted, van Neck left Mauritius with two of the birds, one of which stayed in the Netherlands where it posed for fourteen portraits, while the other one travelled to Germany to amuse emperor Rudolf II. The journal van Neck kept during his voyage was published in 1601. After his description of the dodo he added: '*We called these birds Walghvogels* [disgusting birds] *for the reason that the more and the longer they are cooked, the less soft and more unpalatable their flesh becomes.*' Hungry sailors from the second expedition found the breast meat tasty enough, and their ship left Mauritius with forty-four of the birds, enough meat to last them for the rest of the voyage.

• Soon Dutch settlers were hopping off ships with their dogs, monkeys and pigs, and several seasick rats would also scurry ashore at each docking. While the colonists were eating the adult birds, the animals they had brought with them were feasting on the eggs and the young. What could the dodo do? With the exception of its beak, the bird was defenceless. When it tried to run, its big belly scraped on the ground, and it was physically impossible for it to climb a tree to nest out of harm's way. The last dodo on Mauritius was eaten in 1681.

• When English ornithologist Hugh Strickland declared that the dodo had been a giant dove whose wings had withered away from disuse, his colleagues roared with laughter; but Strickland's theory was proved to be correct. Then the dodo furore died down until 1977, when it came to light that the beautiful calvaria major tree of Mauritius had entrusted the bird with its future and was facing extinction itself as a result of the dodo's demise. The tree's seeds had such thick hulls that they could only sprout after being run through the rigours of the dodo's digestive tract. The calvaria, a long-lived hardwood, had held out for 300 years, but only thirteen dying trees remained on the island by 1977. Dr Stanley Temple, an ornithologist from the University of Wisconsin, came to the trees' rescue with turkeys, whose gastrointestinal systems are capable of wearing down the calvaria seeds so that they can sprout and save the species from the hapless dodo's fate.

QUESTIONS

1 (a) Why did the Dodo become extinct?

(b) Could this have been avoided? Explain your answer.

2 The ecologist John Muir once wrote:

> 'When we try to pick out anything by itself we find it hitched to everything else in the universe.'

How would you apply his insight to the story of the dodo's extinction?

3 What would have happened without Dr Temple's intervention?

Give reasons for your answer.

BIO-DIVERSITY

This refers to the variety of biological forms within an environment. This variety needs to be preserved for a number of reasons:

- Crop diversity is crucial in case our current staples like wheat and maize become diseased.

- Half of all medicines come from plants — morphine comes from poppies, Amazonian trees provide quinine. The destruction of particular plants could deprive us of future cures for serious illnesses.

- All species, including humans, are part of a complex chain, relying and depending on each other. The loss of one plant can result in the loss of animals and insects which rely upon it. If enough links in the chain are broken our own survival may be at stake.

- When a species of plant or animal disappears our world loses a little more of its beauty and richness.

THE DELICATE BALANCE IN NATURE

At the 'Global Possible' conference held in Washington, D.C. in May 1984, it was repeatedly emphasised by scientists that our planet has a frail and perishable environment. They warned of serious long-term consequences as people carelessly damage the delicate and complex network of organisms and plants that make up our world's ecosystem. Thomas Bokenkotter tells the following story:

'We lose a species a day — very bad news, for as science shows, the diverse organisms of the ecosystem live together in an orderly fashion and form a whole whose parts are extremely interdependent. Interference with this smoothly functioning system can have unforeseen and devastating effects. A parable illustrating this point is found in the story of the health workers in Borneo who sprayed the huts of the villagers with DDT in order to exterminate a malaria-carrying parasite. Lizards ingested large quantities of the DDT sprayed on the walls and died. Cats ate some of the moribund lizards and they too died, while the caterpillars, which were kept in check by the lizards, were now free to go to work chewing on the thatched roofs of the huts. As a result, the villagers lost the roofs of their homes and suffered from a plague of rats.'

Rain forest in the Amazon

Essential Catholicism.

THE COST OF ENVIRONMENTAL VANDALISM

In recent times, more and more people have come to realise that the human race can no longer afford to pollute the air and water or wreak havoc on the delicate balance of plant and animal life in our ecosystem.

(1) The American National Cancer Institute estimates that between 60 and 90 per cent of cancer is caused by a polluted environment.
(2) Experts at the Global Possible Conference (1984) stated that environmental pollution accounts for almost 20 per cent of the physical and mental disabilities in newly born infants.
(3) Although the report of the Green 2000 advisory body found Ireland to be still an 'environmental treasure' in the European context, it warned that there is no room for complacency.

During the debate on the Green 2000 report, the Dáil was told that an estimated 155,000 jobs depended on a high-quality environment.

These were in the areas of dairying, meat processing, tourism, chemicals and pharmaceuticals, electronics, aquaculture and forestry. Also since a large number of those in employment worked on the land, the continued success of the farming sector depended on the maintenance of a high-quality and healthy environment.

> *'It is clear that if significant environmental degradation occurs, there will be a resultant loss of existing employment in our natural resource-based activities.'*
>
> *Green 2000.*

QUESTIONS

1   What do you understand by the phrase *'the delicate balance of nature'*?

2   What, in your opinion, are the main sources of pollution in our environment?

   Give reasons for your answer.

3   What are the economic benefits of a clean environment?

CASE STUDY II: THE NUCLEAR ENERGY DEBATE

There are few issues today which have aroused such fierce debate as nuclear energy. There are strong feelings among both its supporters and its opponents.

Here, an argument supporting nuclear power is put forward by *British Nuclear Fuels plc*, a company servicing the UK's nuclear industry. Arguing against it are the environmental groups *Greenpeace* and *Friends of the Earth*.

Given Ireland's close geographical relation to Britain, this is a topic of considerable importance for all of us.

For:	Against:
Today the world obtains three-fifths of its energy from oil and gas. These are fossil fuels which need millions of years to form.	The best sources of energy are those called 'renewable'. They include the power available from the sun, from the movement of winds, tides and waves, and
Oil is being consumed at such a rate	from underground heat. These energy

that known reserves will run out in about 40 years. The Gulf War showed how dangerous it can be for industrialised countries to rely too heavily on oil.

An alternative source is nuclear power. There is no threat of nuclear fuel running out. Uranium exists in large enough quantities to last for at least another 5,000 years.

sources are largely untapped.

At present, renewables supply only about a fifth of the world's energy needs. But if they were developed, renewables could meet all the world's needs in the next century.

For:

Nuclear power is less damaging to the environment than energy generated from fossil fuels because it does not contribute to global warming — a process that is raising the Earth's temperature.

One cause of global warming is the greenhouse effect. This happens when various gases in the Earth's atmosphere form a layer that traps the sun's heat in a similar way to the glass in a greenhouse. One 'greenhouse' gas is carbon dioxide, which enters the air, among other ways, from the emissions of conventional coal-fired power stations. For each unit of electricity that is eventually produced, coal-fired stations release about 25 times more carbon dioxide than nuclear power plants.

Against:

Coal-fired power stations are only one source of carbon dioxide, which is only one of the greenhouse gases. Even if nuclear power produced all electricity, global warming would only be reduced by about 11 per cent.

The solution to global warming is not nuclear power, but cutting energy consumption.

For:

Large amounts of radiation can cause concern, and nuclear power stations use some radioactive materials. But radiation occurs naturally in the air, in the ground, and in food and drink.

Of course, we must still make sure that nuclear power stations are safe. But the history of nuclear power, especially in the UK, shows that radiation can be controlled.

Against:

Nuclear accidents have happened. The British nuclear power programme was troubled almost from the start. A fire broke out in Windscale (now Sellafield), West Cumbria, in 1957. Estimates of the number of fatal cancers caused by the incident range from 13 to more than 1,000. More recently, the British Government accepted scientific evidence of a possible link between the blood cancer leukaemia in children and the fact that their fathers worked at Sellafield.

Other serious accidents have occurred — at Three Mile Island in the United States in 1979, and at Chernobyl in the former Soviet Union in 1986, the worst ever.

For:

Nuclear power may seem more expensive than coal- or oil-produced electricity, but this is misleading. Oil and coal prices are low now. But when they climb, nuclear power will be relatively cheap.

Nuclear plants produce radioactive waste, but it is carefully contained in steel tanks, deep holes or shallow trenches, whichever is necessary.

Against:

Nuclear power is extremely expensive. A nuclear plant costs over £2 billion to build — about twice the cost of a conventional power station. Even more must be spent to dispose of nuclear waste and dismantle old power stations.

There is still no solution to the problem of nuclear waste. Nuclear materials can remain radioactive for thousands of years, and they are lethal.

Adapted from: E. Pilkington, *The Guardian*, 25.9.1990.

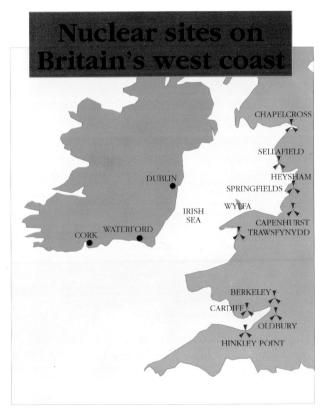

QUESTION

Having studied the arguments for and against the use of Nuclear Energy to generate electricity, which side do you support? Give reasons for your answer.

CASE STUDY III: ANIMAL RIGHTS

Human beings have rights. In recent years, there has been considerable debate on whether or not animals too have rights and, if so, the precise nature and extent of their rights.

The moral debate on animal rights centres on six controversial areas:
- The breeding and killing of animals for food.
- The use of animals in medical research.
- The testing of cosmetics, detergents and non-medical household goods on animals.
- The breeding and killing of animals for fur.
- The hunting and killing of animals for sport.
- The breeding and training of animals for entertainment.

A mouse being used in an experiment

Medical research conducted on animals *has* contributed to several important breakthroughs in the treatment of illnesses:
- experiments conducted on *dogs* were responsible for advances in kidney transplants and open-heart surgery;
- research on *monkeys* led to a vaccine against rubella and the development of life-support machines for babies born prematurely;
- experiments on *rabbits* played an important role in the development of chemotherapy for leukaemia sufferers.

Currently, animals are being used in research into AIDS, cancer and heart disease.

However, to achieve such breakthroughs, animals are subjected to laboratory experiments in which they are injected with drugs, exposed to radiation or toxic chemicals and infected with diseases.

Those in favour of animal experimentation point out that animals are *different* from human beings. Animals act only on instinct. Animals do not have the capacity to use sophisticated language, nor can they make plans or accept responsibility for their actions. Animals are incapable of showing real love or of offering any signs that they are critically self-aware. As a result, many philosophers conclude that they do *not* enjoy the same moral status or deserve the same respect as human beings.

There is ample evidence, however, that animals can feel pain, fear and pleasure. Yet, as Paul Higginson points out:

'Standard international tests include the LD50 test (Lethal Dose 50 per cent toxicity test) where animals are fed a product until half of them die (most detergents are tested in this way). The Draize eye test involves dropping products (like shampoo) in the eyes of rabbits for seven days and recording the results. As rabbits cannot blink this is an effective way of measuring damage to the eye. Painkillers are rarely used in such tests.'

A CHRISTIAN PERSPECTIVE

Christians do not deny the factual differences between humans and animals. However, this does *not* mean that they consider this justifies the mentality that we can do with animals whatever we please. In *Genesis* (2:15) God commanded us to care for and cultivate the earth and *all* the creatures on our planet. We are *not* entitled to callously exploit animals, as they are part of the rich diversity of God's gift of creation to us. In his book *The Moral Status of Animals*, Stephen Clark argues that we ought to show greater respect for animals precisely because they *are* different from human beings. We must show a greater sensitivity to other forms of life on our planet if our planet and, by implication, the human race itself are to have a future.

QUESTIONS

1   Describe the ways in which animals are different from human beings.
2   Examine each of the six areas of concern regarding animal rights listed above. Which of them, do you think, are justified or unjustified? Explain your choices.
3   Explain the Christian attitude towards the treatment of animals. What kind of restrictions does it seek to place on the treatment of animals? Explain your answer.
4   What point does Clark make? Do you agree/disagree? Why?
5   If someone you love was in danger of dying if doctors did not use a drug tested on animals, what would you want them to do?
    Give reasons for your answer.

PROJECT

Design a poster illustrating any of the following:

(a) the advantages of a clean environment;

(b) the causes of pollution;

(c) the impact of environmental damage;

(d) the protection of animals.

CHANGING COURSE WHILE THERE IS STILL TIME

If the human race is to have a future, changes will have to take place. The most important will be the general adoption of a new outlook on how our species relates to the fragile environment of this small oasis of life.

J. Barr offers the following advice which he hopes will persuade people to change course:

'(1) *Human beings need more time to learn.* In the week of creation (using *Genesis* time) the human race arrived only three minutes before midnight on the sixth day. The world had worked quite well without us all the previous week.

(2) *Progress does not need ever-increasing speed,* whether it be in air travel; in using up coal, oil and gas; in polluting the air; or in broadcasting poisonous chemicals the environment cannot cope with.

(3) *There are limits.* We cannot let technology grind up the last natural beauty and wilderness before we turn around to repair our damage. As rational beings we can turn around sooner, while there is still natural beauty and wildness around us, serving purposes we may one day be wise enough to understand.

(4) *In diversity is strength.* Biological wealth and stability are dependent upon complexity. For example, had we somehow simplified our national forests to chestnut trees only, the immediate advantages might have been numerous, but a chestnut blight could have wiped the landscape clean of trees. The lesson is unheeded too often. We can learn it now.

(5) *Human beings can remember their greatest attribute.* Through the ages they have aggressively manifested their territoriality to which there are limits. They have less often shown their capacity for *love,* the one resource that *increases with use.*'

WHAT PEOPLE CAN DO TO HELP

Groups promoting environmental awareness advise people to take the following practical steps:

(1) Where possible, use public transport, car pool, bicycle or walk.

(2) Use unleaded petrol.

(3) Do not purchase products made from tropical hardwoods.

(4) If feasible, plant a tree for each family member, native species such as ash, beech or oak.

(5) Save energy by properly insulating your home.

(6) Buy CFC-free products.

(7) Use only biodegradable soaps and detergents.

(8) Use Rehab bottle banks.

(9) Recycle paper, cans and plastics.

(10) Where possible buy recycled products.

(11) Avoid unnecessary packaging when shopping. Bring your own bag!

(12) Where possible use products that can be re-filled. Try to limit your use of discardable ones.

(13) Conserve drinking water.

(14) Use litter bins where provided, and where there are none, bring the rubbish home and put it in your own bin.

EXERCISE

Take each of the above suggestions for practical action and explain the positive benefits of each of them in turn.

Give reasons for your answer.

REFLECTION

- In what way does my daily life show my respect for the oneness of creation and my care for the environment?

- Do I live simply, mindful of how my life affects the earth and its resources?

- What am I doing to reverse environmental damage?
- Do I dispose of waste products in ways that are regenerative or at least do no harm?
- Do I encourage others to care for our world by my example?

CHAPTER 33

The Reality of Death

THE PARABOLA OF LIFE

Some time ago, a mathematician calculated that the dead outnumber the living on earth by approximately thirty to one. The many silent graveyards dotted across the country almost seem to shout out:

'Memento mori': 'Remember you shall die.'

But thanks to improvements in public health and diet, most people in the developed world can look forward to reaching at least 70 years of age. Women, on average, enjoy a longer lifespan than men.

Yet sociologists have noticed that hand in hand with this improvement in life expectancy, there has been a considerable change in public attitudes towards death. Fewer people are willing to discuss the subject openly. Sooner or later, however, every person must face the reality of death. When a close relative or a good friend dies, people are shocked. If the person dies young, they say:

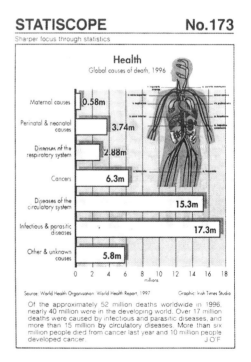

STATISCOPE　　　　　**No.173**
Sharper focus through statistics

Health
Global causes of death, 1996

Cause	Deaths
Maternal causes	0.58m
Perinatal & neonatal causes	3.74m
Diseases of the respiratory system	2.88m
Cancers	6.3m
Diseases of the circulatory system	15.3m
Infectious & parasitic diseases	17.3m
Other & unknown causes	5.8m

0 2 4 6 8 10 12 14 16 18
millions

Source: World Health Organisation: World Health Report, 1997.　Graphic: Irish Times Studio

Of the approximately 52 million deaths worldwide in 1996, nearly 40 million were in the developing world. Over 17 million deaths were caused by infectious and parasitic diseases, and more than 15 million by circulatory diseases. More than six million people died from cancer last year and 10 million people developed cancer.　　　J O'F

'It simply doesn't make sense! How can an accident/disease cause the death of someone I love?'

And even if the person was elderly and died peacefully, people often say:

'Only the body has died: it was just worn out. Surely that can't be the end. Will I never see this person again?'

All things in our universe, from stars to snowdrops, have a certain, limited lifespan. All are subject to decay and will eventually cease to exist.

'There was an experiment taken to its depressing conclusion some years ago by the medical faculty at Stanford University. Specimens of human cell culture were isolated, kept under ideal conditions, nourished with a perfect mix of proteins, salts and vitamins. At first it seemed as if the culture was flourishing, would last indefinitely. Then, gradually, the first signs of degeneration began to appear. The scientists responded, boosted the dosage, varied the mix. The culture "stabilised", but, after a bit, started to deteriorate once more. The team responded with bigger and riskier chemistry. But the recoveries became feebler, and more shortlived; the periods of degeneration came round more frequently. In the end, the culture died — of old age.

The experiment seemed to show that, while you can mitigate the onset of senility, you cannot, in the end, avoid it. Death is "programmed"'.

The Sunday Times, 1995.

Within all living things there seems to be an internal mechanism, something like an 'age clock' which, in the case of human beings, seems to stop one's further growth at a certain age by limiting one's cells' ability to divide and regenerate. (Read *Job* 14:1-10).

The great psychologist C.G. Jung believed that life is like a *parabola*. A person reaches the peak of his/her physical and mental powers in life's noonday, which in the diagram (on page 285) is between 35 and 40 years of age. From this point onwards, the curve slopes downwards as a person approaches death. Needless to say, this diagram is not an accurate representation of every person's life.

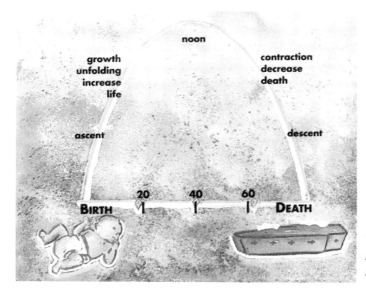

The parabola of life as expressed by Jung.

THE MEANING OF DEATH

But what is death itself? In answering this question it is important to distinguish between death and dying.

Death has been defined as:

> 'the permanent ending of all the functions that keep an organism alive'.

The word 'dying' refers to the *way* in which a person's life comes to an end.

How can we know if a person is dead as distinct from being in a coma?*

> 'Death used to be pronounced when a person's breathing and heartbeat stopped. The advent of mechanical aids has made this point sometimes difficult to determine, and in controversial cases a person is now pronounced dead when the brain ceases to control the vital functions, even if breath and heartbeat are maintained.
>
> For removal of vital organs in transplant surgery, the World Health Organisation in 1968 set out that the donor should exhibit

---

* A coma may be defined as 'a state of deep unconsciousness from which the subject cannot be roused and in which the subject does not respond to pain'.

no brain-body connection, muscular activity, blood pressure, or ability to breathe unaided by machine.'

Webster's New World Encyclopaedia

QUESTIONS

1 What is the scientific definition of death?

2 The film director, Woody Allen, has commented:

   'It's not death I'm afraid of; it's dying!'

   (a) How representative of people's feelings is this statement?

   (b) Do you share in the sentiment expressed? Why/why not?

DEATH AND THE MEDIA

In a survey conducted into violence on American television in the early 1980s, it was discovered that during one hundred hours of prime-time viewing programmes broadcast by the three major networks, there were:

Twelve murders, 16 major gun-fights, 21 persons shot, 21 other violent incidents with guns, 1 stabbing with a butcher's knife, 37 hand-to-hand fights, 4 attempted suicides, 3 successful suicides, 4 people pushed or falling off cliffs, 2 attempts by car drivers to run over people, and so on.

Peter Thornton, 'Television Violence', *Kairos* (1989).

Although Irish and European television programmes are generally less violent than their American counterparts, they, in conjunction with widespread video viewing, have resulted in most people seeing thousands of 'deaths' each year. Some are real, most are fictional. But in each case, death happens to someone else, to *other people*, not oneself. Death can become sanitised. Death can become *unreal.*

Read the following article:

A Tale That Was All Too Real

LIVE ON TELEVISION, A THREE-DAY CHASE LEADS TO DEATH

On the screen, it looked like prime-time police drama. A man steps off a bus holding a pistol to the head of a little girl. 'Hey!' he screams, 'I'll blow her away!' Next scene: the bloody corpse of a dark-haired youth is dragged from the bus. Finally, a bearded gunman stands at the door of the bus and puts an automatic pistol in his mouth. 'The last bullet goes here,' he says.

Gunmen Rösner and Degowski with hostages on a hijacked bus

But it was not make-believe, and the gunman was no actor. He was Hans Jürgen Rösner (31), one of two ex-cons who led police and TV crews on a deadly three-day chase across Germany and the Netherlands. Fleeing a bank robbery that went awry, Rösner and a companion, Dieter Degowski (32), hijacked a bus with some thirty passengers, killed a teenager and held live interviews on German television before running into a police ambush that left a woman hostage dead and one of the bandits wounded.

The botched bank robbery took place in Gladbeck, a gritty Ruhr Valley town near where the robbers lived. After an all-day police siege around the bank, the robbers fled towards Bremen in a car with two hostages, stopping to pick up Rösner's girlfriend on the way. With police shadowing them, they next hijacked a city bus with its passengers and headed towards the Dutch border.

The chase, until then bloodless, turned into a nightmare when the hijackers stopped the bus at a service station south of Bremen. Rösner's girlfriend, heading for the rest room, encountered two police officers hiding inside. When the gunmen heard her shouting, Rösner dragged a young girl from the bus and threatened to kill her if the police did not free the woman.

Inside the bus, meanwhile, Degowski put a pistol to the head of a 15-year-old Italian boy, Emanuele de Georgi, and pulled the trigger. Moments later journalists carried the dying youth from the bus, which was then forced to the Dutch town of Oldenzaal, where authorities provided the gunmen with a car in exchange for the freedom of all but two of the hostages. With the girlfriend and two young women hostages, they drove back to Germany.

In Cologne they stopped in the middle of a pedestrian mall to conduct a bizarre series of TV interviews, before racing away towards Frankfurt. When they reached the nearby autobahn, however, police in armoured Mercedes sedans rammed the car and forced it to halt. Hostage Silke Bischof (18) died in the ensuing shoot-out. Rösner and the second hostage were wounded.

Germans were transfixed by the blanket media coverage provided by a cavalcade of journalists trailing the desperadoes in cars, television vans and even taxis, largely unhindered by police. Once a taxi approached so close that a nervous bandit shot at its windshield, spraying glass fragments over the driver and his fare, a reporter for Deutsche Presse-Agentur, the German news agency.

Degowski with hostage Silke Bischof, who died shortly afterwards in a shoot-out.

At another point, in the Cologne mall, a crowd of about fifty journalists pressed five-deep around the bank robbers' car, yelling for interviews. Reporters shoved cameras and microphones through the windows of the BMW as Rösner, gun in lap, declared that the killing of De Georgi was the fault of 'the cops with their dirty tricks'. Cameras zoomed in on the faces of the two frightened women hostages in the back seat and took close-ups of Degowski's hand thumbing back the hammer of a revolver aimed at the cameras. Earlier near Bremen, Rösner had stepped off the hijacked bus for interviews while Degowski sat inside, counting 520,000 Deutschmarks stolen and extorted during the bank robbery. 'I can tell you for sure, if it comes to it, there'll be a shoot-out, and my pal there is very dangerous,' he said. 'I've done eleven years inside, and I'm not going back.'

If television viewers were riveted, politicians were outraged. 'I *don't think it is responsible to offer a public forum for the wild demands of violent criminals,' said Johannes Gerster of the Christian Democratic Party. 'With this kind of reporting, a life-and-death affair becomes a public spectacle, degraded into prime-time police drama. Sure, the public has to be informed, but not at the cost of the hostages' safety.' Other leaders agreed. A front-page editorial in L'Osservatore Romano, the Vatican newspaper, denounced the media as 'unscrupulous' for giving the renegades a forum.*

Time Magazine, 29.8.1988.

QUESTIONS

1   It has been said that there are two kinds of stories:

(a) those that are *in the public interest*; and

(b) those that are *of interest to the public*.

How would you classify this story? Give reasons for your answer.

2   Do you think the activities of the news media in this story were justified/unjustified? Why?

3   Were the relatives and friends of the hostages given due consideration during the 'blanket coverage' provided by the news media? Explain your answer.

4   What does this story say to you about prevailing attitudes among *certain* sections of the international news media, and their viewing public in general, towards situations of life and death? Give reasons for your opinion.

IGNORING THE REALITY OF DEATH

A man who was shot through the skull with an arrow by a friend trying to knock a fuel can off his head has survived with no brain damage.

Surgeons removed the arrow from Anthony Roberts's head by drilling a larger hole around the tip at the back of the skull and pulling it through.

Roberts (25) was shot last Saturday at a friend's home in Grants Pass, about 200 miles south of Portland, Oregon.

Paramedics saved his life by restraining him when he tried to pull the arrow out himself in the helicopter on the way to hospital.

Roberts, an unemployed carpenter, lost his right eye.

At a hospital news conference, Roberts initially told reporters he was walking through a park when he heard a bow fired, then felt the arrow hit.

Later, he said his friend was trying to knock the can off his head as an initiation into a rafting and outdoor group called Mountain Men Anonymous.

Evening Herald, 6.5.1993.

Even when faced with proof positive that a certain kind of lifestyle will endanger life, some people seem merely to shrug it off and adopt an attitude of 'it will never happen to me'.

QUESTIONS

1 Some social commentators believe that the following are examples of how death has become *unreal* and *distant* to some people:

(a) A person who continues to smoke cigarettes despite evidence that he/she is exposing him/herself to a high risk of lung cancer.

(b) Every year hundreds of people die in motor vehicle traffic accidents. Yet, some people persist in driving in a reckless fashion placing both their own and other people's lives at risk.

(c) The indifference with which some people view issues such as the environment and nuclear proliferation (spread of nuclear weapons technology).

(d) Patterns of sexual activity do not appear to have changed very much despite the danger of contracting AIDS.

Why do you think that this is so? Explain your answer.

2 **Read the following extract:**

One morning Alfred Nobel awoke to read his own obituary. The obituary was printed as a result of a simple journalistic error ... Any man would be disturbed under the circumstances, but to Alfred Nobel the shock was overwhelming. He saw himself as the world saw him — 'the dynamite king', the great industrialist . . . None of his true intentions — the breakdown of barriers that separated people and ideas — was recognised or given consideration. As he read his obituary with horror, Nobel resolved to make clear to the world the true meaning and purpose of his life. (This could be done through the final disposition of his fortune.) His last will and testament would be the expression of his life's ideals . . . The result was the most valued of prizes given to those who had done the most for the cause of world peace.

N. Halasz, *Nobel.*

(a) Why was Nobel shocked when he read his own obituary?

(b) What was his lasting reaction to this strange experience?

(c) How would you wish to be remembered? Why?

FACING DEATH

Most people are anxious about death, dreading the prospect of dying, whether theists or atheists.

'Belief in the resurrection does not remove the anguish and suffering of death. To pretend that there is no pain in death is to trivialise our human condition.'

Michael Simpson, SJ, *Death and Eternal Life.*

Human beings are the *only* creatures that *know* they must eventually die. At the same time, in common with other creatures, human beings have an instinctively powerful drive for self-preservation. It is hardly surprising, therefore, that people react strongly against the threat of personal extinction.

In her book, *On Death and Dying*, Dr Elizabeth Kübler-Ross presented the fruits of her many years of experience working with the dying. She shows that, once they have been told that their condition is terminal, they usually go through five psychological stages:

(1) Denial and isolation — refusal to accept the fact that they are dying.

(2) Anger and resentment — *'Why me?'*

(3) Bargaining with God — *'If you will only save my life, I promise to do . . . in return.'*

(4) Depression — the realisation that there is no hope of a cure and that they are powerless can cause people to turn in on themselves.

In most cases they move on to:

(5) Acceptance and Hope.

Grief at a funeral in Croatia during the civil war.

QUESTIONS

1 If death were the end of human life would all the characteristics of the human condition, namely suffering, pain, guilt and evil, have any meaning?

   Give reasons for your opinion.

2 Alan Paton has written:

   'Jesus suffered on the cross not to save us from suffering but to teach us how to bear suffering.'

   What do you think he means by this? Explain your answer.

CHAPTER 34

Suicide

INTRODUCTION

The death of a loved one is always a tragedy. An even more traumatic experience for those who are left to mourn their loss, however, is where their deceased loved one has committed suicide, i.e. *intentionally* taken his/her own life.

> *'If those who complete suicide had any idea of its devastating effects on their families it would probably act as a powerful deterrent. First there is the trauma of the discovery. Then there is the silence at the funeral. Normally talkative neighbours are temporarily tongue-tied. Well-meaning people can say hurtful things in awkward attempts to be helpful.'*

Dermot Clifford, *Suicide: A Permanent Solution to a Temporary Problem.*

The recorded suicide rate in Ireland has increased four-fold in the past two and a half decades. According to official figures, more than 1,500 people have committed suicide between 1993 and 1996. Some 378 people committed suicide here in 1996 alone.

Irish Times, 10.10.97

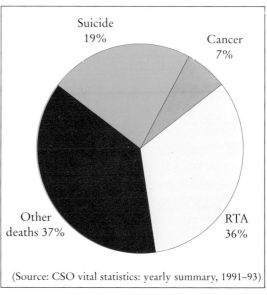

Cause of death for 15–24 year-old Irish males, 1991–93.

(Source: CSO vital statistics: yearly summary, 1991–93)

293

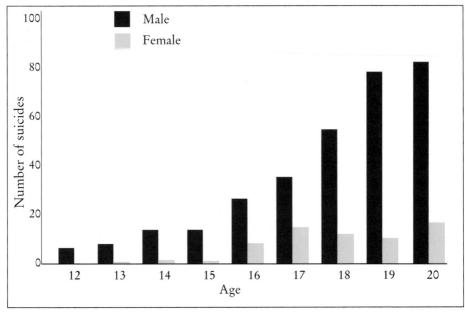

Irish male and female suicide by each age up to 20 years, 1976–93. (Source: CSO Dept of Vital Statistics)

Many social commentators believe, however, that the actual suicide rate is higher than that reported in the official figures. This tendency to under-report may partly be explained by a well-meaning consideration for the feelings of the bereaved families and friends. However, one fact clearly emerges from the statistical evidence: men outnumber women by three to one in successfully completing suicide. Why this is the case is a matter of some debate.

THE MORALITY OF SUICIDE

The Catholic Church taeches that the act of *rational* suicide, where a person *knowingly* and *freely* chooses to end his/her life is always wrong. It does so because rational suicide:

- contardicts our natural human inclination to preserve and perpetuate our own lives;
- rejects any just and proper love of oneself and embraces self-destructiveness instead;
- unjustly inflicts damage on others, particularly those who are left to mourn their loss.

The Catholic Church teaches that God is the Author of Life and is the *only* one who should determine when life should end. No human being has the right to play God with either his/her own life or that of another. We have a responsibility to cherish life, both our own and that of others, until the natural processes take their course and death comes.

However, the Catholic Church believes that a person who commits suicide should *not* be morally judged by other people. *None of us can be sure of all the physical or psychological pressures influencing our actions.*

At times, certain psychological factors can hinder or totally remove a person's responsibility for his/her suicide. God alone knows what occurs in the mind of a person who takes his/her own life.

The rational or clear-headed form of suicide is quite rare in Ireland. Depression, where a person is in the grip of intense mental anguish and pain, is believed to be a key factor in the majority of suicides.

QUESTIONS

1 What is '*rational*' suicide?
2 Why does the Catholic church teach that the act of rational suicide is morally wrong?
3 Why does the Catholic Church teach that we should not pass judgment on someone who commits suicide?
4 What is '*depression*'?

N.B. While the Catholic Church has traditionally opposed suicide, it has always respected and upheld the belief that a person may choose to sacrifice his/her life for a good and just cause (*John* 15:13). For example, Fr Maximilian Kolbe volunteered to take the place of another prisoner in the death cells of Auschwitz concentration camp during World War Two. He sacrificed his own life to *save* that of another person (see chapter 19).

SUICIDE AND THE IRISH

Read the following extract adapted from the Thomas Davis lecture by Dr Tom Fahy, Professor of Psychiatry at UCG.

'*Even in high suicide countries, self-homicide is a rare event and correspondingly hard to predict. The modern view is that victims are caught in the cross-fire between serious mental illness on the one hand, and extreme personal vulnerability at a point of time, on the other Contrary to popular belief, the suicidal state of mind is not something which persists over weeks or even days: the impulse comes on suddenly and does not last for long. Severe depressive illness brings with it psychological effects which distort perception. Very depressed people feel worthless and alone even in the midst of family and friends. The illness can cause extreme anguish.*

However, not all suicides have major depressive illness, especially when the victim is young, and it is amongst the young that suicide rates are rising most quickly. If one recalls that the child's idea of death is one of a temporary adventure, childish remarks such as 'you'll be sorry when I'm dead' are not reasons for great alarm in parents. But this kind of magical thinking can persist into adulthood in persons who fail to mature and who suffer from chronic lack of confidence. Such individuals are over-represented amongst those who attempt suicide. The ambivalence of young suicide victims about death as a terminal event is reflected in remarks, threats and notes which are often worded in such a way as to give the impression that the victim expects to be a witness at the discovery of his own body and looks forward to the consternation of the finders. It is this quality of resentment and hostility in pre-suicide communications which confers so much guilt and frustration on family survivors and makes it so difficult for them to come to terms with suicidal death.

Nowadays rational intellectual suicide no doubt occurs, but is rare in this part of the world. The majority of cases are now seen as problems for medical scientists and needing support and care rather than censure. Vulnerability is increased by chronic debilitating illness; single or divorced men over fifty-five years are most at risk, and drug or alcohol abuse may facilitate the act. Lack of a strong personal philosophy of the sanctity of human life combined with instability of personality also weakens resistance.

Suicide seldom occurs completely out of the blue. Warnings are given, threats made and notes left. Nobody is left untouched.

Ireland is somewhat unusual in that our suicide rates are higher in rural than in city areas. In most industrialised countries the reverse is the case. Whatever the benefits of country living for healthy people with a good family life, the availability of open water, poisons and shotguns make the Irish countryside a dangerous place for the isolated depressive.

Modern medical studies of suicide usually find evidence of severe depression preceding the act. Often depressive illness has gone untreated.

The story of suicide is not told without reference to the current global epidemic of non-fatal deliberate self-poisoning by prescribed drugs, sometimes called parasuicide. *The invention of safe sleeping pills in the 1950s presented the community for the very first time with a relatively painless opting out for a while from the troubles of life. For some years now deliberate self-poisoning has been the second commonest cause of admission to British general hospitals and it is not uncommon in this country.*

At first, self-poisoners were seen as failed suicides, but the psychiatrist Erwin Stengel, who carefully interviewed hundreds of parasuicide survivors, has shown clearly that they are different in many important respects from failed suicides. Parasuicides, for example, are younger, more often women and have no clear-cut intention to die, although some miscalculate the odds, and a substantial minority finally dies by suicide. There seems to be a muddled motivation amounting to a wish to sleep. The act may follow a difficult, inter-personal crisis and is often facilitated by alcohol: one English survey recently showed that St Valentine's Day is a peak risk period. The principal motivation is seen as a cry for help.

The latest chapter in the story of suicide is still being written. It has always puzzled psychiatrists that only a small minority of mentally ill persons, even those at greatest risk, actually take their own lives. Very recently it has been found that the brains of suicide victims are depleted of an important chemical messenger. This substance, called serotonin, *is one of the most important neurotransmitters in the nervous system. It has for some time been suspected that lack of serotonin is one of the main reasons behind the development of severe depressive illness with its attendant risk of suicide. This suspicion has been strengthened by the finding that successful treatment restores the supplies of serotonin to the brain.*

Although this country still ranks as one of the lowest suicide countries in the developed world, it would be naive to expect that we can withstand indefinitely the worldwide trend towards secularisation, the break-up of the nuclear family and the abandonment of traditional values, factors which are increasingly cited as prime causes for rising suicide rates. It is certain that medical scientists alone cannot *solve the problem. Ironically, and paradoxically,* what seems to be needed now is a return to basic Christian virtues. *If the sanctity of life is really worth all we say it is then surely the life of the would-be suicide is worth saving? Here, the example of the* Samaritan *organisation shows the way in the provision of emergency telephone helpline services for the lonely, the despairing and the suicidal.'*

Colm Keane (ed.), *Mental Health in Ireland.*

QUESTIONS

1 What are the effects of severe depressive illness on a person's outlook on life?

2 Is it the case that *all* suicides are caused by major depressive illness? Explain your answer.

3 Why do close relatives and friends have difficulty coming to terms with the death of a loved one by suicide?

4 What kind of person is considered most likely to think that suicide offers the best solution to his/her problems? Explain your answer.

5 What is the danger of a depressive illness going untreated?

6 What is *parasuicide*? How does it differ from attempted/failed suicide? What are its most common forms?

7 What does Dr Stengel believe is the principal motive for parasuicide?

8 (a) What is *serotonin*?

   (b) What role do some psychiatrists believe serotonin may play in the severe depressive illnesses that can contribute to suicide? Explain your answer.

9 Can medical scientists alone solve the problem of suicide? Give reasons for your answer.

SOMEONE WHO LISTENS

'The overwhelming urge to commit suicide generally does not last for very long and if someone can buy time for the victim it can pass over and the person can be saved.

The Samaritans give a wonderful service at this point through their hot-line telephones. Many owe their lives to their skill and dedication.'

Dermot Clifford

The Samaritans were founded by Rev. Chad Varah, Rector of St Stephen's Anglican Church, London, in 1953. He had discovered that befriending by 'ordinary' people was often more acceptable than professional counselling for those who were considering suicide. This befriending service is available 24 hours a day, every day of the year, and has spread across the globe, with over 22,000 volunteers in some 200 branches.

In 1996 the eighteen branches in Ireland received over 220,000 calls, and 23% of callers expressed suicidal feelings. Dublin branch is the second busiest after London.

A Samaritan counselling

All Samaritans obey the same strict rules:

- *Absolute Confidentiality*

The Samaritans guarantee complete secrecy about the identity of callers and anything they discuss.

Even if, for instance, a husband and wife or a parent and child contacted the Samaritans separately, each can depend on total confidentiality.

Any request for information about callers is refused. Answers to letters are in plain envelopes and do not mention the Samaritans, and personal callers are not acknowledged 'outside' by the volunteers.

- *Non-interference*

The caller is always 'in charge', and will never be contacted by the Samaritans or mentioned to any other agency or person unless he or she specifically requests it — and then only if the Samaritans' intervention is clearly needed by the caller.

- *Acceptance of the caller's own beliefs and standards (no preaching)*

The Samaritans have no 'message' except that there is somebody ready to listen and befriend you, day or night.

The Samaritans seek to offer sympathetic and concerned friendship to callers.

The volunteers are ordinary people from all walks of life — from those in their twenties to senior citizens — who give up some of their free time to befriending others. Usually only their immediate family know they are Samaritan volunteers, and they are known to callers and volunteers only by first names — Michael 24, Nuala 6 etc.

Primarily, the Samaritans are there to help those who are suicidal or feel overwhelmed by feelings of loneliness and despair. But *there is no problem that they will refuse to discuss.*

The Samaritans offer callers *time*, treat them with *respect* and take what they say *seriously*. They do *not* offer material help in cash or in kind but will help people to contact those organisations which provide concrete help. They do *not* try to minimise people's problems nor do they offer vague assurances that things will work out easily. However, they do believe that talking things over in absolute confidence and privacy with someone who accepts you as you are can help you to solve problems — or to discover new ways of living with an insoluble situation.

The Samaritans believe that, by really listening to another human being in distress, they can help increase his/her sense of self-worth, gain insight into his/her situation and reduce feelings of isolation and despair. They aim to help people see their problems in a new light and encourage them to find answers or to develop new attitudes that may help them to cope with their problems.

QUESTIONS

1 Who founded the Samaritans? Why did he do so?
2 (a) What do they offer?
   (b) What do they not offer?
3 What are the three strict strict rules which the Samaritans obey?
4 What do you think is the value of the service provided by the Samaritans? Explain your answer.

THE CHRISTIAN PERSPECTIVE

Christians believe that Jesus understands the pain of those who are intensely lonely and tempted to despair.

'In the garden of Gethsemane Christ suffered intense mental anguish. He suffered alone. His disciples slept when he needed them most. At that moment he was at one with all human pain and anguish. Again on Good Friday, as he hung naked on the cross, his mission was in ruins, his apostles scattered, his enemies seemed to have defeated him while his clothes were raffled. Even his Father in heaven seemed to have forgotten him. "My God, why have you abandoned me?" he cried out.'

Dermot Clifford

Jesus understands us and wants us to turn to him in prayer, drawing strength and inspiration from his example (Read *Luke* 22:39-46 and 23:44-46).

Jesus loves *each of us* so much that he gave his life for us. He lived a life which testified to God's concern for each and everyone of us. The Christian believes that life is worth living despite the hardships and tragedies which may befall us. When we are tempted to lose hope and give way to despair, that is the time we must remember that each of us has infinite worth in the eyes of God, and seek help from those who want to be our friends in time of need.

QUESTIONS

1 Why do Christians believe that Jesus understands those who suffer intensely and are tempted to despair?

2 What is the Christian perspective on the hardships and suffering which many people have to endure in this life?

CHAPTER 35

Dying with Dignity

WHAT IS EUTHANASIA?

'Many people today are afraid that an unnecessarily long and agonising process of disease and dying will be forced upon them against their will. They are afraid of a phase of lingering, harrowing sickness at the end of their lives, attached to many machines, largely immobilised, isolated and with minimal human contact.'

K. H. Peschke, *Irish Theological Quarterly*, 1992.

Euthanasia is *the act of intentionally killing a patient, usually someone who is incurably ill and in great pain, by means of a drugs overdose and sometimes suffocation.* It is usually advocated for reasons of compassion, to liberate a patient from extreme suffering.

In some countries, the Netherlands in particular, euthanasia is advocated as the *best* solution to such a tragic situation.

Read the following article:

DUTCH ARE 'BULLIED' INTO EUTHANASIA

It seemed the perfect way to die. When Frans Swarttouw decided to give up his fight against lung cancer, his doctor agreed to administer a lethal injection.

'I want to be able to draw the line myself,' said Swarttouw, 64, the flamboyant former head of one of Holland's largest companies, in a television interview recorded just days before his death.

However, the apparently civilised nature of the 'Dutch way of death', which has turned the country into the euthanasia centre of the world, is being undermined by alarming new findings.

Herbert Hendin, a New York psychiatrist who works in suicide prevention and has spent several years studying so-called mercy killings in the Netherlands, claims almost 3,000 Dutch people are being 'terminated' each year without their consent.

Others, Hendin claims, are being cajoled or even bullied by their doctors into seeking euthanasia rather than being given adequate palliative care. His controversial findings, which are bitterly contested by Holland's euthanasia advocates, are due to be published in the Journal of the American Medical Association.

'We are talking about occasions when the doctor is taking active measures to end a patient's life and the patient has not given his consent,' said Hendin. 'Euthanasia is becoming much more of a habit and routine. I even had one hospital doctor complaining to me that a colleague had killed one of his patients because he needed the bed.'

Under a typically Dutch compromise, euthanasia remains technically illegal, carrying a penalty of up to 12 years in jail. But if doctors stick to strict guidelines, they are not prosecuted. Chief among these is that the practice should be carried out only at the 'informed and repeated request of patients who suffer from unbearable and irremediable pain'.

Official figures for 1995, the latest available, show 3,600 reported cases of euthanasia or assisted suicide in which a doctor either administered a lethal injection or gave patients pills to take. In another 19,000 cases — 19% of all deaths — doctors ended treatment or administered potentially life-shortening dosages of pain-control medicine.

The government has admitted there have been cases of what it described as 'termination of the patient without explicit request', but insisted that the figure was 900 rather than the 2,900 claimed by Hendin. More than 50,000 Dutch now carry a 'euthanasia passport' which tells medical staff that the carrier has written a 'living will' setting out the circumstances in which he or she should be allowed to die.

But according to Hendin, many of those who give formal consent were pushed into it *by the doctors, partly because of the lack of hospices for the dying or other palliative care.*

Worse still, Hendin claims, in other cases doctors simply make the fateful decision on behalf of *patients without even seeking their opinion. 'An attorney from a pro-euthanasia group gave me the example of a nun who was dying of cancer and was suffering, but because of her religious belief she could not request death,' said Hendin.*

'So, out of compassion, the doctor put her to death. That's the mentality that doctors get after they practise euthanasia. They feel they know best whose life is worth continuing and whose isn't.'

The rules governing euthanasia do not specify, for instance, that a patient must be suffering from a terminal disease. This, critics say, leads to cases in which doctors have agreed to requests by people to be put to death, even though they could have gone on living healthily for years.

Sunday Times, 16.3.1997

QUESTIONS

1 What is the meaning of *'euthanasia'*?

2 Who is Dr Herbert Hendin?

3 What is the purpose of the document known as a *'living will'*?

4 What is meant by the phrase *'termination of the patient without explicit request'* attributed in the above article to Dutch government sources?

5 What are the claims made in this article by Dr Hendin? Do you think that he is justified in voicing his concerns? Give reasons for your answer.

THE MORALITY OF EUTHANASIA

Catholic Christian teaching has consistently opposed euthanasia, stating that to *purposely* put a patient to death is an *act of murder*, because:

• God alone is the creator of life and human beings have a special worth and dignity because they are made in the 'image and likeness of God'. (Read *Genesis* 1:26-27).

• Therefore, all Christians should maintain great respect for human life and avoid any action that unjustly seeks to destroy it.

However, Christian teaching acknowledges the plight of the tormented, incurable patient and, while admitting the complexity of the issue, offers guidance for action that respects his/her human dignity.

The Catholic Church teaches that there is a moral obligation on the patient, his/her family and the medical staff to take all *reasonable* steps to preserve and to protect his/her life.

However, in cases where recovery is excluded *beyond doubt*, and where prolongation of life by extraordinary, painful therapy will only inflict *suffering* on the patient *without any corresponding benefit*, medical carers are said to have no obligation to continue such treatment when it is judged to be futile. They may administer pain-killing drugs in order to relieve the patient's pain even if this has the side effect of shortening his/her life. But the patient's death is *not the intended end* of their action.*

QUESTIONS

1   Why does Catholic Christian teaching oppose euthanasia?

2   In the light of the Dutch experience of euthanasia, K. H. Peschke has written:

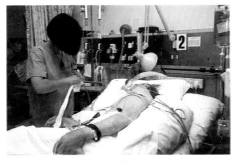

Hospital patient on life support equipment

> 'The admission in principle of euthanasia can easily lead to the crevasse effect, inasmuch as such a step will create a precedent to extend the practice also to handicapped and sick individuals, who do not suffer so much themselves, but rather are a burden to society.'

(a) According to Peschke, what would be the implications of the availability of euthanasia in our society for the following people:

• the disabled, both physically and mentally?

• those requiring long-term care and attention due to progressive, debilitating illness?

• the senior citizen, especially those who are poor and without any living relatives?

(b) Do you agree/disagree with Peschke's point of view? Explain your answer.

3   What is the Catholic response to the plight of a tormented, incurable patient?

---

*   **N.B.** We affect other people's lives and our own by what we *do* and what we *fail to do*. When deciding whether doing or not doing something is morally right or wrong, we should take into account

• the nature of the action itself,

• the circumstances in which it occurs,

• the consequences of the action, and

• the intention behind the action.

DYING WITH DIGNITY

Cicely Saunders launched the mother ship of the modern hospice movement in London in 1967 but still sees death as 'an outrage' and seeks ways to soften its sting.

For the doctors and nurses at the south London hospice it has been a wrenching weekend. Twelve patients had died between Friday and Sunday nights, and by Monday morning death's wide swathe had left the staff physically and emotionally exhausted. It was time for a tall, white-haired woman to provide the reassurance of her presence: standing in a stairwell, in the path of grief-bruised nurses and doctors, greeting each with a jovial smile and concerned questions: 'How was your weekend?' 'Are you exhausted?' 'Are you coping?'

Cicely Saunders

If there is one thing that Cicely Saunders knows about, it is coping. This much-honoured 70-year-old physician has devoted much of her life to caring for the dying, and in doing so has changed the way of death for millions of people. She has made herself death's interlocutor, bargaining away the pain and isolation in return for peace and acceptance. She has done this as much through the strength of a very forthright character as through good medicine.

In 1967, inspired by a gift from a dying patient and armed with an indomitable determination, Cicely opened St Christopher's, the world's first modern hospice. In doing so, she changed the impersonal, technocratic approach to death that since World War II has become endemic in overwhelmed Western hospitals. No heroic efforts were made to prolong life. There was no operating theatre; no temperatures were taken or pulses. Instead of specialists mumbling into charts, there were doctors sitting at bedsides holding patients' trembling hands. When death came, it was not with the accompaniment of I.V. drips and respirators but with tranquil normality. Above all, through the skilful and unobtrusive administering of drugs, there was control of the agonising pain that is often bound to terminal cancer. 'What I did,' says Cicely, 'was to allow patients to speak for themselves, to suggest what we ought to do to give them safe conduct.'

Why would such a woman, an Oxford graduate and the daughter of a wealthy London real estate agent, choose to devote her life to death? One answer is her religion. Converted from atheism as a young woman, she went through a period of evangelistic fervour, during which she was a Billy Graham counsellor, before she finally settled into the Anglican Church. Her faith created much apprehension among doctors when St Christopher's first opened. 'We suspected she wanted to produce deathbed conversions,' says consulting psychiatrist Colin Murray Parkes. 'How wrong we were.' Insists Cicely: 'There's an absolutely built-in rule that there are no religious pressures here.'

Saunders did not invent the hospice. The Greeks probably originated the concept of a place to go to die before 100 B.C. It has its modern roots in a home for the dying opened in Dublin in the late nineteenth century by an associate of Florence Nightingale. Not long after, the Sisters of Charity opened a similar home in London. It was largely at that home, in the 1950s and 1960s, that Cicely developed her ideas for a modern hospice that would bring physical and spiritual peace, in the face of death. The end of life 'can turn out to be the most important part', says she.

One powerful reason why that is true at St Christopher's is the system of pain control developed by Cicely and others. The hospice only admits patients with terminal cancer or amyotrophic lateral sclerosis (ALS), the motor-neurone illness. Fully 60 per cent of new arrivals suffer from pain that has been consuming them, sometimes for weeks. With a combination of morphine and other drugs such as tranquillisers administered every four hours, the pain is quickly eliminated for most patients. But other components of pain are, in their way, equally agonising. 'I would put at the top of the list just anxiety and fear,' says Cicely. 'It's very frightening to be very ill and feel you are losing control.'

The nurturing begins the moment the ambulance arrives with a new patient. Madeleine Duffield, the matron (nursing director), is at the door with a warm bed covered with a colourful afghan. Questions like 'Doctor, am I going to die?' are answered honestly. 'Deception is not as creative as truth,' says Saunders firmly. 'We do best in life if we look at it with clear eyes, and I think that applies to coming up to death as well.'

It is not hard to find patients at St Christopher's who will complain about the lack of honesty when they were in hospital previously. Or of the suffering because medication was only given when the pain became too enormous to bear. Or of the indignities forced on the dying. 'I saw a man die full of wires and plugs and little bleeping things,' says cancer patient Ted Hughes (56). 'He was treated like an embarrassment and put in a side room with curtains around his bed.' By comparison, says patient Phyllis Sadler (87), 'I am looked after with such love and kindness here.' So well does St Christopher's revivify its new patients, physically, mentally and spiritually, that 15 per cent of them are soon well enough to return home, even though they seemed only days from death when they arrived. At home they are looked after by the hospice's team of five visiting nurses and a doctor on 24-hour call. Even after a patient dies, St Christopher's offers bereavement counselling to relatives.

The other aspect of her personality, the humorous, tender side, is reflected not only in the devotion of her staff but also in the lively, casual air of St Christopher's. Visitors, even small children, are admitted at all hours. Dogs stroll around, visiting their sick owners. Some patients sip whiskey with their visitors. 'It's like a five-star hotel,' says an elderly patient. More, perhaps, it is a throw-back to the early days of the century, when care from birth to death was delivered at home. As Matron Duffield observes, 'A hospital would insist on a strict diet for a dying diabetic patient. We serve chocolate cake.' Saunders calls it creating an ambience of safety. 'We make it possible to face the unsafety of death.'

She has never lost her sense that death 'is an outrage' for those left behind. 'It's an outrage when a young father or mother dies, leaving two kids, or when two old people who have spent fifty years together are parted.' She is sustained by her belief that 'this isn't the end, and parting isn't forever'. For those who take a more secular view of death, there are very practical reasons for the hospice philosophy. 'We must not lose the chance,' she says, 'of making good on a great deal of untidiness in our lives, or of making time to pack our bags and say, "Sorry, goodbye and thank you."' There are many in

Hospice care

the world today who, after watching death come calmly and peacefully to relatives, have good reason to say thank you to Cicely Saunders.

Time Magazine, 12.9.1988.

QUESTIONS

1 What are the main ideas of the hospice movements?

2 What is the source of Cicely Saunders' commitment to care for the dying?

3 Compare and contrast the aims and practice of the hospice movement with the Dutch experience of euthanasia.

Which, in your opinion, offers people death with dignity?

Explain your answer.

4 The average lifespan of a patient in a hospice treatment is just three weeks. While admittedly expensive, it is no more so than treatment in an intensive care unit, where most hospice patients would otherwise end up.

Imagine you are a hospice administrator seeking partial funding from the Department of Health. Write a letter to the minister seeking to convince him/her of the merits of your case, especially that any resources made available will be money well spent.

CHAPTER 36

Near Death Experiences

WHAT ARE NEAR DEATH EXPERIENCES?

Over the past three decades, scientific research into the experiences of people who have tottered on the very brink of death, only to be restored to life at the last moment, has produced fascinating results. A number of doctors and philosophers believe that their *Near Death Experiences* (NDEs) may help us to finally answer the age-old question:

'What happens to human beings when they die?'

Two pioneers in this field are Dr Elizabeth Kübler-Ross and Dr Raymond Moody. Both were simultaneously but *independently* investigating the same area and reached remarkably similar conclusions.

It is only due to recent improvements in medical technology that NDEs have become a matter for investigation at all. People who in earlier times would have died could now be saved. What intrigued both Kübler-Ross and Moody was that people who had been momentarily declared 'clinically dead', but were resuscitated, *complained* about being brought back to life because their experience of a life beyond this life was so exquisite.

Both doctors sifted through hundreds of interviews with people who had had such an experience. *But in virtually every case, the interviewees stated that human language is simply inadequate as a means of describing what happened to them.* As one woman stated:

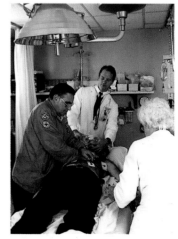

> *'This is a real problem for me because all the words I know are three dimensional. As I was going through this, I kept thinking, "Well, when I was taking geometry, they always told*

me there were only three dimensions and I always accepted that. But they were wrong. There are more." And, of course, our world — the one we're living in now — is three dimensional, but the next one definitely isn't. And that's why it's so hard to tell you this. I have to describe it to you in words that are three dimensional. That's as close as I can get to it, but it's not really adequate. I can't really give you a complete picture.'

R. Moody, *Life After Life*

Thanks to the co-operation of hundreds of 'NDErs', however, Moody eventually derived a set of common elements that define a Near Death Experience and proceeded to construct the following account of a complete or ideal NDE, with each aspect in the order in which it would normally occur:

'A man is dying and, as he reaches the point of greatest physical distress, he hears himself pronounced dead by his doctor. He begins to hear an uncomfortable noise, a loud ringing or buzzing, and at the same time feels himself moving very rapidly through a long dark tunnel. After this, he suddenly finds himself outside his own physical body, but still in the immediate physical environment, and he sees his own body from a distance, as though he is a spectator. He watches the resuscitation attempt from this unusual vantage point and is in a state of emotional upheaval.

After a while, he collects himself and becomes more accustomed to his odd condition. He notices that he still has a "body", but one of a very different nature and with very different powers from the physical body he has left behind. Soon other things begin to happen. Others come to meet and to help him. He glimpses the spirits of relatives and friends who have already died, and a loving, warm spirit of a kind he has never encountered before — a being of light — appears before him. This being asks him a question, non-verbally, to make him evaluate his life and helps him along by showing him a panoramic, instantaneous playback of the major events of his life. At some point he finds himself approaching some sort of barrier or border, apparently representing the limit between earthly life and the next life. Yet he finds that he must go back to earth, that the time for his death has not yet come. At this point he resists, for by now he is taken up with his experiences in the afterlife and does not want to return. He is overwhelmed by intense feelings of joy, love and peace. Despite his attitude, though, he somehow reunites with his physical body and lives.

Later he tries to tell others, but has trouble in doing so. In the first place, he can find no human words adequate to describe these unearthly episodes. He also finds that others scoff, so he stops telling other people. Still the experience affects his life profoundly, especially his views about death and its relationship to life.'

Life after Life

QUESTIONS

1   What is meant by a *'Near Death Experience'*?
2   Identify the various stages of a Near Death Experience.
3   Do you find Moody's claims, regarding NDEs as a glimpse of the next world, as comforting and reassuring or not? Give reasons for your opinion.

OBJECTIONS TO NDEs: A RESPONSE

(1) The *'tunnel experience'* is simply the memory of one's experience of being born (i.e. the passing from the womb to the world outside), that is buried in one's unconscious mind, but is jolted into one's conscious mind by a major trauma such as a heart attack or near-fatal traffic accident.

• This sounds plausible and would explain why people of different races and religions have a similar NDE. But Moody replies that recent medical research has shown that new-born babies are unable to understand and define their experience of being born, so they could not store such a memory and be able to recall it later.

(2) The tunnel experience is caused by an increased flow of carbon dioxide to the person's brain when the heart stops pumping oxygen. Research conducted in the 1950s revealed that people exposed to large doses of CO_2 gas had similar tunnel experiences.

• Moody responds by saying that their inhalation was *not* accompanied by such experiences as meeting a *'being of light'* or by *'life reviews'*.

(3) NDEs are hallucinations caused by the person being placed under great stress due to a serious illness.

- Moody states that research shows the experience is had *exclusively* by a person literally at death's door and *not* by someone who is merely very sick.

(4) Only religious patients, who believed in life after death, had such visions. Their expectations of such an experience caused them to have it. They only experienced a hallucination boosted by 'picture images' of what they believe God and the next world to be like.

- Moody denies this, saying that people with *no* religious beliefs whatsoever have recounted their experiences of leaving their bodies, having tunnel trips, meeting a being of light and having life reviews.

- In his book *Life At Death* (published in 1980) Prof. Kenneth Ring, University of Connecticut, reported on a study of 102 cases of women and men who had had close calls with death. Using three different methods of analysis, he found that religious belief seems to have *nothing at all* to do with what people experience in NDEs. Further, he concluded that:

> *'physiological or neurological interpretations of NDEs are so far inadequate and unacceptable.'*

THE IMPACT OF NDES

In the face of criticism, Moody remains steadfast that NDErs get a glimpse of the life beyond. He points to the fact that people's outlook on life is dramatically changed by their experience.

> *'I don't know what to make of these things, but there is no doubt that people's beliefs and lifestyles are dramatically changed by them. As a psychiatrist, I naturally want to know what it is that turns many of those who have had them into better people. Whatever causes them — chemicals in the brain or talking to God — here's something that can happen in a flash which we can't achieve in ten years of treatment.'*
>
> Bruce Greyson, Professor of Psychiatry,
> University of Connecticut Medical school,
> *Irish Independent*, 8.7.1993.

Those who have had a Near Death Experience naturally find it difficult, at least initially, to settle back into the mundane routine of life in this world, having experienced what C. G. Jung described as something:

'so unspeakably glorious that our imaginations and our feelings do not suffice to form even an approximate idea of it.'

More importantly, the evidence shows that those who have undergone an NDE demonstrate a greater appreciation of life as a gift to be cherished, and many have stated that their NDE changed their whole way of life for the better.

At the conclusion of his book on NDEs, Prof. Ring writes:

'It is obvious that my own interpretation, though I tried to keep it grounded in scientific theory and research, occasionally was forced to stray into the spiritual realm. I confess that I did so with considerable intellectual reluctance, but also with a sense that it would have been intellectually cowardly to avoid doing so. In my opinion - and I could be wrong - there is simply no way to deal with the interpretative problems raised by these experiences without confronting the spiritual realm.'

Kübler-Ross, Moody and Ring do *not* claim that NDEs offer certain proof of life after death. However, they do claim that NDEs provide us with evidence which points us in that direction.

QUESTIONS

1 What, in your own words, are the positive effects of Near Death Experiences on the lives of those who have had them?

2 Do you believe that NDEs are a genuine glimpse of a life beyond death or not? Give reasons for your opinion.

3 If NDEs were to be *disproved* would it affect your views on life after death? Why/why not?

CHAPTER 37

Life After Death

THE SOURCE OF HUMAN UNIQUENESS

The philosopher Aristotle once observed that all things that exist belong to either of two categories:

(1) *animate* (i.e. *living*); and

(2) *inanimate* (i.e. *non-living*).

He reasoned that a thing must have a special quality, therefore, to be considered animate, a living thing. This special quality is called its '*life principle*'.

Every human possesses a distinct, individual life principle which forms the core of his/her being and which sets our species apart from all other life forms on our planet. Christians usually refer to this as the *soul*.

From conception to old age

Christian psychologists view the soul as the constant, unchanging centre of each individual man and woman's personality. This can be seen, they argue, in the mysterious process of personal maturity undergone by every human being during the course of his/her life. As one psychologist has noted:

'In spite of the passage of years, in spite of change and development, I am the "I" of twenty or thirty years ago. So many things have happened, travel, thought, adventure, the myriad of daily experiences. Nevertheless, I am myself, I have retained my identity. My body has changed, my mind grown, but the soul by which I am what I am, abides.'

Prof. Peter Dempsey, *Psychology for All*

N.B. Students may recall Kate's poem, 'What do you see?', which illustrates this point (see Chapter 29).

Christian psychologists state that:

• through a mysterious union begun at the moment of conception, the soul infuses life into the body to produce a completely new and unique human being

• the soul is *non-material* (i.e. not physical but *spiritual*).

• The soul is the *source* of the unique gifts of the human *mind*, i.e. our *ability* to understand, to imagine, to remember, to reason, to choose and to love.

THE MYSTERY OF THE HUMAN PERSON

When Christians say that a person is composed of body and soul, they do not mean that he/she is put together, body and soul, like a sandwich of bread and jam is put together. A human person, Thomas Aquinas argued, is *one unified being*, not an amalgam of two parts.

The contents of the soul, a person's own individual thoughts, memories and feelings, are intricately and intimately linked to the body. We know that there is a close, intimate connection between a person's ability to reason and choose, and his/her brain functions. The human mind is dependent upon the nervous system since all our knowledge is derived from reflection on our experience of the world in which we live. But it would be a *mistake* to think that the mind can be simply identified with the brain. While the proper functioning of the brain is a necessary *pre-condition* for our being able to reason and to make choices, what happens in the mind *cannot* be fully explained by what happens in the brain. Human mental life is a much more *mysterious* thing than many

316

people realise. Jostein Gaarder tells the following story to illustrate this point:

> 'A Russian astronaut and a Russian brain surgeon were once discussing religion. The brain surgeon was a Christian but the astronaut was not. The astronaut said, "I've been out in space many times but I've never seen God or angels." And the brain surgeon replied, "And I've operated on many clever brains but I've never seen a single thought."

Sophie's World

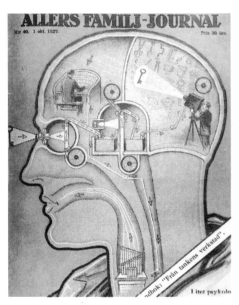

It's a mystery: scientists are still arguing about the brain's role

The surgeon makes it clear that thoughts are *not* things that can be seen or operated upon. The relationship between thought and the brain is *not* like the relationship between gall and the liver or urine and the kidneys. Gall and urine are purely *material* products of our bodily organs. Thought has both a material and a *spiritual* dimension.

While human beings are very much a part of the physical world, there *is* a spiritual dimension, a mysterious aspect to our nature, which is the source of our unique capabilities for rational thought and free choice.

However, while one can mentally draw a distinction between the body and the soul, one knows that *in reality* neither is by itself a human being. To illustrate, consider how water is composed of hydrogen and oxygen (both gases). Taken separately, neither is water, but when *combined* they form an entirely new thing that is liquid, not gaseous.

If we say that 'Maura' has the capacity to think, choose and love, we do *not* mean that it is her soul which does these things but the *whole person*: Maura, a spiritual (psyché) *and* physical (soma) being. She is a *psychosomatic unity*.

QUESTIONS

1 Explain the difference between things which are: (a) *animate* and (b) *inanimate*. Give examples of each.

2 What is meant by the terms: (a) *soul*, (b) *mind*, and (c) *psychosomatic unity*.

3 In your own words, express your understanding of the Christian view of the human person.

4 Do you consider this to be a plausible or implausible explanation? *Give reasons for your answer.*

CHRISTIANS AND THE MATERIALIST CHALLENGE

One of the most pervading and universal beliefs found in every culture is the hope that somehow and in some way the person continues to exist after physical death.

Every year, Christians all over the world visit cemeteries on All Souls' Day (2 November) to pray at the graveside of their departed loved ones, usually placing flowers on the grave as a mark of remembrance and respect. *This is also a sign of their trust in Christ's promise that death is not the end and that he invites all people to share eternal life with him.* Christians believe that the human soul survives the death of the body, that it is *immortal*.

Some leading atheists have had no difficulty in accepting the reality of the human soul, but they do *not* believe it to be immortal. For them, a human being is so totally identified with his/her physical body that any continued life by the soul after the death of the body is considered unthinkable. This view is called '*materialism*'.

Christians argue that the materialists' vision of what it means to be human is *too limited*, that they do not show due respect for the spiritual nature of the human person, that their vision of life is *too narrow*.

> '*We are still very much at the sand castle stage in understanding the physical world, and we find that the more we understand, the more progressively appears over the horizon of discovery. To deny, on the basis of modern human knowledge, that there cannot be a future life, would be like denying the existence of those ranges of the*

spectrum invisible to the eye, or to maintain that there cannot be a fourth dimension simply because we have become used to living in three.'

M. Ledwith, The Furrow, 1977.

Christians argue that *materialists reach the wrong conclusion because they adopt the wrong approach*. For materialists, the question of whether or not there is life after death is a *problem*; if there is not a scientifically proven answer in favour of it, then it is deemed to be either impossible or, at best, unknowable and not worth discussing.

Christians argue that the question of whether or not there is life after death is a *mystery*, to which religion, not science, provides the key to greater understanding. Science can be of great assistance in the search for an answer, but it is *not* the only tool of human inquiry.

QUESTIONS

1. What is meant by saying that the human soul is *'immortal'*?

2. What is *'materialism'*?

3. *'Materialism is inhuman, a prophecy of desolation and despair. What a destiny for humankind, a flat aimless thwarted existence where pain and agony rule, and joy is but a shadow. If there be no personal immortality then the human person of all beings is the most cruelly frustrated, his/her actions, his/her aims, his/her life a colossal mockery.'* Prof. P. Dempsey.

   (a) What point does this writer make?

   (b) Do you agree/disagree? Why?

4. What is the Christian response to materialist objections to life after death?

THE CHRISTIAN VISION OF LIFE AFTER DEATH

Christians believe that a loving God would not create us with a capacity for growth and happiness, and then entirely destroy us. It would be out of character for a God who is love to give us these gifts and then to annihilate us.

Over the centuries, Christians have reflected on the life, death, and resurrection of Jesus. They believe that he rose not only for his own sake, but for the sake of all of us. His rising is the guarantee of our rising to a new life.

'Christ Jesus. . . not only died for us - he rose from the dead, and there at God's right hand, he stands and pleads for us.' Romans 8:34.

Unlike the Buddhist or Hindu, however, the Christian believes that human beings survive bodily death with their individual identities *intact*, retaining the very characteristics and memories that make up their separate, unique personalities. Their belief is firmly rooted in the truth of Christ's resurrection. The risen Jesus is a sign from God of what will happen to *everyone* (read *1 Peter* 1: 3-4).

Reflecting on the experiences of those who witnessed the risen Jesus, early Christian writers sought, with understandable difficulty, to express what it means to survive bodily death in a *personal* way. They concluded that:

(1) God offers all people the opportunity to share a new life after death that is *spiritual* and *eternal*, i.e. beyond the restrictions of space and time.

(Read *John* 3:16; *Matthew* 6:19-20; and *2 Corinthians* 4:16-18.)

(2) Since the soul of each person requires a physical body:

- to recognise others and be recognised; and
- to express oneself and communicate with others;

upon the death of the physical body everyone receives a *spiritual body* as Christ now has. It will belong to the spiritual world, just as one's physical body belongs to this world.

(Read 1 *Corinthians* 15:39-44 and 49-53; 1 *John* 3:2).

QUESTIONS

1   How does the Christian vision of life after death differ from that of Buddhists and Hindus?

2   Having reflected on their experiences of the risen Jesus, what conclusions did the early Christians reach about life after death?

CHAPTER 38

Reincarnation?

WHAT IS REINCARNATION?

In 1987, the American actress Shirley MacLaine caused quite a stir in the British tabloid press, when she declared that she had had an extra-marital affair with a senior British politician. The excitement died down rather quickly, however, when she explained that she had had the relationship in a *previous* life.

Ms MacLaine is but one of a number of people who believe in reincarnation, namely:

> *the belief that after death, the human soul may live again by being re-born on earth in a new human or even animal body.*

Reincarnation is also known as the 'transmigration of the soul' or 'metempsychosis'. It was believed by the ancient Egyptians and is accepted by Hindus and Buddhists today.

In Hinduism, the soul (called 'Atman') is said to survive the death of the physical body and wanders through the centuries in a perpetual cycle of re-birth (called 'samsára'). The kind of existence a person will have, whether it will be as a person, an animal or an insect, depends on how well or how poorly the individual has grown in goodness and self-awareness. If a person does good deeds, he/she *ascends* the ladder of existence; if he/she does evil, he/she *descends*, being born into a lower social class or as a lesser kind of creature in his/her next life.

According to Hindu belief, a person must expect to undergo repeated reincarnations until he/she reaches a state of *'enlightenment'*, i.e. the realisation that his/her belief that he/she has a separate identity is actually an *illusion*.

Whereas Christians believe that, when a person dies, he/she will retain his/her individual identity and share eternal life with God, the Hindu believes that once he/she has recognised the illusion of his/her individuality, the soul is re-absorbed into Brahman (the impersonal world spirit), just like a raindrop returning to the ocean from which it originally came.

QUESTIONS

1 What is 'reincarnation'?

2 Why, in your opinion, is reincarnation an attractive idea to some people? Explain your answer.

3 Compare the Christian with the Hindu view of the afterlife. In what ways do they differ?

EVIDENCE FOR REINCARNATION

A small but growing number of people in Western society are beginning to believe in reincarnation. They do so, apparently, for two reasons:

(1) The testimony provided by people who have undergone hypnotic regression:

In a number of well-documented cases, a person was hypnotised and was able to talk at length and in detail about what it is claimed he/she did in a previous existence. Sometimes these individuals *appear* to have lived more than one previous life.

(2) The experience of déjà-vu (French expression meaning 'already seen'):

This is the feeling some people experience of having encountered some place or situation before, in what they believe to have been a previous life.

PROBING THE UNCONSCIOUS

Psychology is the science which *studies human behaviour and development*. One of its most important discoveries has been the realisation that the human mind (i.e. our ability to reason and choose) has two distinct but interacting aspects called: (1) *the conscious* and (2) *the unconscious* (sometimes called 'the subconscious').

The following extract explains what is meant by the 'unconscious' and will provide the key to understanding why some people sincerely believe they have been reincarnated, when there is another, *more plausible* explanation.

'Have you ever had the experience of not being able to remember something when you wanted to, and then suddenly remembering it later when it was no longer useful? It was there all the time; you just could not grasp it.

When a person is unaware of something it is said to be unconscious. *When he becomes aware of it, then it becomes* conscious. *Unconsciousness means unawareness; consciousness means awareness. Of course, not all the things buried in our minds are equally unconscious. Some things can be brought to consciousness quite easily, such as your address, date of birth or a good friend's telephone number. Other things would be very difficult to bring to consciousness, maybe impossible under ordinary circumstances, such as childhood experiences before the age of two.*

Impressions of sounds, sights, touches, smells and tastes pour into us all the time. We remain unconscious of most of them because they are unimportant. For instance, right now you are receiving impressions from your feet touching the floor, from your eyes seeing your hands and catching glimpses over the top of this book, from your ears hearing little background noises and so on. While you were concentrating on reading, all kinds of little sense impressions were unnoticed. They were unimportant. You became conscious of them only when your attention was drawn *to them.'*

A. Panzarella, *Growth in Christ*.

QUESTIONS

1   What is *'psychology'*?

2   What is meant by *'consciousness'* and *'unconsciousness'*?

3   In your own words, explain the role of the unconscious in human life.

EXAMINING THE EVIDENCE

A. Hypnotic Regression

Case One

In 1952, an American woman named Virginia Tighe was placed under hypnosis and appeared to recall a previous existence in which she had lived as a 19th century Belfast woman named *Bridie Murphy*. Her story convinced some people that they had found proof positive for reincarnation.

Careful investigation by psychologists revealed that Virginia Tighe was merely *the unwitting victim of her own unconscious memories which she had recalled in a garbled/confused manner.* The investigators discovered that the Belfast house she described in great detail bore a very close resemblance to the house in Philadelphia where Virginia had herself lived as a small child. Further, while living there she had a neighbour named Bridie Murphy with whom, when Virginia was a little girl, she used to spend a lot of time. Bridie was an elderly woman who had emigrated to America, but who was homesick for Ireland, and loved to tell Virginia stories about her life there.

Case Two

In 1956, Canadian psychiatrist Dr H. Rosen revealed that, when placed in a hypnotic trance, one of his patients had written down a full page in Oscan dialect, a long dead language once spoken in central Italy before it was conquered by the Romans, more than two and a half thousand years ago.

Again, detailed investigation revealed that Rosen's patient was *not* recalling some knowledge that could only be derived from a previous existence. It was discovered that, many years before, the patient had been working in a library where he saw displayed in an open book the only written example of Oscan language known to exist. He possessed what could be called a *'photographic memory'*, which accurately recorded this information but which afterwards slipped from his consciousness into his unconsciousness. There it remained, until it was *recalled* when he was placed in a hypnotic trance by Dr Rosen.

B. The Experience of Déjà-Vu

Case Three

In 1906, an Anglican clergyman named Forbes Phillips published an account of a strange experience he had had while holidaying in the city of Rome. While there he had visited a number of the leading tourist attractions. When he visited three particular places: the Thermae of Caracalla, the Appian Way and the Tivoli, he had what he could only describe as a most peculiar feeling. He had never been there before, yet these locations seemed unusually familiar to him. It was as if he had lived there before, long ago.

Subsequent investigation revealed that when Rev. Phillips visited other tourist sites in Rome, he did not have the same experience, even though they belonged to the same era as the others. Psychiatrists believe that as an avid reader, Rev. Phillips had most likely *read* about those locations several years earlier, but that the actual sight of them brought the buried memory of them *back* into his consciousness.

Sometimes another reason for the feeling of déjà-vu is advanced: that some people have an as yet inexplicable facility for *pre-cognition*, i.e. being able to *anticipate* what he/she is about to experience. A person might have a dream in which he/she seems to get an advance warning of some event or impressions of the layout of some place he/she has never before visited, such as, for instance, a rival football team's stadium.

Some researchers believe, however, that the phenomenon of déjà-vu may have its roots in the minuscule time lapse which occurs between our initial experience of some person, place or thing, and our subsequently becoming *aware* of what we are experiencing. We have not really recalled an earlier experience, merely misinterpreted our present experience and drawn the wrong conclusion!

QUESTION

Having examined these case studies, what is your assessment of the idea of reincarnation? Give reasons for the opinions you express.

ARGUMENTS AGAINST REINCARNATION

Peter Kreeft and Ronald Tacelli S.J. offer the following reasons for rejecting reincarnation:

- It involves a very low opinion of the body, presenting it as a prison or punishment for the soul. This implies that God has only put us here on earth to punish us, and contradicts the Christian belief in a loving God.

- Reincarnation claims that we are really pure spirits imprisoned in our bodies and so denies the psychosomatic unity of the human person.

- The idea that we are reincarnated in order to learn lessons we failed to learn in a past earthly life runs contrary to both common sense and sound educational psychology. We cannot learn something if there is no continuity of memory. We can learn from our mistakes only if we remember them! People do not usually remember these past reincarnations.

QUESTIONS

1 Read *Hebrews* 9:27–28. Then, in the light of the above arguments, consider the following statement by an acknowledged expert in the field.

   'For a Catholic, it should be clear that one's faith has no room for theories of reincarnation.'

   J.H. Crehan, SJ, *Reincarnation.*

   Do you agree/disagree? Give reasons for your answer.

2 What effects would the widespread acceptance of the idea of reincarnation have on such issues as poverty, women's rights, unjust imprisonment and so on? Explain your answer.

CHAPTER 39

Ghosts: Evidence of the Afterlife?

INTRODUCTION

'From ghosts and things that go bump in the night — the Good Lord preserve us.'

Old Cornish Prayer

Some people think that ghosts offer proof of a life beyond the grave. But this begs the question: Do ghosts exist? And if they do, what are they and from where do they originate?

According to the *Oxford English Dictionary*, a ghost is defined as:

> *'the supposed apparition of a dead person or animal; a disembodied spirit.'*

Some people are only too willing to believe in the existence of ghosts, while others reject the very idea out of hand.

QUESTIONS

1   Do you think that it is possible or impossible for ghosts to exist? Give reasons for your answer.

2   Dr Samuel Johnson once remarked about people's attitudes to ghosts:

> *'Some who deny it with their tongues, confess it by their fears.'*

What do you think he meant by this? Explain your answer.

THE SOCIETY FOR PSYCHICAL RESEARCH

In 1882, the Society for Psychical Research (SPR) was founded by a group of scholars from Cambridge University in Britain, to examine the subject of ghosts and other unusual (i.e. *paranormal*) events in a detached, scientific manner. Since then its researchers have scrutinised hundreds of reported sightings of ghosts. Most have been revealed to be either deliberate frauds, mistaken interpretations of natural events or the over-heated imaginings of psychologically disturbed persons. But a *few* occurrences have apparently defied rational explanation and continue to puzzle psychic researchers.

CONFLICTING EXPLANATIONS

- Some psychic investigators believe that all ghosts exist only in the mind of the beholder. If a person is of a nervous disposition and given the right set of circumstances (e.g. being on his/her own in a dark house with a reputation for being haunted), his/her imagination will conjure up a ghostly apparition which is not actually there. The person sees what he/she *expects* to see. It's merely an illusion, but seems very real to the person experiencing it.

- Other investigators admit that, while this explanation is true of many cases, it does *not* apply to all reported incidents of ghostly apparitions. They argue that some alleged ghost sightings are genuine because in a few authenticated cases there was (a) more than one reliable witness present and (b) more than one sighting by other credible witnesses. In other words, these 'apparitions' seemed to be there *independently* of any observer.

These investigators offer what they claim are the authenticated experiences of people who have witnessed the ghost of a relative or friend at the moment of the latter's death, even though that person was far away.

QUESTIONS

1 What is the Society for Psychical Research?
2 Why do some paranormal investigators insist that ghosts exist?

POSSIBLE ANSWERS FOR PUZZLING CASES

If, in a few genuine cases, ghosts *can* be said to exist, what are they?

- Supporters of reincarnation claim that ghosts are simply a memory of our experiences in a previous life. But this does not explain how different people from different places can apparently witness the same ghostly apparition at the same time.

- Others believe that ghosts are the spirits of the dead, returning to visit us from the next world.

The *problems* with this idea are that:

(a) there appear to be no discernible reasons why they should return to visit us, and

(b) these ghostly apparitions are unable to communicate with us or we with them.

- A growing number of those investigating these unusual or *'paranormal'* events are convinced that ghostly apparitions have some rational explanation. Some investigators claim that they are a natural phenomenon, possibly caused by some, as yet unknown, force left behind after a person's death. They believe that when a person dies in some violent or tragic way, he/she gives off some kind of 'energy discharge' which creates a photographic image at the place of his/her death. This, they claim, can *only* be seen by those people gifted with certain psychic abilities.

The *problem* with this explanation is that it does not explain why some images are selected while others are not, especially since countless millions have died violent and tragic deaths over the centuries.

- Another theory by those favouring a scientific explanation is that which suggests that ghosts are the result of a 'time slip', i.e. a kind of *'action replay'* where people catch a glimpse of some past event.

Bishop Dominic Walker, an Anglican psychologist, tells a story about a young couple who started seeing a ghostly figure after they had combined two small cottages they had bought into one dwelling. One evening, as they were watching the Nine O'Clock News, a woman seemed to appear from nowhere and began walking up the wall in the place where some stairs had been *before* renovations were carried out. The same thing happened at regular intervals. The couple became very uncomfortable and they decided to sell their house. The new owners also witnessed this apparition, but felt in no way threatened as their ghostly visitor seemed *totally unaware* of their presence.

Question

Do you find any of these possible explanations plausible or not? Give reasons for your answer.

Poltergeists

Curiously, however, investigators of the paranormal point out that some ghosts *do* make their presence felt. But these do *not* visibly manifest themselves. These are called '*poltergeists*', a term derived from the German words 'polter' meaning '*noisy*' and 'geist' meaning '*spirit*'.

The presence of a poltergeist is indicated by such otherwise inexplicable phenomena as bottle caps popping of their own accord, lights being switched on and off by what seems an invisible hand, or objects which appear to hurl themselves through the air.

In July 1988, the *Liverpool Echo* reported how one family was forced to flee from its home after objects had inexplicably been hurled at family members and their local curate.

Most alleged cases of poltergeist activity, however, have been revealed to be frauds perpetrated by clever hoaxers, such as that well-documented case by the SPR at the Woods' Farm, near Shrewsbury, England in 1883. A servant girl named Emma Davies was revealed as the cause of all the havoc experienced by her employers and co-workers. She had mastered the art of flicking objects in her vicinity while simultaneously screaming, so as to give the impression that she was reacting to some incident *rather than causing it.*

A few reported instances of poltergeist activity are thought to be genuine. They are *not*, however, believed to be the work of a 'playful spirit'. But if not, why then does there appear to be some kind of intelligence behind these occurrences? If they are not some mischievous spirits or the angry ghosts of dead persons returned to persecute the living, what are they?

Some psychologists believe that poltergeists have a *human* rather than a supernatural origin. They claim that some people have untapped natural psychic abilities which they may never either become aware of or normally use. But under certain circumstances they might tap into these abilities without ever realising it.

In what are considered the few genuine recorded cases, poltergeist activity seems to occur only where a child or teenager is under great emotional stress, which he/she either will not or cannot discuss with anyone. Some parapsychologists claim that these hidden emotional problems well up inside the young person and demand some form of expression. This can culminate finally in a release of emotional tension by means of his/her projecting objects through the air without any physical contact with them, i.e. *psychokinesis*. The person is usually quite unaware that he/she is causing objects to move apparently of their own accord, because, this is a product of his/her *unconscious mind*. Poltergeist activity does not appear to involve a 'ghost' at all.

QUESTIONS

1 What is the meaning of the term '*poltergeist*'?
2 What is '*psychokinesis*'?
3 Do you find the above explanation of the poltergeist phenomenon credible or not? Give reasons for your answer.

CONCLUDING REMARKS

After reviewing the available evidence, paranormal expert J.H. Crehan SJ concluded that there is no reason to believe that the existence of ghosts offers any evidence for belief in life after death. He argues that while they are some kind of unusual manifestation, they are actually *natural phenomena*. He believes that their occurrence is of a non-religious nature and may one day be explained.

QUESTION

J.H. Crehan SJ has written:

> '*The Christian belief in an afterlife where each person is rewarded on the basis of how he or she has lived his/her life, seems more consistent with the idea of an intelligent and loving God than vague and meaningless hauntings which appear bound to this world.*'

(a) What point does Fr Crehan make?

(b) Do you agree/disagree with him? Explain your answer.

CHAPTER 40

Our Reason for Hope

WHAT DOES ETERNITY MEAN?

'High up in the North in the land called Svithjod, there stands a rock. It is a hundred miles high and a hundred miles wide. Once every thousand years a little bird comes to this rock to sharpen its beak. When the rock, has thus been worn away, then a single day of eternity will have gone by.'

This old Scandinavian legend imagines eternity as if it were the same as earthly time but just went on and on for ever without end. This is *not* the Christian idea of eternity.

Christians believe that a clue to what eternity is like can be found in the scriptures.

In the Old Testament account where God appeared to Moses in the form of a burning bush, God told the latter that his name is *'I am'* (Read *Exodus* 3:14), in other words, that God lives, knows and acts always in the present tense. For God there is no past or future, *only now*. The *'life everlasting'* Christians pray for in the Apostles' Creed is not a reality with a past or a future but only a present — *an everlasting now*.

However, because this world is dominated by the passage of time, where people's lives are ruled by the ticking of the clock, there will always be great difficulty in trying to imagine what eternity will be like. Human language is designed to describe *this* world and it is of limited value when trying to describe things that go beyond anything within human experience. The best one can do is try to offer images produced by *drawing analogies* as to what heaven and hell will be like, based on one's experience of goodness and wickedness respectively in *this* world. But they are only intended to act as helpful images and *not* to be taken literally.

Further, it is important to remember that one should *not* regard heaven and hell as physical realities. There is a story about the Russian leader Khrushchev which illustrates how earth-bound some people's thinking can be.

A foreign diplomat once mentioned the word 'heaven' in a conversation with Khrushchev. The latter gave him a look of disgust and remarked: *'For goodness sake, don't talk about heaven. We sent cosmonauts up into space and they couldn't find any trace of it!'*

Christians believe that heaven and hell are *spiritual*, not material realities. As Sean Goan has written,

> *'We are not talking about places so much as experiences, experiences of total love or of its complete absence. Anyone who has known the joy of being in love or the anguish of a broken heart knows that the images we use only serve to give an idea of the experience. This is truer when we come to talk about union with, or separation from, God.'*

The Word, 1995.

QUESTIONS

1 (a) Write a brief essay based on an experience you have had where words seemed of little help in expressing your thoughts and feelings about someone or something important to you.

(b) What does it say to you about the limitations of language? Give reasons for your answer.

2 What do Christians understand *'eternity'* to mean?

3 Given the limits of language, how can we meaningfully talk about heaven and hell?

TALKING ABOUT THE HEREAFTER

> *'We'd love to know what it is like beyond the grave. But the images we were taught as children don't help. Take that business about heaven having cotton wool instead of floor tiles and people playing harps. George Bernard Shaw has a vicious piece where he says Christians have made heaven sound so dull that no one with a bit of life in them would want to go there.*
>
> *But this shortage of detail has one great advantage — we are free to imagine what Heaven or Hell are like from the minor heavens and hells we experience on earth. Life beyond the grave is always casting shadows over this life.'*

Colm Kilcoyne, *Sunday Press*, 1992.

Christians believe that human life is divided into two phases. Death is not the end but *the moment of transition* which marks the end of a person's earthly life and the beginning of a *new life* beyond the grave. The kind of person he/she is or has developed into at the moment of death is the kind of person he/she continues to be in the next world. Each person is accountable for the consequences of his/her actions. In effect, a person chooses his/her own fate for all eternity. God does not judge people, rather, by their moral choices, they judge themselves (read *Galatians* 6:7–10).

'The Last Judgment' by Michelangelo

QUESTION

1   What is the Christian view of life and death?

2   Read *John* 15:10–17 and *Matthew* 25:14–30.

What, in your view, is the standard Jesus sets against which people are called to judge their own lives and actions?

Explain your answer.

I HEAVEN

'The tongues of angels, the tongues of glorified saints shall not be able to express what heaven is.'

John Donne

Christians believe that those who have tried to love God and their fellow human beings to the best of their ability will be brought immediately into the community of perfect love that is heaven. There all our human needs will be answered and our hopes fulfilled. People will enjoy perfect happiness and peace in the presence of God.

Read:

Matthew 5:8, *John* 10:10, *Luke* 23:43, *John* 14:3, *2 Corinthians* 5:1–10, and *Revelations* 21:1–5.

QUESTIONS

1   What do Christians mean by '*heaven*'?

2   *'The moment I am sorry and am forgiven is a taste of heaven. Whenever we want a moment to last forever, we are experiencing the vocabulary of heaven.'*

Colm Kilcoyne.

(a) In which life experiences do you catch a glimpse of heaven?

(b) Explain what it is that you find so special about them.

II PURGATORY

For some people there will be all kinds of barriers in their lives that obstruct their entry into heaven. They will have to undergo a process of rooting out/*purging* all those things that get in the way of completely loving God. This process of purification is called *'Purgatory'*.

As with any experience that helps a person to grow in genuine love it involves pain, but not of a physical kind. The pain of purgatory will, Christians believe, be the realisation of how far short one has fallen from loving God and one's neighbour, coupled with a great desire to enter heaven. Once a person has purged those things from his/her life that prevent him/her from loving others as a Christian should, God will draw him/her to share eternal life in heaven.

Once again, however, a problem arises. There is no way of knowing how long a person must remain in purgatory. The afterlife does not measure time in the same way as this world. It is beyond our ability to know the answer.

QUESTION

What do Catholic Christians believe about *'purgatory'*?

III HELL

> *'God wants everyone to be saved.'*
> 1 *Timothy* 2:4.

Yet, this is beyond even the power of God. Human beings are uniquely gifted by God with the power to choose between good and evil. If a person *freely* and *knowingly* pursues his/her selfish desires by indulging in a destructive lifestyle, rejecting any involvement in making this world a better place, choosing to cut him/herself off from God and other people, then they have *chosen* the alternative to heaven. Consider the following story:

> *An architect, who had worked for a large company for many years and who was soon to retire, was called in one day by the board of*

directors and given plans for a fine house to be built in the best quarter of town. The chairman instructed him to spare no expense, using the finest materials and best builders. As the house began to go up, the architect began to think, 'Why use such costly materials?' so he began to use poor materials and to hire poor quality workmen, and he put the difference in the cost into his own pocket. When the house was finished, it looked very fine on the outside, but it certainly would not last long. Shortly after it was finished, the board of directors held another meeting to which the architect was called. The chairman made a speech, thanking the architect for his long service to the company, as a reward for which they were making him a retirement present of the house!

The *contrast* between heaven and hell is clearly illustrated by the following story:

'A long time ago in a place far away, a small group of people were being led on a tour by a messenger from God.

As they travelled down a long corridor, the messenger opened the first door and said, "This is heaven".

They looked inside and saw a huge banquet table full of delicious foods. All the men and women who sat around the table looked healthy and well fed. And the room was filled with joyful noises. In the hands of all the people were four-foot-long forks that they used to feed one another.

Then, the messenger led them to a second door and said, "And this is hell".

The door opened. Inside was another huge banquet table filled to overflowing with all sorts of delicious foods. But all the men and women who sat around the table looked horribly gaunt and emaciated. Whining, groaning, and angry shouts filled the room. Again, each of the people held a four-foot-long fork; but this time each of them was trying to feed only himself or herself.'

Christians believe that if a person has no room in this life for anyone but him/herself, then so it will continue in a future life beyond the grave.

QUESTIONS

1 What do Christians believe about hell? Use the two stories above to help you answer this question.

2 Read *Matthew* 25:31–46, *Luke* 16:19–31 and *Romans* 2:6–9.

  • What are your reflections on these scripture passages?

  • What do they say to you about the consequences of one's decisions in this life on one's eternal destiny?

3 Christians today do not believe hell to be a physical place 'full of fire and burning sulphur', but they do believe hell to really exist and that the experience of evil in this world can give some idea as to what hell is like.

> *'When I let what is dark and jealous in me control me,' self-destruction. When I am cornered by sin and haven't the generosity to arise and go and take my proper place at the feast of the forgiven. When a home is controlled by brutality. When money is short. When life has taught us to hate who we are. Hell on earth is the experience of life unravelling, of the crushing of what is beautiful in us. The other hell is that for eternity.'*
>
> Colm Kilcoyne.

(a) In which life experiences do you catch a glimpse of hell?

(b) Give reasons for your answer.

CONCLUDING REMARKS

When someone dies, those who are left behind don't stop loving him/her. Human love refuses to accept division by death. Christians believe that this is all the more true in the case of God's love.

God wishes to share eternal life with all people. This is the *destiny* God offers each of us. It is an *invitation*, not a command. Human beings, by their moral decisions, choose their eternal destiny. Yet even if they have spent their entire lives turned away from God, God is ready to forgive, even in the final moments of a person's life. God's love has no limits, it is forever. As St Paul writes:

'I am convinced that there is nothing in death or life — nothing in all creation that can separate us from the love of God in Christ Jesus Our Lord.'

Romans 8:38–39.

Alpha and Omega are the first and last letters of the Greek alphabet. They are used as symbols of the eternal God in the Book of Revelations.

Further Reading

GENERAL:

Butler, B. C. *An Approach to Christianity*, Fount Books.
Hinniells, J. R. (ed.) *Dictionary of Religions*, Penguin Books.
Pasco, R. and Redford, J. *Faith Alive: New Catechism Edition*, Hodder and Stoughton.

WORLD RELIGIONS:

Catoir, J. A. *World Religions*, Guildhall Press.
Pastva, L. *Great Religions of the World*, St Mary's Press.

FAITH TODAY:

Cassidy, E. (Ed.) *Faith and Culture in the Irish Context*, Veritas.
Gallagher, M. P. *Questions of Faith*, Veritas.

LOGIC AND PHILOSOPHY:

Adler, M. J. *Aristotle For Everyone*, Collier-Macmillan.
Gaarder, J. *Sophie's World*, Phoenix Books.
O'Donnell, R. *Hooked on Philosophy: Thomas Aquinas Made Easy*, Alba House Publishers

RELIGION AND SCIENCE:

Polkinghorne, J. *Serious Talk: Science and Religion in Dialogue*, S.C.M. Press.
Poole, M. *A Guide to Science and Belief*, Lion Publications.

MORALITY:

George, S. *How the Other Half Dies*, Penguin Books.
Hannon, P. *Church, State, Morality and Law*, Gill & Macmillan.
Keane, C. (Ed.) *Mental Health in Ireland*, Mercier Press.
Miller, M. *Making Moral Choices*, Twenty-Third Century Press.

Smith, D. *Life and Morality*, Gill & Macmillan.

Varga, A. C. *The Mains Issues in Bioethics* (2nd edition), Paulist Press.

RELATIONSHIPS:

Bausch, W. J. *Becoming a Man*, Twenty-Third Century Press.

Dillon, V. *Becoming a Woman*, Twenty-Third Century Press.

Dominion, J. *Passionate and Compassionate Love*, Darton, Longman and Todd.

THE MEDIA:

McMahon, B. and Quin, R. *Real Images: Film and TV*, Macmillan Publishers.

Tierney, M. *The Media and How to Use It*, Veritas.